The Accredited Witness

The Verdict is In

The Accredited Witness

The Verdict is in

Deborah Harvey Wynder

Copyright © 2024 by Deborah Harvey Wynder

All rights reserved. No part of this publication may be reproduced, distributed, or transmitted in any form or by any means, including photocopying, recording, or other electronic or mechanical methods, without the prior written permission of the copyright owner and the publisher, except in the case of brief quotations embodied in critical reviews and certain other noncommercial uses permitted by copyright law. For permission requests, write to the publisher, addressed "Attention: Permissions Coordinator," at the address below.

ARPress
45 Dan Road Suite 5
Canton, MA 02021

Hotline: 1(888) 821-0229
Fax: 1(508) 545-7580

Ordering Information:
Quantity sales. Special discounts are available on quantity purchases by corporations, associations, and others. For details, contact the publisher at the address above.

Printed in the United States of America.

ISBN-13:   Softcover   979-8-89676-307-9
                     eBook   979-8-89676-308-6

Library of Congress Control Number: 2023909606

TABLE OF CONTENTS

SECTION ONE

Chapter 1 Introduction 1

Chapter 2 The Beginning 5

Chapter 3 Deliverance 21

Chapter 4 He Called 28

Chapter 5 Census 32

Chapter 6 Say It Again 35

Chapter 7 History 43

Chapter 8 Poetic, Prayers and Psalms (Songs) 61

Chapter 9 Principles To Live By 73

Chapter 10 God's Wisdom (What's life) 80

Chapter 11 A Love Song 81

Chapter 12 God's Spokes People 83

SECTION TWO

Chapter 13 All About Yahshuah 113

Chapter 14 The Model Church 159

Chapter 15 Letters to live by 172

Chapter 16 The End 233

Chapter 17 Footnotes 248

Chapter 18 Legally speaking 263

"Your inheritance is the Holy Spirit.
Everything yields to the Holy Spirit.
So grow up your spirit man." – Deborah E. Wynder

There aren't many paragraphs or chapters in my book because there were no chapters or paragraphs when people were inspired. The translators put that in. My book won't be for everybody but the ones who want to wake up spiritually.

Chapter 1
Introduction

The accredited witness. The verdict is in. Is a book about the journey of the bible through the eyes of a seer. God calls me the Prophetess in the plans. God's name is YHVH, pronounced YOD-HEY-VAV-HEY or Yahveh in Hebrew. Meaning, I am —He exists by himself, never increasing, never decreasing. The Torah is the foundation of the bible . Vision allows you to see so your not distracted. Yahshuah means Yahveh will save. Yahshuah is Jesus's name in Hebrew. Jesus is Greek. Might of fact if Jesus was walking down the street he probably wouldn't answer you. The bible is the written rule of faith. A revelation of God. Canon is the rod of measure. God told me the bible is the last will and testament. The bible is a will. Which is a legal document. Which we received everything when he died. It's amazing to me how every other belief wants to pull from our bible but won't admit God died. The word testament means deposition. So actually the old deposition rolled into the new deposition. Deposition meaning you get something when someone dies. The Ark of the Covenant means death contract. God is legal so God honors his contract. Ark means coffin and a coffin represents a death. It also means bed and burial. Covenant means contract . Israel knew this so they kept the Ark of the Covenant until God honored his contract and died. The Mercy seat was laid in gold to represent a king. This is where God laid his blood so he could be the mediator for sinful man. Then he showed two angels one on each side to guard the coffin. The Old Testament was called the Scriptures or the Word of God. The Old Testament is also called the Torah which is the law. What is so hard to believe he put his spirit in a body. The bible is the sword holder- When it comes out of your mouth it's a sword. The word of God sustains your spirit , soul, and body. If you skip the word it's like missing a meal in the natural. Your malnutritioned in the spirit. I can see so I am going to take you *through the bible through my seer eyes. YHVH God's name in Hebrew inspired me to write this book. Many believers don't know what they believe. God says my people perish because of a lack of understanding. Understanding meaning you can see what's going on. God has graced me with several spiritual gifts seeing being one of them. God calls me the Prophetess in the plans and the accredited witness. The bible's food for the spirit man. Just as natural food is for the body. So I am going to take you on a journey through the bible through my eyes. Did you know you see with your mind through your eyes upside down and your brain has to turn it right side up? First let me give you a little history. Israel knew God as Yahveh which means son in Aramaic. God told me you know someone by their name and their face. God is a title not a name. So I told myself I better find out God's name because I probably won't see his face until I get to heaven. The bible doesn't tell you what God's name is. The bible tells you who God is and what he has done. The original Hebrew alphabet consists of twenty two letters. The JWX and I are non existent. You can take the bible back to the millennia. Hebrew would be spelled Hebrev. I'm only going to single out what God wants me to . The bible reads like a complete story except it's not in chronological order. I guess what gets me no one else sees what God showed me. You know God calls seed spermazoan. God's seed is his word. So why couldn't he speak his word into a womb. Check this out we have the protein laminin in each one of our cells and it's shaped like a cross. When I saw this I said how can they say God's word isn't true.*

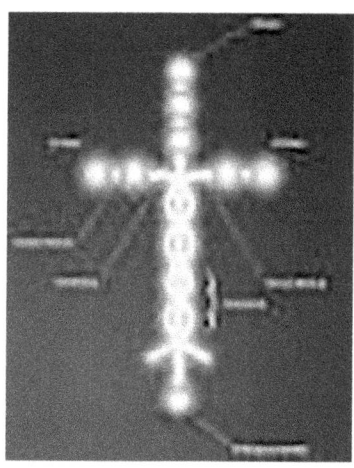

Life is in the blood

I thought this was pretty interesting. The bible is one story. The last part of the book in the bible reads like the end of the story begun in the first part of the first book in the bible.

The first word in Genesis is almost the last word in Revelations. I wrote the number to represent Genesis and the alphabet to represent Revelation.

1. In the beginning God created the heavens and the earth. Gen 1-1
   A. I saw a new heaven and a new earth Rev 21-1

2. The gathering together of waters he called sea. Gen 1-10
   B. the sea is no more Rev 21-1

3. The darkness he called night Gen 1-5
   C. there shall be no more night there. Rev2-5

4. God made the two great lights (sun and moon) Gen 1-16
   d. the city has no need of the sun nor the moon Rev.21-23

5. In the day you eat there of you shall surely die Gen 2-17
      e. death shall be no more Rev

6. I will greatly multiply your pain Gen 3-16
      f. neither shall there be no pain anymore Rev

7. Cursed is the ground for your sake Gen 3-17
      g. there shall be no more curse Rev 22-3

8. Satan appears as the deceiver of man kind Gen 3-14
      h. satan disappears forever Rev 20-10

9. They were driven from the tree of life Gen 3 22-24
      i. the tree of life reappears Rev 22-2

10. They were driven from God's presence
       j. they shall see his face

11. Man's primeval home was by a river Gen 2-10
       k. man's eternal home will be beside a river Rev 22-1

Chapter 2
The Beginning

This is how the bible is broke down.

- *First you have the five books that make up the Torah which is the law written by Moses. Torah means teach.*
- *Then you have the history section*
- *After that the poetic*
- *Next the prophets (God's spokes people)*
- *The gospels which speak of Yahshuah*
- *The Church*
- *Then you have the letters which tells us how to live this life*
- *Then there's Revelations the end. This book reveals Yahshuah*

The Old Testament speaks of a nation. The New Testament speaks of a man. Israel was founded and nurtured to bring Yahshuah into the world.

One God manifested in three personalities to redeem man. The bible teaches us how to be one with God. The devil teaches us the bible is a religious book. The devil taught us to be busy.

The bible is a form of government for his people. Might of fact God talks like a judge. You figure everything is ran by the government. The military, court system, your life and how you deal with your family and each other. God gave us the best possible way to live. You can say the bible is in code for the spirit man. The natural man will never see it. Every other belief system changes the book so the spirit man will never grow up to be a mature believer. The bible allows you to see the real you. It's like looking in the mirror.

Religion is like cancer it mimic's something good but kills the body of Christ. Religion's like giving natural man chemo. Religion is man's way to reach God. Relationship is God's way to reach man.

God's easy. Religion consists of rituals, self effort, doing works, and manifests nothing. God never told us how much to read. God said get understanding which most believers don't have any. They think because they can quote scripture they're doing something. The only way you know you understand something is if you do it. If you quote scripture it tells me you're a parrot. A parrot can repeat what you say but it doesn't mean it understands. One day God told me to go into a book store and take a look at how the books were written. God informed me that these books were written by the natural man the body part of man's exsistence. Which is the flesh part of man not the spirit and that's not the one God wants writing. God also assured me that I would be the perfect candidate to write this book. I look pretty stupid to the secular world. I am a woman, black, uneducated and have no husband. God said you are ordinary like Peter and John. Once they hear you they will know you spent a lot of time with me. We as believers should ask questions. I asked God why is the church so broke? When he has everything. It's like our Dad owns the electric company but we are sitting with the lights off. God told me it's to much natural man or the church looking like the world. Which church means ecclesia called out ones. The church is the people not the building. Church should be like boot camp. We made church into a social club. God's a spirit so how can the natural man receive from God. God said the natural man is a opposition and receives nothing from him. Every other belief system operates in the natural man and denies, God's power. It's something how all these other beliefs take from our bible but they don't want God's spirit. Which is the Holy Spirit. I just wonder how can a defeated man whip a demonic spirit. What do we think? They just went away. Tell me how do you go to church by observation(you think it's the right thing to do ,culturally) or do you go by revelation (because God revealed himself) As believers our focus should be Yahshuah(Jesus) not us. The objective should be the cross and the source should be the Holy spirit not the world. God always tells us to change the way we think and act. It's pretty bad when the church looks like the world. God doesn't prosper us solely to have a better western life but to bring his kingdom. God needs nothing. He wants to express himself and fellowship with his man. Everyone needs God but God comes where he's desired. Everything God tells us to do is for our benefit. There's no mystery in what God does. God does everything by his word which is his law and his government. I just wonder how believers take cute little clichés that mean nothing and run with them. Instead of saying what God said. Example believers will say God is good all the time. When God says he is good and his mercy endures forever. Well I guess I could go on but I want you to read my book. We all know the book of Genesis but let me show how the spirit would tell the story. God is explaining what he did. Just like someone would explain something in court. Notice God commanded light twice in the bible. The first time he spoke of light he was dealing with a spirit (devil). That's a different dispensation. The story I believe's in Ezekiel and Revelations. He was also introducing Yahshuah. The light of the world who expels darkness. You see the Holy Spirit was hovering over the water which is God's power. God was actually dealing with the enemy when he was hovering over the water. Yes he is one God with three distinct personalities in one substance. Just think of a person with multiple personalities housed in one body. Just take away the perverseness. When a person with multiple personalities does something all the personalities did it because they are one just like God's one. God can release himself because he's God. God had to release himself to redeem his man. We are also three in one. The spirit which is the Holy Spirit is also God. The soul is our ability to make a decision and the body allows us to touch this earth. When God is spoken of as father it means everything originated from him. The Holy Spirit guides us and it's his power. It's the same spirit that was in Adam, Eve and us. God had to give them his spirit so the enemy would be under their feet . The devil has power but God's spirit has more. Everything on this earth was made to yield to the Holy spirit. God came as the son to show us relationship. Besides he wanted more sons not fathers. Just look at it this way a man can be a father, a son , and a husband so why can't God. So God is still one God but we see him in different roles. Why do we limit God? We make him so small or limit his power. God needed nothing to make this earth. He didn't use needle or thread. He made it so everything knows what it's suppose to do . Everything can hear. Did you ever wonder why the moon never fell out the sky or how the sun knows when to rise? God tells time from evening to morning 6pm-6pm. So we would always be prepared and ahead of everyone else. His days go day one day two day three etc not Sunday, Monday, Tuesday etc. God would go by the full moon to tell a new month. We aren't on God's calendar. I really wanted to get this book out before 2016 on man's calender because man has Yahshuah resurrecting before he dies. How's that? God's new year would be around August or September in six month intervals. God's redemption plan or I like to call it his seven step plan for man. Now God has appointed times which he calls his feasts. These feasts allow us to know where God is and when he is going to be there. So why wouldn't we want to meet with God on his schedule? So why do we wait till something bad happens then we unite? We need to know the seasons of the Lord. Which are his feasts, not winter, spring, summer or fall.

God's feasts are;

1. Passover which is where he died for our sins,

2. Unleven bread is where, he was in the tomb(unleven means sinless) Yahshuah was made sin.

3. First fruits (not easter) he rose and God had to get him first. God had to make sure his assignment was complete and the evidence wasn't tampered with.

4. Pentecost, God came to bring the power, not give us a religion . The Fall Feasts are prophetic and haven't happened yet.

5. Trumpets means Awakening or coronation of a king. The Trumpet will sound we just don't know which one.

6. *Atonement is where the books are closed. We need to examine ourselves. So we can be reconciled back to God. We have ten days to atone for our oneness with God.*
7. *Tabernacles. We will be together with the Lord. It's a engathering with us dwelling with the Lord.*

Yahshuah did four of these feasts you can best believe he will come back and do the other three. I hear believers say they are Jewish feasts but God says they are his feasts. God tells you exactly where he is. So why wouldn't we meet with God at his appointed times when we know he's there? Besides Yahshuah is Jewish. One of the problems with the church is we were cut from our roots. Think of it this way if a tree is cut from it's roots it dies. The church was cut from it's Hebraic roots. After the apostles and disciples died the enemy infiltrated the church. The devil can teach church he spent a lot of time with God before he fell and he had so many thousands of years to study man. What we see today isn't God's church. God's church is the church in Acts. A full grown church. God made everything full grown so you would know the end result. God goes from the end to the beginning. Stop looking at the church down the street and take a look at God's model church. Constantine made Christianity a state religion but the people never renewed their minds so their hearts weren't in it. So he changed God's government into religion. The Romans didn't care much for Jewish people so they threw everything Jewish out and threw Yahshuah in with their pagan traditions. The church is modeled after the pagan churches in Rome. They even threw out the way God's people worshiped. Hebraic people are expressive. We made worship a spectator event. What we see in church is that Roman Greco thinking. That no movement is good. What we need to do is find out what God really wants and do it. What we need to know is what God says it is that's what it is. God just doesn't talk like we do saying any old thing out of our mouths. Now we all know the story God finished everything by the sixth day. That means everything was finished and complete so the time the man came he had to do nothing just maintain what God given him. Now I will start by breaking down the books of the bible. I may spend more time on some books. The bible is repetitious. When you meditate on God's word you start to see. This I believe was done to wake the spirit man up. That's one reason why the enemy changes the book. The bible's food for the spirit. Remember the bible isn't in chronological order. The Torah represents the law and was set in place until Yahshuah came. Moses wrote the Torah. The law was set in place to show us what sin is. Genesis means beginning which means bring forth . In the beginning we didn't have religion we had light. In Gen 1vs1 the original intent was for everything to yield to the Holy spirit. The Holy spirit is called living water. In the natural our bodies are over 90% water. If you feel like something's missing more than likely it's the Holy spirit. The Holy Spirit is the deep spirit of God moving. There's power in words. In the New Testament Yahshuah calls himself the light of the world. Light dispels darkness. God doesn't consider darkness meaning he doesn't think about it. The spirit of God works in the natural world. God ordained his spirit to be involved in every day activity. Yahshuah came back to restore things back to order and correct his finished work. How can man have a concept of God? God is above man's comprehension. Glory is the full expression of a thing. The full expression of God came in Christ. God's goodness leads to repentance. What else is God going to be besides good. We see when God made vegetation it was full grown. The seed was in itself. So when Adam came around he knew what he would get when he planted a seed. If he planted a watermelon seed he knew he would get a watermelon. He knew what it looked like. Then God talks about the light to separate the day and the night which he says will be signs in the sky. Signs are to show the way. Like the four blood moons. Creation talks loud but we have to pay attention as believers. When these four blood moons came two were on Passover and two were on Tabernacles. God was saying beginning and end. He said it twice because it's important. God told Moses after he brought them out of Eypt and they had Passover this is the beginning of months for you. I already discussed how God tells time previously. We are time bound people. God's not bound to time. God sits outside of time and isn't subject to it. We don't know what's going to happen the next second. How can we wonder about the way God marks time? Where do you think the military gets the idea? Every idea or thought was taken from God even if the world perverted it. God set up boundaries for us. God gave everything instructions. When God says let us make man this begins man's time. Remember the Holy spirit was to influence man. Natural man can do nothing without the spirit. Adam was lying there until God blew his spirit in him. Think of a body in a casket no spirit. The Image –Who God is   Likeness- What God does   Dominion- To have ownership. How God made us three in one. There are two hundred and fifty seven accounts of seed in the bible. If God says something a lot it must be important. When God says give a account he's giving a explanation or a reason.

Man's three dimensions. You are a spirit that possesses, a soul that lives in a body

God allows us to have freewill. He didn't want us to be robots. How would somebody know they really loved you unless they could decide for themselves. God pulled Eve out of Adam's side not out of his backside, like some men believe. God called them both Adam. Adam named Eve. When God blessed them he was giving them a instruction. Adam and Eve were together in the spirit. God didn't make Adam's body until chapter two. So why don't we live from the source we were created from? Adam had the Holy Spirit in him. He was a man who was made to walk in the spirit. When he fell Yahshuah came another man walking in the spirit. Fish live in water. Take them out of water, they die. Trees live in the ground take them out of the ground they die. If we don't walk in the spirit we are spiritually dead. God gave us the best possible way to live. God made us, thinking and reasoning like him. So I don't understand how people trip over Christ becoming the word. He was together with God in his mind. God released his thoughts in words and we all know what God says comes to be. Just like our words are with us. We release are words when we talk. We have a enemy that's fighting our words. God told me to study out his finished work for ten months straight. I only heard one pastor teach this and I've attended church all my life. People really ought to ask themselves why they go to church? God finished his work and on the seventh day he rested. God didn't rest because he was tired. God rested because he was finished. Now the word created means he made something from something that was non-existent. The word formed means he made something from something that was already here. God formed Adam from dirt. The dirt was already here. He blew the breath of life (Holy Spirit) in Adam not oxygen. Jewish wisdom says God blew everybody's spirit in Adam. So that's how all of us became decendants of Adam. Adam was drawn off the blueprints in God's mind. Which is Yahshuah. It's just like when you build a house. You look at the blueprints before you build the house. The natural man would have me talk about physical land as territory. I'm taking you for a walk through my spirit eyes. The spirit man's territory moved from land to souls. So I'm more concerned about souls. When God told me the soul has no color

I ran with it. God just jumped in a body because he had to do his assignment. When you see Black, White. Asian or Hispanic, it's just a colored suit. Just like a brown, blue or black outfit. The body is just a earth suit. So we can touch this earth. If we make it about color we missed God. God showed me how he's making disciples. And they are all colors and sizes. God will use anybody, look at Abraham. Abraham was a rich man. Then you have Rahab who was a woman and a prostitute. Only God can bring people together for his work. In the world you won't see a person making twenty thousand fellowship with a person making one hundred thousand. We put so much into the natural man. We pump him up and he's not even the real you. Adam is God's highest creation. There were two trees in the garden. The tree of life and the tree of good and evil. There was no sin in the garden until they came into agreement and ate. Adam had God's wisdom. He named all the animals and knew not to have sex with the animals. There was no perversion at this time. He knew none of these animals were like him. He knew you could only fellowship with someone like yourself. So God put Adam to sleep and pulled Eve out of him. The man with the womb. The man is the head and carries the seed but the woman has the power. In the spirit everyone's the same. Adam had such wisdom how did he know about a mother and a father and he didn't have one. Adam and Eve were naked and unashamed. I wonder how that was? They were both covered by God's Glory. They were at the spirit level of their exsistence. They both had to be at the same level to be higher than the enemy. Walking in the spirit. Now people live from the lowest part of their existence, the body.

Chapter three the enemy got Eve to question herself. The enemy can come in any form. God told her not to eat but she began to wonder. The tree looks good.(sike) Looks can be deceiving. The tree of knowledge. A choice maybe you don't want all of this. They chose to give up everything to work. The tree brought in another idea about themselves. Adam was there he didn't stop her. He probably was curious to. Eve was deceived. Deception is worse then finding out something is wrong and dealing with it. Deception appears to be something it's not. The sin was magnified in the garden. Don't be deceived after God gives you something. Deception is really worse than the sin because it goes on but if you realize the sin you can correct it. It's not where you start it's where you finish. Can you fight through who you where told you are? God is no respecter of person's. So why are so many believers?

If he was, Eve wouldn't be talking. When they sinned, the Holy spirit left them. They spiritually died. The natural man woke up. Now the only place the natural man can get his information is from this world. The spirit will not be housed with sin. The snake who was the devil knew he had to separate the man from God's spirit, so he could defeat the man. The devil is evil with intelligence. Sin entered everywhere even in the man's nature. When sin entered it opened the door for sickness, lack, suffering and everything else came in. None of these things were in the garden before. Adam was nine hundred and thirty nine years old before sin killed him. Making me to believe God never wanted us to die. Imagine a whole earth filled with spirit filled people. The enemy wasn't having that. God said to me if the spirit is sleep will he hear the trumpet? The trumpet will be blown in the spirit. God designed prayer so he could communicate with his man. We made prayer a religious obligation. IF it's a conversation why don't we like talking to God? Adam started dying when the Holy spirit left. Adam was all about self preservation which was all about him. Adam said heck with his wife. When Adam and Eve clothed themselves with figs that was self effort which is never good enough. Especially when God has done it all. It's a gift and he wants intimacy with us. When they sinned it created a problem. God is Holy and he is not going to have sin or flesh glorify in his presence. So he made a way in predestined time to fellowship with his man. He solved the problem before the foundation of the world. The only remission of sin is blood. He shed his blood before the foundation of the world. That's how he could be in Adam and Eve's presence after sin. So when he looked at them he saw the blood. When they sinned they became disconnected from God. God dealt with the snake first. God's a judge and he follows his laws in his bible . His form of government. Look around a court room. In God we trust and placing the hand on the bible. All that came from God. Now they want to take God out of everything. The believers are losing their rights. In chapter three God talks of the virgin birth. .The seed of a woman, when we all know a seed comes from a man. So if it's not man's seed, whose is it? We all know that God didn't have sex with the earth to make Adam. So why is it so hard to believe God became a man? He talks about crushing satan's head. Meaning he will break satan's authority. And he will bruise his heel meaning we will tread on satan. The serpent allowed satan to use his body. So God sentenced the serpent. So now being a judge, God sentenced Adam and Eve. Their sentence, community service and God took the wrap. Now since the Holy Spirit was no longer in the man the earth no longer yielded to the man. He had to physically work the land which now produced thorns and thistles. Yahshuah redeemed the land when he put the crown of thorns on his head. When man sinned God had no right to be on earth. Adam gave up his contract to satan until the end. That's why God doesn't intercede because he's legal. Where do you think the world gets it's stuff even though it's counterfeit? What people fail to realize is a third of the angels fell which is a infinite number. Nobody knows how many that is. God had to do everything like the man to get the Holy spirit back to his man. If he didn't come through a womb he would have been here illegally. He had to do everything like a man or it would result in a mistrial. So the enemy was always looking for the seed. The blood from Adam was tainted so how could any man that was a descendant from Adam redeem us? A defeated man can't redeem a spirit which is the real us. You know how a baby in the womb gets addicted to crack but had nothing to do with it? It's the same with us, Adam and our sinful nature. I bet you guys didn't know you get your blood from your father? So God and Yahshuah were the only two whose blood wasn't tainted. A perfect sacrifice. The mother's blood never touches the baby's blood while in the womb. So Yahshuah's blood never touched Mary's. God did the first natural sacrifice when he cut the coats for Adam and Eve while they were in the garden. What people fail to realize God had to put them out to get them back. If they would of eaten off the tree of life after eating off the tree of knowledge, they would have been immortally corrupt forever. God would not of been able to redeem them. Remember the soul never dies. After God put them out he placed a sword there to guard the tree of life. God had to make the way back to him. God's plan answers fallen man. We need to have a biblical world view. When we work God's plan we will destroy the works of the devil. We don't work or ask God about his plan we just want it to work. We are always looking to be fixed when God gave us a new life.

    Now we all know the story of Cain and Abel. The enemy thought Abel was the seed so he influenced Cain to kill his brother. Cain left room in his heart for sin to enter. That's why God said sin is crouching at the door. Sin is always looking for a way to get in. Cain was prideful meaning he was about himself. God wants us to be about him. Cain's sacrifice wasn't accepted because it was vegetables out of a cursed ground. There was no blood in his *offering meaning there was no sacrifice or remission of sin. God cursed the ground not the man. On the other hand Abel's sacrifice was accepted. He gave God a lamb which we know would be sacrificed. There's life in the blood. The lamb represented Yahshuah. God gave me a telescopic eye so I see where others might not. Where the word is concerned. I just want to bring other believers some sight. It's important how and what you see. So it is amazing how some people can say they can come in the presence of a holy God without a sacrifice when the pattern has been set. When God asks Cain where is his brother it is a rhetorical question. It's for us. We need to examine ourselves. So we can see who and where we are.*

Then God talks about a man named Lamech who committed murder. His fate was set because of Cain. Cain set the order. It's something how Lamech's wives names were Adah and Zillah. Then God talks about the blood of Abel and Zachariah. Which refers to the beginning and end. You best believe God's going to finish everything. Then God gave Adam another son which lineage Yahshuah comes out of. God always gives us a list of descendants . God always wants you to know where you came from so you know where you are going.

Chapter four God talks about how the people start to worship him. Maybe we should define worship. Worship means worthiness, respect, reverence, paid to a divine being expression of extravagant respect or admiration or devotion. Now let's define rejoice. Rejoice means to give joy , gladden, feel great delight. Now what's the meaning of praise. To express approval to glory. Glory is a full expression of a thing. Where do we get clapping? From man and we associate this with God's greatness. So why is it we sit in church and don't move? We just sit there like a bump on a log. We give more to a football game or a entertainer. You bless someone with your mouth. While God our creator has given us everything. God's a great king. It's baffling to me how we can't express ourselves in the presence of a king. Hebraic people are very expressive. David danced right out of his clothes in the presence of God. So where did we learn that just to sit in a pew and say God look at me here I am? I made it. Like we accomplished some great feat. Do you think he honestly died for us to be able to sit in a pew? Since God had no right to be here he had to get people to come into agreement with him.

The first man was Noah which means relief. He came into agreement with God and his plan. Yahshuah would come out of Noah's son Hashem's line. Hashem meaning the name. Out of Shem came Hispanic people (maybe that's why so many Hispanic men value marriage) and people of Asian desendant. Japheth produced White people and Ham produced Black people. God knew we would try to make it black or white when it isn't. God knows us well. During this time evil increased. The devil taught the people how to sin. Remember we are dealing with evil with intelligence. The Nephilim were on the earth which were half angel and half human. The angels were sleeping with the women and producing children. When God says sons of God he's talking about walking in the spirit. So God decided to cleanse the earth. So Noah built a ark. Noah was 600 years old when he finished the ark. Noah's name means preacher of righteousness meaning he was in right standing with God. Man's number is six. God closed the door to the ark. It was eight people in all that went into the ark. Eight represents eternity. Now I am going to ask a question most people get it wrong. How many pairs of animals got into the ark. Most people say two of every kind. There were one pair of unclean animals and seven pair of clean animals. There were more pairs of clean animals so sacrifices could be done. Nobody plays the numbers game better than God. Every time you hear of someone going to the altar you know they are doing a sacrifice.

Chapter 8 vs 20 to 22 God said man's heart is set on evil because of his sinful nature. Heart meaning mind. God promised as long as there's a earth there would be seed and harvest time. This implemented sowing and reaping. In chapter 4 God gave Noah a instruction to be fertile, increase in number and fill the earth. God implemented the first form of government. Then in 9 vs 12 God promises never to destroy the whole earth by flood waters again and uses the rainbow as a sign of his promise. God always seals his contracts. Isn't it crazy how the world steals from God. When God's people should be using the things of God. God's people are pretty clueless. The children of this world are much wiser. The enemy tells the world the things of God. So the world claims them as their own. Noah's sons populated the whole earth. Noah was a farmer. He planted a vineyard. What do you think comes from a vine? You got it wine. So Noah got drunk . His son Ham went and mocked his father's nakeness. The other two brothers covered him up. Noah cursed Ham(caanaan) This is a natural example of disconnection. Noah and Ham became disconnected and in *the spirit God and man became disconnected. God showed me that man is always trying to clothe himself with cultural identity instead of clothing himself with God. For all of you who didn't know Abraham came out of the line of Shem not Ham. God told me to learn Genealogy. If you don't know where you came from you don't know where you are going. Noah's descendants scattered because of the tower of babel. The nation of Israel started with Abram (Abraham).*

Gens. Chapter 12 Abraham's name means called by God. When God called Abraham out he was worshipping the sun god Tammuz . Tammuz is linked to Allah in the epic of the flood which I will explain later in my book. Abraham had a encounter with the one true living God. Abraham knew God as God Almighty. Almighty meaning power which God's power is the Holy spirit. God revealed himself to Abraham whatever he showed Abraham impacted his life. God revealed his glory. Abraham believed. The job of the believer is to believe. In that day people worshipped Gods for all different things such as water, land, air , breath, moon, sun ,dirt etc. Here's a little history lesson in some papers called the epic of Atrahasis and the epic of Atrachasis coneform which tells of a flood and is older than the physical bible talks of a deity named Tammuz. Whose name is also Allah they didn't even cover the name up. It represents him as a transvestite deity. The coneform speaks of Ishtaran frequently represented as a snake. Then it speaks of Ishtara a Hittite goddess of love war fertility etc. Then it speaks of the planet venus and sin which are both linked to Allah. This coneform talks of a account of a great flood in Mesopatamia. Where Abraham was from. It said the gods were fighting over head deity. Then it says the God Enlil (God of breath) came and took care of Tammuz. Breath means spirit. The God of breath being the one true living God. The breath being the Holy spirit. Tammuz is named in the bible . In the book of Ezekiel chapt 8vs 14. Ezekiel being the book for the spirit man. Every body is in the bible. Believers need to do their homework. You know the spirit is here. Just because you can't see it doesn't mean it doesn't exsist or it isn't moving. Just like air. Muhammad was affiliated with the church in Rome. Rome wanted the land in Jerusalem from the Jewish people. So they built Muhammad up and he went south on them. That's where Muhammad got the one god idea from. In Abraham's time they worshipped many false gods. Islam got the idea flesh was bad from Rome. They also got you have to work and qualify to get to heaven. God use to fellowship with man before the fall. When you think you have to work it's like you are saying God owes you something. Like you are working for a paycheck. We all know God will not be a debtor to any man.

Chapter 12 We see God changing Abram's name to Abraham. Meaning he changed Abraham and left his past in the past. How much are we connected to our past? How much are we connected to the world? Are the generational curses and works of darkness severed? Is our receiver damaged? God told Abraham he would bless him. We are Abraham's spiritual children. Believe Christ's message. God wants to bless us so we can be a blessing to others. Yahshuah became a curse so we could be blessed. When Yahshuah died he gave us salvation and predestination. We all believe in salvation but we never think about our destiny. The second time God spoke to Abraham, he told him he would give his descendants the land. So Abraham built a altar meaning he was doing a sacrifice. Abraham traveled and God made him wealthy. God's presence would come after the sacrifice was done. Then Abraham and Lot separated because they had to many possessions. Lot chose Sodom because the land was rich and plentiful. Most people ask why would Lot move there? It's just like a straight man moving to Atlanta. God came to Abraham again and told him he would give the land indefinitely to his descendants. When we see dust over earth that refers to our natural existence. When we see stars that refers to heaven. Now we know Lot got captured. Abraham came and rescued Lot. The king of Sodom wanted to give Abraham money and keep the people. Abraham didn't take any money because he didn't want the king to be able to say he made him rich. He didn't let him keep the people either because as long as you have people they can work and make you more money. Then Melchizedek king of God Most High having no genealogy(meaning he had no parents) met with Abraham he brought bread and wine. Sounds like communion to me. Melchizedek was a king and a priest. Before the law. He established the order. We all know priests come from Levi and kings from Judah. Then the king blessed Abraham. Abraham gave the king a tenth. This was a form of tithing. This was 430 years before the law. You can say Levi was in Abraham's loins. So this supercedes the law. Some time later in a vision God told Abraham his reward would be great. Then God made a blood covenant with Abraham. God had to show Abraham that Abraham believed. God already knew. Abraham brought a three year old heifer, a three year old female goat, a three year old ram, a mourning dove and a pigeon. He cut them in half except for the birds. Then birds of prey came and Abraham had to fight them off. We always have to do our part in God's plan. It's not us earning anything. It's us partaking. Then a flaming torch walked through the animals which was God. God's seal of the contract making it legal and binding. No one can see what you believe in your heart. Sarah, Abraham's wife was barren so she gave Hagar to Abraham. God didn't tell Abraham to do that. That was Abraham's self effort thinking he can help God. God hadn't spoken to Abraham for some time but that doesn't mean you do what you think. God was finished talking at that time. When we don't see anything we have to think back to the promise instead of jumping ahead. So we have to live with the results of our actions. Ishmael was the child of the flesh. God said no flesh will glorify in his presence. Also Hagar was a Eyptian slave. Why would God use her when God's all about his covenants? She wasn't married to Abraham. God blessed Ishmael even though he was a product of Abraham's self effort. So if you make a mistake repent. When the bible speaks of Ishmael being a wild donkey it was God seeing his future not God cursing him. In our self effort we have no peace and humility. Nothing in Yahshuah is bondage. So why would Yahshuah use a woman in bondage to bring peace and freedom to his people. Then God gave Abraham his fifth promise which is Yahshuah. Then God confirmed his promise and made a covenant with Abraham. The covenant of circumcision. God made Abraham a Jew outwardly. Throwing that Abraham's a muslim out the window. Then God appears to Abraham again by sending three men to him which represents the trinity. God had to do everything in the natural so we would understand spiritual things. Everything that happened in the Old Testament is a foreshadow of the New Testament. The three men told Sarah she would become pregnant. She laughed.

Next you have the story of Sodom which I won't go into. Now we know Issac was born and his name means laughter. We see Abraham getting ready to sacrifice his son Issac. When we see his son carrying the wood prophetically speaking that's Christ carrying the cross. People wear crosses but when you carried a cross it meant you were going to your death. Abraham was willing to sacrifice his son because he knew God could raise him up. God provided the ram in the thicket. God sees a need and he provides. This was so Abraham could know he trusted and believed God. Then Issac grew up. Where it says Issac dug the wells of his father it means he did what his father did. Issac made pretty good decisions we see him meditating. Issac married his wife Rebekah first then he loved her. Showing me marriage is a decision. We do it backwards in this society. When Sarah died Abraham married again and had a son named Midian. Lot had two sons by his daughters named Ammon and Moab together with Ishmael became the fore fathers of Islam.

Now time goes on and Issac has Esau and Jacob. You see where Esau gives up his birth right for a meal. Showing he has no regard for spiritual things and rather fill his belly in the natural. That's a poor man's mentality. Then time goes on and Jacob gets the blessing, Esau was suppose to get. We see manipulation working. Time goes on and Rebekah never sees Jacob again. Jacob's name means trickster .Jacob treasured the things of God. God changed Jacob's name to Israel. This is a example of going from the old man to the new creature. The changed condition. Jacob also means planter while Israel means prince. Planter means works while prince means son of a king. So it doesn't matter what condition you are in. God can still help you. Inspite of your behavior God still loves you and wants to show affection towards you. Then Jacob has his first encounter with God and speaks of giving God a tenth which represents tithing. Then you see Jacob rolling a stone away for Rachel who was taking care of the sheep. Prophetically the stone being rolled away from the tomb for Yahshuah. Now this is for the men who say women can't be pastors. Pastors just take care of the sheep . If Rachel and Rebekah were in the New Testament they would be pastors. Then Jacob goes through life has kids and God tells Jacob to go back to his land. He only has a shepherd's staff when he crosses the Jordan. This represents Moses. The bible is prophetic. For the spirit eyes. Then we get to Jacob's fourth encounter with God where he wrestles with the man of God all night. Jacob got punched in the leg and it left him with a limp. Meaning if you have a encounter with God your walk should never be the same. Jacob strived. God wants us to rise up. God made us kings and Priests, so go to work. Then Jacob goes on has a couple more encounters with God. Then the story goes on to Joseph. Joseph is sold into slavery by his brothers. His brothers were jealous of him. The whole time God was preparing him. He never spoke bad about his brothers. Imagine if he did . Pharoah might of killed them or not given them any food because of how they treated Joseph. Even though Joseph was a slave he walked with God and God made him prosperous. He was Pharoah's right hand man.

Chapter 3
Deliverance

Now we move on to the book of Exodus which means deliverance and Redemption. Israel is God's nation. God chose Israel because they were weak compared to the rest of the world. God could show his power through Israel. They were to exalt God's name, uphold his reputation and obey his ways. God had to get his people ready for him to come back. Since God was out legally he had to get people who are in the natural man to know him. Now in this book we learn of the story of Moses. God had Moses raised up in Pharoah's house so he would be able to stand up against Pharoah. If he thought like a slave he would of felt intimidated by Pharaoh. Slaves had no power over Pharoah. Moses didn't have the mentality of a slave he thought like a prince.

So we go on to chapter three. Here we see that God is self existing. God introduces himself to Moses. So we should celebrate and recognize the fight and stand for God. When we get down to vs 15 we see that God is who he is, will be whatever he needs to be when he needs to be. Abraham knew God as God Almighty by his power. Moses knew God on a more personal note. God is God of the living .God said he is the God of Abraham, Issac and Jacob meaning they are living in eternity. God is past, present, and future all at the same time . God tells them how they are going to go out even though they are slaves. When they left Eypt, God gave them Eypt's wealth, showing God is more than enough. Might of fact the women knocked on the doors and Eypt turned over 400 years of wealth. God sent the women cause women know how to shop. Their pockets were full. The church, just sees being delivered from sin. The church has to learn the patterns and come out of the world. Abraham came out. They came out of Eypt. They came out of Babylon and Peter said save *yourself from this corrupt generation. Meaning come out of the world. We the church have to come out as a unit. We have to be unified but churches make church like college. For self. The church says Pastor teach me something to change my life. God's about corporate success then it trickles down to individual success. I looked at the casinos closing it trickled down to where the little businesses closed and then the individual was out of work. We have to resist from what we were taught from the world to save ourselves. Constantine with that Roman Greco thinking which is God is mad at you so you sit, be still and listen. That's Stoic Catholics. Moses use to stutter so he sent Aaron with him. With God there are no excuses. God called Israel his first son meaning they were in covenant with him. A covenant is a agreement . A legal contract. We all know the story but I bet you didn't know when Moses was on the way to meet the elders, God was going to kill him because he didn't circumcise his son on the eighth day ? The number eight represents eternity. If you don't follow the law you are suppose to die. Moses wife circumcised her son and threw the foreskins on Moses feet. Just like a woman to save the day. When Christ came it became circumcision of the heart. Yahshuah cut sin away from our hearts. We can meet God in covenant ,have a relationship with God and know Yahshuah as our father. It doesn't matter who are natural parents are . God had to get us here. Make it personal with God and watch what he does. Do you know God's done it all for you? Do you honor, praise,and give your service? What's restricting you from moving? Passover removed that yolk. Yolk meaning what holds you to the burden. The burden means sin. Natural man doesn't bring the kingdom. Acting and thinking like God does.*

Then in Exodus chapt 6 vs 6, God takes Israel through his cycles. I am Yahveh. I will bring you out from out of oppression of the Eyptians. I will free you from slavery. I will rescue you with my powerful arm and with my mighty acts of judgement. Then I will make you my people and I will be your God. You will know that I am Yahveh your God who brought you out from under the forced labor of the Eyptians. I will bring you to the land . I solely swore to give Abraham, Issac and Jacob. I will give it to you as a possession. I am Yahveh. See how God keeps saying bring. God's cycles in the spirit are tied to God's feasts. Festival means cycle(circle). Every year tied to the cycle of the moon. Sowing and reaping are tied to the agricultural cycle. Just go through God's cycles which are cycles of blessing.

Satan mimics God. Satan's a law breaker. He takes the things of God by force and doesn't respect the things of God. God taught us to fight with our mouths and satan taught us not to speak. Things work in this world by speaking. We rather follow the cycles of destruction which consists of rebellion, oppression, captivity, and deliverance. Then we repeat this cycle over and over again. The people didn't want to listen to the spirit on Moses they wanted to continue in works. Does that sound familiar? We always want to make it about what we can do. Which points to self effort. God wants to work through us...... God gives us freedom of choice. Pharoah thought of himself as God. Then we see where God sent all these Plagues and we finally get to Passover. Passover was a sader meal. That they ate before they left Eypt. The lamb represented Yahshuah and the bitter herbs represent the bitter life, they were leaving behind. Everything on that plate meant something. The Matzah is made with no yeast meaning it was unleven. Leven is a type and shadow of sin. The haroset represents the mortar which was used to make bricks. The Karpas (non bitter vegetable dipped in salt) represents a new life and the tears of slavery. Then you have the cup of wine which I will discuss later. The blood on the door from the lamb was the remission of sin in all Eypt. The first born and the lamb were a foreshadow of Christ. He was the sacrifice that brough salvation. Why was the blood on the door instead of the floor? Can't thread on the blood. Anything on the floor is unworthy. That's why the devil is under your feet. God brings us back in harmony. Man's suppose to be in harmony and unity with God. God began the beginning of months for us and established a New Year for us when he took them out of Eypt. The New Year was established on what he's done and a specific way of doing things. God brings you out full, walk in the transfer. God did all this. God brought them out at night, showing your victory over darkness. God brought Pharaoh to his knees, people were wailing and crying. God gives us a instruction for every attack. Slow down in this world so you can pick up speed in the spirit. God told them if they listen carefully and do what is right he wouldn't make them suffer the diseases of the Eyptians. God commands us because a command is the best possible way to live. God should know and we have a enemy out there. God did everything for us because of grace. Which is God's loving kindness. We had to do nothing. Passover was before the law and so was grace. Grace did what the law couldn't do. Grace is like a life insurance policy that you get after someone dies. Believe in the blood. We always focus on satan. What does the kingdom of God have to do with the world? There's no sin in the third heaven. If anything the world is hindering you. Especially when you mingle it with God's kingdom. The vineyard is our heart and you grow what you plant. Grace has to be displayed for it to abound. You do that by being gracious. The grace of Yahshuah, he became poor so we could be rich when he died on the cross.

Add God –you=fullness of grace Israel says grace after a meal. God says if you have eaten and you are full you ought to bless the Lord. To bless somebody you have to say something.

Here's some food for thought.

Yahshuah our Passover lamb. The lamb was a male of the first year---Yahshuah was raised before the fourth day.

The lamb had no blemish—Yahshuah was without blemish

The death penalty was imposed when the lamb was chosen—Christ came to receive the death penalty to free us from the bondage of sin

The lamb was killed at three-Yahshuah died at three

The lambs bones weren't broken—Yahshuah's bones weren't broken

The lamb was eaten the same night—Yahshuah was crucified, suffered and died the same night

The blood on the door saved the Israelites firstborn—The blood of Christ shed on the cross which saves us all

No work done on Passover—The blood saves us not our works

The Israelites left Eypt quickly so their bread didn't have time to rise. So it was unleven which is a type and shadow of Christ in the tomb. Christ was made sin and he took that sin to the grave. A sinful man couldn't carry the weight of sin, it's to heavy. A dirty rag can't clean dirt, it would just spread it around. You need something clean to remove dirt. Then you have the Feast of first fruits which represents the source of Israel's light which is God.

God will always direct your life. After firstfruits they started counting the omer. Then we come to Pentecost. I will discuss the feasts later in my book.

In chapter 14 we see Pharoah chasing the Israelites meaning death is always chasing you. Most of us live from the tree of good and evil. Just because something is good doesn't necessarily mean God thinks it's good. There was some good on that tree of knowledge but we have to live by what God says is good. God provided manna for them. Their shoes and clothes didn't wear out. So you know God was super naturally providing for them. Even after all this the people still complained and turned back in their minds to Eypt. Eypt is a type and shadow of the world. Meaning they wanted to go back to their old lives. When God wanted to take them to the promise land. Another incident the people cried for water and made Moses strike the rock more than once and cost him going into the promise land. God told him to speak to the rock not strike the rock. The rock represented Christ.

Then in chapter 19 God spoke in seventy languages all at the same time at Mount Sinai. So why would God send a book from heaven by Gabriel. How did they know it was Gabriel nobody knew what Gabriel looks like it could have been Lucifer. Lucifer masquerades as a angel of light. Ezra translated the bible in Aramaic way before the Quran. He was a Jewish Priest who came from captivity in Babylon. The people adopted some of the culture while in captivity. They said Aramaic should be a Jewish Language. I understand when they say God inspired the writers of the bible. I constantly hear God in my heart talk. My spirit bears witness with God's. Acts chapter 2vs2 God spoke to seventy nations. God moved from the mountain to men. We are God's masterpiece.

Now God brings the law. The law came in so you know what sin is. God doesn't need anything when God wants something it's for us. Sin we have to deal with. If we look at what or father did we would know we overcame. The devil will throw sin at you. The devil presents your life to you. We need to forgive so we can be set free .God gave us the ten commandments which is a outline. There are 613 laws. Now how are you going to keep all those laws? If laws were really in their hearts, you would see it in the way they live. When they say God is jealous. It's just like you have a mate who cheats on you. How would you feel? You always have to flip the script.

Now we get to chapt 23. About Passover. So everytime there is a feast God tells us not to come empty handed. If we come empty handed we are saying God didn't do anything.

Exodus 26vs16 talks of the ark of the covenant. The ark was a chest which carried the tablets with two angels engraved on the side. Now ark means coffin in Hebrew. The tablets represented Yahshuah and the angels were guarding the way back to God. We all Know Yahshuah said he was the way not a Christian. The word Christian came a 100 years after he died. Coffin means burial and bed. I thought about Yahshuah in the ground. I just found this a little interesting. Believers have been cut from our Hebraic roots. . Then God talks about the throne of the mercy seat that covers the chest. This is where Christ's, Blood was laid on the mercy seat. So every time God looks at us he sees what Christ done. The tablets are the word of the promise. The promise is Yahshuah. I just wanted to add this where it says never cook a goat in it's mother's milk it's because that's the source it came from. When the priest represented us they would go into the holy of holies once a year. If they didn't do the sacrifice right they would burn up. The priest would have a rope around him in case they had to pull his body out. Everything had to be just right. We all know the story when the people made the calf 3000 people died. I guess it was interesting cause 3000 people were saved in the book of Acts. .By the sacrifices sin was covered but with Yahshuah are sins were taken away. We have to understand the heart of God and make it personal. No human effort. Moses could only go so far. Moses didn't have the Holy spirit. Moses wanted to be special. Moses saw God's glory. Where God says he will be kind to anyone he wants to God's talking about saved people, people connected to him .

God revealed himself to Moses 33 vs 23 God put his hand in the way so Moses could see his back side. God was to powerful he would of consumed Moses. Two ways you know someone by their name and their face. Then God tells Moses what his name means. A compassionate, merciful El, patient always faithful and ready to forgive. He continues to show his love to thousands of generations, forgiving wrong doing, disobedience. and sin. God's about justice he never lets the guilty go unpunished, punishing children and grandchildren for their parents sins to the third and fourth generation. (people who don't love or obey God) The cycle goes on. The people were disobedient and didn't have God's spirit.

Exodus 34 vs 32-33 Is where it talks about Asherah which is a pagan goddess which means wife . God tells us not to worship other Gods. When you see a Ashrah pole that's a altar for a sacrifice different then our God. Ashrah is a form of ashtaroth which is a form of Astarte. Astarte is where easter comes from. She was a fertility goddess. That's where you get the eggs and the rabbits. There were also prostitutes that practiced their rituals in the pagan churches. God warned them not to do what the neighboring people did. God knew that men chase skirts. The woman will take the man away from what he believes. A man's lust will take over. I say the man's the head but the woman has the power. Besides what does easter mean? When God says something it means something. So I say skip those easter outfits and invest in God's Kingdom. The church has no power. Do you think God's going to share his altar with something else? Then God tells them how to sacrifice and what feasts to participate in. As you read down the number 40 represents a preparation and a pruning period. Example Moses was on the mountain for forty days, and Yahshuah in the wilderness tempted by the devil for forty days. Then we go on and God tells us how to come to him. Then we come to the end of Exodus. Which you can read for yourself.

Chapter 4

He Called

The Feasts are God's seasons and they are a constant reminder of our deliverance. God meant for the Jewish people to teach his plan so shouldn't we look at what they did. Instead of Roman Greco philosophy which tells us the body is evil and must be silenced. Jewish people are 2% of the population but hold 24% of the wealth. Might of fact the Jewish people helped America become a nation when they broke off from Britain. America ran out of money and the Jewish people came through for them. America's the spiritual Israel. That's getting ready to go into captivity . I will explain a little farther in my book.

Now we get to Leviticus which means law and God called. God showed the people how to come to him. Life is in the blood. The people no longer had the spirit of God. The Holy spirit was in Adam and Yahshuah. God had to show Israel how to atone for sin. So they could come in his presence. Sin came about because of man's disobedience. This disobedience was put on Christ. All scripture is geared towards Christ. The law leads to Christ. Christ came to fulfill the law. Man could never keep all 613 laws. The ten commandments were called the ten words. These ten words were the outline for the laws. These words allowed us to know what sin is. All the feasts that Israel participated in represented Christ. God had to show them visually so they would understand. I call them God's seven step redemption plan for man. Which I listed them in the beginning but here we go again.

Passover-died for us

Unlevenbread-made sin in ground

Firstfruits-rose up first of many brothern not easter

Pentecost-power

Trumpets-awakening

Atonement-one with God, self examination

Tabernacles-together with God

Yahshuah did four of the feasts we better believe he's coming back to do the other three

The animals they used were innocent and without blemish. Those animals didn't do anything but God used them in our place like Christ. The priest washed the animals and cleansed the temple. John the Baptist washed Yahshuah. The lamb had to be washed. Yahshuah did everything. When God took them out of Eypt, he began their months, in two six month intervals. This was considered their spiritual birth because they already had a natural birth . God's spirit use to come on people back then now his spirit comes in us. God plays numbers to show us something. When satan plays numbers it's for lustful reasons. God was showing us, he would make a way for us to come back to him. You couldn't come to God any old way. God is holy. Which means sacred and set apart. God is everywhere but he won't be anywhere. God's calling us. Prayer is the response to the call. We have to recognize we are sinful and God is holy. We always want God to come down to us. When God is always trying to raise us up. In the New Testament God wrapped those 613 laws into two. Everything is God's. So God asks us to bring the choice parts, which is the best. These sacrifices represented Christ.

Chapt 3 vs 9 This is where the principal came of how they would do the altar. After all these sacrifices, God tells them to send out a scapegoat to see if their sins were forgiven. Yahshuah's our scapegoat, so we know our sins are forgiven. Then God goes through all the different laws. 12 vs 11 talks about the blood making atonement for the soul. So how do those other beliefs deal with sin? Leviticus 18 God made man to rule over the earth, but when man sinned, he became one with the earth. This made nature sick and confused. So when we don't live a certain way the earth doesn't respond the way God ordained it to. The earth rejects our behavior. God shows us how to live in all areas of our life. Like I said the bible is the government for the spirit man. The spirit realm is the realm for us. We were made from God who is a spirit. We were made to live from the Holy spirit. So why do we put so much into the natural man who is defeated. We are concerned about us when we should be concerned about Yahshuah. When the priest did the sacrifices for the people he didn't get any land but shared in what God had. So what happened? Constantine made the priest take a vow of poverty. Constantine changed the state religion to Christianity but he never renewed his mind. Christianity was the minority, so how can you change a majority with a lie? It's not going to happen. That's natural man's always trying to figure it out if it doesn't make sense to him. We will never be able to figure God out. Never in all eternity. God called his feasts appointed times so what better time to meet with God. During his feasts you know where God is. Every seven years was a year of rest. Even the land was to rest. One reason Israel went into captivity in Babylon was because they didn't let the land rest. So every year the land didn't rest they spent seven in captivity. The seventh year was called the Shiemitah year. The year of release. Then you had the year of Jubilee. Which happens every fifty years. Everything is released and goes back to it's original owner. Teshuva is Yom Kipper God's New Year. We follow God's feasts so we can remember. Teshuva ties in with Tabernacles so if we remember, we know we will be scooped up. We just don't know which one. In Thessalonians it says we won't be caught off guard like the rest of the world. Because we know what we believe and know the order of things on God's calendar. We celebrate the feasts according to the spirit. God said they are his feasts so why do we say they are Jewish feasts?

Leviticus 22 through 26 God talks about dedicating. We should partake in winning souls and releasing these souls from bondage. Those that want to sit don't need the anointing. Learn to pursue the enemy. When the enemy increases the anointing increases. When the assignment increases the anointing increases. God is Christ centered not man centered. Focus on his son. Satan gets you to focus on you. Focus on the shining in your heart, anointed with power. God's not about feelings but his plan. Look for the truth God shows us how to overcome death. Israel didn't have the full affect because they didn't have the spirit. Partake of the call. This is a type and shadow of us coming out of the world. Live from the harvest. God put disobedience on his son. Yahshuah broke the power of sin. Tithing -give

God the first part so the rest is blessed. The ten gives God the right to empower the other ninety. God has a system for everything in our lives In 26 vs 27 God talks about discipline then seven times in the New Testament it talks of how Yahshuah put all this on himself.

In chapt 31 Israel wasn't a nation but a desert and they, didn't hear God. God's faithful. God doesn't need to be our God we need him to do it in their face. In the Old Testament it was a lot of physical labor. We need to be committed to the things of God. Vs 26 All about Yahshuah. Why do we handle the word of God like man is talking.

Chapter 5
Census

Now we get to the census. The duties of the priest, military, and going to the promise land. Kings go to war. All this is government. Then God talks of all the tribes.

Chapter 4 How Yahshuah paid the price. We need to look at the bible prophetically. God explains everyone's specific duties and jobs.

Chapter 6 vs 22 God put his blessing and name on his people. The blessing is a empowerment to succeed. The Lord bless you and keep you (In all your endevors) The Lord make his face shine upon you and be gracious to you (care and loving kindness) The Lord turn his face towards you and give you peace. God established Israel as his people.

In chapter 9 God allowed them to have a second chance . It was the second year from their deliverance from Eypt and the second represented some who missed the first passover because of uncleanness. He's the God of second chances. When God brings you out it's with prosperity. We need to partake of what God has done and do what God tells you to do. We have to take responsibility for the atmosphere. Hint-Hint church. The second Passover showed God's mercy and grace. God's willingness to meet you and give you a chance to offer to him. This shows the goodness of the lord. Remember the first part of the spiritual year on the calendar carries you through the year. If he doesn't get it first what does that mean? God's determined for us to get it. After we are taken up in the rapture 144,000 will evangelize the world. The Holy spirit loves you in spite of you. So we ought to lay down our lives for the brothern. The enemy just presents the life we think is ours to us. We should never act like *our job adds to our life it should be the other way around. The Father never cuts you off but still blesses you. It's us recognizing the move of God.*

Chapter 10 Who God is? Blowing the Shaphar over our offering . When we do this it is to remind us , God remembers our giving. Then in chapter 12 tells where Miriam and Aaron oppose Moses. God showed me that his audible voice over rides a vision. It's like God himself. The word. God looked at Moses as a friend . Moses got it straight from God's mouth so all the prophets had to line up with what Moses said.

Then in chapter 13 the spies were sent out to scope the land. Only two Caleb and Joshua knew they could conquer the land. The other people doubted because the enemy was bigger and they were scared. So the only ones that made it to the promise land who were over twenty years of age were Caleb and Joshua. They had a different kind of spirit and God didn't give us a spirit of fear. All God scriptures link together. They forgot who God is.

Chapter 15 It speaks of grain and wine which is another form of communion. Then it talks of Koran's followers who were against the man of God. God had the ground open up and swallow them, their families, and all their possessions. Then God allowed Aaron's staff to bud so they would know who God put in charge. Everytime you see water it represents the living water. The Holy spirit.

Chapter 20 Water from a rock. Moses was leadership and responsible for the people who aggravated him. Moses struck the rock twice which represented Christ. The rock should only of been hit once. This cost Moses going into the promise land. When much is given much is required. It's not that you do something, it's how you do it. Isn't that like us thinking we have to do something when God's already done it. God gave Moses the instruction to speak but he chose to hit the rock instead. God said that rebellious spirit is not going into the promise land like sin is not going into the new heaven. God took care of all the enemies on the way to the promise land. Self was the greatest enemy so the ones who were about self didn't enter the promise land. Balak the king of Moab hired Balaam, a seer to curse Israel, he felt there were to many Israelites. Balaam ended up blessing the people instead of cursing them. God wouldn't allow Balaam to see sin in any of the Israelites. God was covering them. All those people and no sin? In the Old Testament God was always covering the people since the spirit was gone. God had to make sure the fight was fair. Like the Father and his children. You figure man was defeated and lower than the demonic forces that ruled the earth.

In Baalam's fourth prophecy Numbers 24:37 talks of a star. That star is Yahshuah. The star is a sign for us to see where we are going. Then it talks of crushing the heads of the Moabites. That's Yahshauh's authority. So Balaam had the spirit of compromise. He told the king he would have to get the people out of covenant with God. He told him to bring the Moabite women to the camp. So the men slept with those foreign women .So God sent a plague where 24,000 were killed .Remember the wages of sin is death .So you had to die. So Phinehas killed the man and woman who started it. There are many voices in the the land. Spirits speak to you. So if you listen to that spirit you claim that thought as your own. That's why Yahshuah tells you to take every thought captive. Hold it hostage and interrogate it and see if it lines up with God. Then there's another census. Zelophehed's Daughters fought for their rights. Four sisters united who had no brothers or a father. Moses had to give them their land after he consulted with God. God always provides, we just have to keep going. It's power in numbers. Ladies in Christ we have to stand together. Then he talks about the sacrifices all 7,14,21 meaning completion. You can read that.

Chapter 32 Shows if you don't do what you are suppose to judgement always follows.

Now we get to the end of chapter 33 .Number 33 vs 8 They complained of water, they only had a three day travel and they would of ran into 12 palm trees . One for each tribe. So if you see trees you know there's water. Lesson here patience .God gave the Israelites a form of government. Can't say that enough. God told the Israelites to push the enemy out. They didn't do it . So the enemy became a everlasting thorn in their side . It's going to be like that till Yahshuah comes back. Some people say God was mean but God had to show his power so they would listen to him and know he is God. Remember the spirit was gone. God gives us boundaries.

I thought this was interesting chapter 35vs 36 speaks of a hit man.

Chapter 6

Say It Again

Now we come to the book of Deuteronomy which is the last book of the Torah. This book means the say it again laws. Maybe God says it again because we didn't get it the first time.

Chapter 1 vs 9 What God said to Abraham. He is faithful. He who promised is faithful. God always wants you to have a better life. Who wants a bad life? Vs 5 talks about empowering the man of God. Talks about making life a 1000 times better. Then it talks of when God told them to go fight and they didn't do it. Then they wanted to fight without God's okay and got whipped. When you don't do what God tells you to when you are suppose to it's a missed opportunity. So when God tells us to do something it's for our own good. God doesn't hold anything against us . God faith is right now. David eventually defeated the giants when he came on the scene.

This book is a book of rememberance in chapter 3 we see how God can be in manifested time. God's not subject to time we are. God is telling Moses to look at the land because he won't enter. Then God told Moses to go up the mountain and die. Moses was still strong and he still had good eyesight. Moses was 120 when he died. In chapter 4 we see God as our wisdom. We should be a example for the world .So they can see God's glory through us. Fear means respect . God wants us to leave a legacy for our children. He never meant for it to die with us. How are our kids going to be able to stand if we don't teach them? Then he talks more about the ten commandments so the people wouldn't make a idol.

Chapter 5 vs 4 Talks about the people being scared when God spoke on the mountain. If they were really scared they would of did what God said. Children will be punished if they keep doing what their parents did. Hopefully you will recognize what's happening and not go down that road. So history won't repeat itself. Now you get to chapter 5 vs 20 It speaks of why there's a curse. They were under the curse because they left God and were disobedient. The only thing they had was the law. So that was all they could get was the penalty for the law. When they were disobedient they weren't covered by God. Once God commits, it becomes law. God is bound by his law. God is a judge and he does everything by his book. There's no mystery in God.

Then chapter 6 speaks of the Shema(the Jewish confession of faith) which God expects us to hear and do. Then it will go well with us. We have to do it after we hear it ,so it can go well with us. God's desire for us is to leave a legacy .God says he's one God. The people worshipped many gods so they didn't know the real one. They had gods for the moon, sun, air ,water etc. If you hear you increase prosperity. God is more than enough. So we should prosper the way God ordained us to. Outside of division . We are always going somewhere God isn't. Where God says might he's talking about money. God's going back over what he gave us. It's all in the way you see. If you don't get it in your heart your never going to get it on the outside. It gets in by what you see and hear. In chapter 6 vs 14 God's explaining how he's devoted and Israel is like a adulterous wife. God is jealous. How would you feel if your wife cheated on you? God's like a consuming fire and he is always trying to lift us up. At this time God could only deal with them in the flesh. In the end of this chapter God tells us to obey the law of the land. For he gave us the best possible way to live. He wants us to be in proper alignment so we would eat off the tree of life. The tree of life is what God says is good.

Chapter 7 vs 5 talks about destroying the pagan holiday easter. In 14 talks about Israel being blessed. God also talks about not taking something bad and using it for good . Example using drug money and doing something for God.

Chapter 8 The land God gave Israel was plentiful in minerals and resources. Live and increase. You live by being careful of what God said to do. When you live it causes you to obtain certain things and promises. The word of God sustains you. We should see Israel's mistakes so we don't make the same ones. God sent manna, spiritual food from heaven. God doesn't want us to live by natural means. Things we associate with us we think bring life. We have to understand natural things so we will understand spiritual things. The church is suppose to be the ground and pillar of the truth . So why does the church look like the world? If we don't live the word we are no different then the world and living a lie. God gave us something we weren't capable of getting on our own. For specific reasons we have to live by God's word. No ability from us. So we need to stop living off what we can do and live by God's word. Manna didn't exsist in this world. The Word can bring you the impossible. The word can handle situations and circumstances. You can't afford to miss the word like you can't afford to miss a meal. If we rightfully divide the truth we show wisdom of the church. The word gets in our minds and changes our behavior. Then transformation occurs. God's inside out. If we understand we can live out –then prove it out . Which is proof of application. Stop looking for a miracle. Live by obeying God's word. People are lazy. The devil can do miracles but he can't do the word. Pharoah's magicians did miracles. The devil can trick you. The Word will expose you. The Word is God. Anybody can preach the word. But can they do it. It shows in their life after church.

Sinner------saint

No name-----name

Old -----new

By the word of God

If the word of God can do this what makes you think it can't change your finances. As we go on we are to glorify our Lord. If we do what God says it will come to pass. God's not subject to time we are. God calls the people stiff neck meaning they were unmoved, stubborn. They didn't listen. If you don't listen life will destroy you. Are you like Yahshuah or the devil? There's nothing bigger then God . God's finished work cancelled out our debt and made us forgiven. People are cursed because they left God. God put all 613 laws on

Yahshuah when he died on the cross. One law was whoever is hung on a tree is cursed. Why do you think God said you can't love your life? The enemy will use anything in your life against you.

Chapter 16 God is the best. Blood represents Life. No remission of sin without blood. God gave us a new life line when he came as Yahshuah. Celebrate. The feasts are a type and shadow of Yahshuah. The feasts tell us what Yahshuah has done. The church broke away from God's feasts and picked up their own holidays that mean nothing. If you follow God's system everyone is blessed. By the church following the world's system you have the have and have nots . In God's church everyone has. Passover established the wealth transfer. You manifest the wealth transfer by having a biblical world view. Live from the source you were created from. Magnify corporate success. Believe the message. People believe for salvation but not predestination. When Yahshuah was on the cross , he emptied himself out, so we could have back what the enemy took from us. We should follow God's order. I had to go back and put this in. God knows everything. God's church is suppose to be nailing stuff. Through the gifts of the spirit. What do you think word of knowledge and word of wisdom are? The world mimics God pretty well. Man if you nail what people are going through, they will know you are the real deal. Now with prophesy anybody can talk. Vs 9 talks about detestable practices. About mediums, and fortunetellers. This is for all of you guys who enjoy the horoscopes. What word is in there? Horror. Why would you want to talk to the dead to find out what's happening in the land of the living? Now I want to point out vs 18 Moses says God will send a prophet like me. Meaning the prophet would be Hebrew, Muhammad's not Hebrew. Someone tried to say Muhammad's essence was around God in that case all of us were. God blew everybody's spirit into Adam. So if people don't believe this are they calling Moses a liar? Deuteromy is a part of the Torah. Ishmael was the son of the flesh not of the promise. Born of a slave woman , who wasn't in covenant and had no husband.

Chapter 21 vs 23 talks of a grown son who lives with his parents. This son is giving his parents a hard way to go. So God tells Israel to stone him. In the spirit , when you think stoned , you think of having it hard.

Chapter 22 vs 23 God placed a high value on women. Women came from the man's side not dirt .It talks about hanging sheets to prove if the girl was a virgin . They called this her tokens. God's always atoning for sin and sealing a covenant with blood. God is legal. Then he talks about not dishonoring your name . Names mean a lot to God. Then he talks about not giving your money as a prostitute. You can't take something bad and make it good. Also you make yourself one with everyone you sleep with. Only God can make you one. You attach yourself to all those different spirits. You join those spirits with yours. Every other sin is outside of the body.

Whatever you do for your brother do better, then you do for yourself in 24 it talks about passing women around. God never intended for men to pass women back and forth.

Chapter 25 vs 11-16 Help somebody get delivered , don't take life, from another person to help deliver a person. If you take a man's testicles, It's like robbing him of his future,life. It might have been possible to deliver the man without taking his future. Boundaries. Vs 13 Be consistent in what you do. Weight based on person not the truth. Vs 14 How we make decisions is it based on God or us? How do we use the word? Sometimes we need to stand down from what we want for the kingdom.

Chapter 26 vs 10-29 Wants us to understand when your in relationship with someone you give. At the end of this chapter God says we should be different. We are special and he always wants to raise us up. Why is it God is always trying to elevate us and we are always trying to bring him down to where we are?

Chapter 27 Talks about the importance of the word. The word written to God's people. God's people should listen to him. Blessing in keeping the word. Jacob's children, Abraham's seed. One mountain was for blessing the other for cursing. We have choices. Talks about many voices in the land. Do you know who is talking to you? Everything's calling. Those adamant spirits are always talking. Disobedience brings the curse. Then it talks about property laws, stealing, landmarks, sexually taking advantage,and family messes. Then it talks about uncovering your father's skirt which is sleeping with your father's wife. Corinthians 5 vs 1. Amen means we affirm it to be true . To agree and become people of

God in actions and words. How come we say if it's God's will? God's word is his will. Like I said the bible is the last will and testament. Which is a legal document. So why wouldn't we do his will which is what we get from the deposition of the will. If you don't obey God's word it won't help you no matter how much you love God. vs 25 Talks about a hit man. If you don't agree with God your not in agreement with God Chapter 28 Reaffirming, pick up in Christ. Blessing rolled into New Covenant. Abraham Covenant vs 1-8 vs 14 The law is the spirit of Christ. Yahshuah made us free from the law of sin and death. Flesh is under the curse, and it won't be redeemed. vs16-63 The law dominates the atmosphere. You sit down because of gravity. So you don't fly away. It's something when Yahshuah ascended in a cloud, he defied gravity. Law of light supercedes gravity. Greater law. Yahshuah was before the law. Law of light several forces violates law of gravity. Gravity holds you down. Yahshuah rescued us and is the light. Then he talks about you getting what you sow. Fruits of disobedience. The outer man is dying day by day. So you should obey God so the spirit man will grow and be strong. Allow the spirit man to pick up speed so he will change the outer man. You will see it on the outside. Remember everything can be corrupt but God. Walk by faith because you don't see God. Then it talks of the shaphar being the mouth of a prince. It's also a trumpet which is meant to set the captives free. It says attention to us and occupy until he comes back. He means in the spirit not the natural. We are to link together and hold the enemy back. Business value. Measure you meet. What or how you feel about it. I'm trying to break stuff down, so you can really understand. Understanding is being able to see what's going on. A lot of my writings are notes inspired by God. All my bibles have notes in them. As I was reading God was talking.

Chapter 29 God wants to be in covenant with us but he never forces us. verse 24 That's the end. You have to realize the Old Testament is prophetic. It's what's going to come. Prophesy is what is forseen. When you line up the blessing comes on you in the Old Testament. In The New Testament, you believe. Verse 29 talks about things hidden. There's no mystery in God. He let's you Know. He has to he's a judge and all the evidence has to be disclosed. There's not going to be a mistrial. Then God says choose Life over death. Meaning live from the substance you came from because that's where you came from. God's very repetitious. God wants to wake up your spirit. Trust me if you meditate on God's word diligently and be in hot pursuit of it something in God's word will wake your spirit up. God's word is the substance the spirit was created from. The bible is food for the spirit man. The natural can't receive it . The natural man is the substance of the world. God explains why Moses isn't going into the promise land. Look for joy don't stay in pain. God is before us. Movement doesn't necessarily mean progress. Look at them wandering around in the wilderness 40 years. God wants us to be who he called us to be. When God talks of the nations, he's talking of all those things against us. God's bigger then all that.

In 32 Moses tells them how to keep going with God. Moses is telling the story of the father. How do I make a good decision? By listening to the father .Jeshurun is a pet name for Israel . God's words can be anything. In this song Moses is telling who God is and what God's done. Moses talks of God being dependable, steady. Talks of Abraham and Issac. How he was already here. How he made stuff from nothing. Talks about boundaries and territory. That he gave the tribes. Talks about the people being his inheritance. and him taking care of Jacob. We know God changed Jacob's name to Israel. He says Jacob here because he wants you to know who he's taking about. God said to me all are not Israel. God wants you to know he's talking about Jacob's line not Ishmael's. The song talks about God being supernatural and the best. God says don't insult him by chasing after other gods. How would you feel if your mate were cheating on you? Tells you how nothing has value but him. It also speaks of the causes and effects of things. It's all about the decisions we make. If we put something in front of God, that's what we are devoted to. What gets me people don't want to believe the bible. It's not just words on paper. The people were taught in songs. So you just sing it over and over. You will remember. I bet some of you can remember your favorite song from thirty years ago. You probably remember all the words to.

In chapter 33 Moses blesses the tribes. We have a better blessing in the spirit Yahshuah. Tells Israel they are blessed.(seed) Know why, you are happy. Blessing from Moses Happy, Fortunate and Prosperous. Saved by the Lord. The shield and sword exalts you. God showed Israel naturally how to get a harvest. They had to plant a seed. It's still the same principal in the spirit. The word has to be planted in the heart and done.

In the last chapter it tells how Joseph followed Jacob's footsteps. It showed how he had a relationship with God. When Moses died he was a 120 years old. He wasn't sick, had good eyesight and was strong. God showing us here if you don't do what I say you die. Now it's a spiritual death. Moses name means drawn out .

CHAPTER 7
HISTORY

Now I'm going to leave the foundation books and move on to the history part. If I forgot something I will add it at the end. I'm just trying to give you some of the insight God gave me. Since God's people are so clueless. God says the world is smarter then his people. Joshua means the Lord is Salvation. Joshua took over wear Moses left off. He took the people into the promise land. God gave them. Everything God gives you, you have to go get. Just like Yahshuah says the violent take heaven by force . That's spiritually. Since we moved from the land to the soul. The enemy is not going to give you what's yours. Joshua was a very apprehensive warrior. God gave Joshua authority. God appears to Joshua and tells him to rise up and go. Enjoy the new life I have for you. Don't fear be bold and strong, follow instructions. I need you to meditate day and night on the word. This shows consistency. How you see makes your way prosperous. Joshua didn't think he could do it. He thought Moses was great. Success is in the routine. Diligence. Vs 1-5 Focus on word. Later focus on Yahshuah=success. The people God talks about in chapter one are Iran, and Iraq, It's important for us to meditate. Meditation allows you to see. Like I said earlier you see with your mind through your eyes. We want to see the way God does. Meditation is how you prosper. Prosperity is more than money. If you meditate on God's word , you wll eventually get wisdom. Once you get wisdom , you will make good decisions. Meditate means to mutter. When you keep saying it to yourself ,it gets in your mind and changes the way you think. Meditate, observe to do. (Allows you to see) Look at things not seen. Like I said you see through your mind through your eyes. Actually you see upside down and your mind turns it right side up. So why trust what you see naturally, without seeking God? Live by what you see in your mind. Walk by faith. Not aimlessly.

We all know that Joshua had a great victory with Jericho with the help of Rahab. So why are we so fast to turn our noses up at people. When Rahab tied the scarlet cord in the window , that was a form of Passover. God passed over her house. In chapter five the men who weren't killed in the wilderness made a covenant with God, through circumcision. It was pretty interesting to me Jericho was called sin moon city. Then God steps down in time to talk to Joshua. So how come people trip on God coming as the son? To much of natural man thinking. Always trying to reason.

Then you have some victories and some losses. The losses where because the people didn't listen. Achan stole and the people suffered. Then Israel was deceived by the people in Gibeon and they forever became a thorn in Israel's side. In chapter 10 it talks of the sun standing still. So Joshua could have more day light to fight the enemy. This was a whole book of fighting and conquering the land and the distributing of the land to the twelve tribes. In the New Testament the land changes to souls. It went from a natural fight to a spiritual fight. Everyone in the old Testament could fight. Abraham, Moses, Joshua. Are you fighting?

The next book we have is Judges. God appointed judges as leadership to his people. This chapter deals with disbelief, lack of faith and hyprocrisy. God's against humanism. God expresses early on fight together. It's power in numbers and the blessing is in unity. So why do we always want to be by ourselves. The enemy wants you to be by yourself so you will be a sitting duck. Then it's easy to prick you off. That's a military tactic. The god of this world counterfeited all of God's stuff. Satan gave the people the God of religion. People are ready to die for this country but won't stand up for God. When people carried their crosses they were literally going to their deaths. We made such a fashion statement out of the crosses we know nothing about bearing it. This society makes Yahshuah look weak. There's nothing weak about him. It must of took everything for him not to snatch the devil up or call a legion of angels to fight for him. He was willing to die for the cause. The king and the kingdom. The king is the Holy spirit. They are one and the same. Every disciple died horribly. Peter hung upside down on the cross. Paul beheaded. James skinned and split in half. John was exciled to Patmos. They were unable to kill him until his assignment was finished. Bartholmeow was flogged and hung upside down on the cross. Thomas was martyred in India. Andrew was crucified. We all know what happened to Judas. I don't have to much to say about this book except you had several leaders.

Deborah was a prophetess and went to war.

Then you had Gideon who was terrified. God was with him. God allowed him to get a victory with only three hundred men. God told him to pick the men that ate their food like a lap dog. Meaning they were always watching even while eating. I believe that's how God's remnant will be. God showed me the remnant will be those walking in the spirit. People like this world to much that's, why there's only a remnant (warriors). God's making disciples and uniting churches. It doesn't make a difference of the faith or denomination.

I think the judge everyone remembers is Samson. Samson didn't understand God's character. He was a Nazarene. Meaning he was dedicated to God. His down fall wasn't just his hair, but women, alcohol,and coming into contact with a dead body. His sight was taken just like our spiritual sight. There were a few others but you can read the book. I have quite a ways to go and I want the book to be short enough so you read the whole thing. Just remember the bible's not in chronological order.

The next book in line is Ruth. Her name means friendship. This book is about a kinsman redeemer. How you and your stuff can be redeemed back. God like I said had to show us naturally. He became our kinman's redeemer. God did everything in the New Testament he did in the Old Testament. He was correcting his finished work. We are suppose to pick up where he left off. It's more of us to do his will, which is his word.

I told you I would only say what God wants now we get to Samuel. Samuel was from the tribe of Ephriam not Levi. Melchizedek set the order. This was before Israel divided. Samuel was a prophet, priest and a judge in the natural. Yahshuah was a priest(offered himself up) king and prophet spiritually. Samuel means voice of the spirit. If a person tells you they are a prophet ask them what's the message? Yahshuah is a prophet which is the voice of God. He is a king meaning he rules and reigns like a judge. He was the last and perfect sacrifice. God doesn't look on the external but the internal. Israel wanted to look like the other nations. They discredited the ministry. They didn't want a judge they wanted *a king like everyone else. This book is about Samuel, Saul, Israel's first king and David Israel's most beloved king. In first Samuel Dagon a false God was placed next to God's ark. The first day the statue Dagon fell forward. Meaning everyone will bow. The next day he fell over again with his head and hands broke off. Meaning the authority and strength will be broken. How can we think we can place anything next to God's altar and have power? It won't happen. Then you have the sons of Belial who were covenant people who didn't know their covenant keeping God. Sound's like some church people to me. King Saul's name means asked. We all know the story of Hannah who was unable to conceive and God opened her womb. In chapter 2 we see Hannah praying. She's praising and acknowledging who God is. So how come when we pray we are always asking God for something? Like God doesn't know what we need. Prayer is communication. So how come when we pray it's one sided? Then we see Hannah dedicated Samuel to God. Samuel went to live with Eli .Eli's sons were sinful. They disobeyed God. They took the best part of the sacrifices for themselves. They slept with the women and offered God strange fire. Meaning they gave God what he didn't want. Some say that they were doing sacrifices drunk. Eli didn't correct his family. So God raised up some one else. After that no man in Eli's family lived passed fifty. Both Eli's sons died in war . Eli was fat, fell backwards in his chair broke his neck and died. Fat meaning he was fat in knowledge falling backwards meaning he was rebellious. Knowledge puffs up but love edifies. Knowledge doesn't do any good if you don't do anything with it. No one gets helped. I already spoke of God's altar being captured. Do you honesty think God is going to share his altar with the easter bunny or santa clause. God showed me the altar is for sacrificing so what are we giving up besides our problems. I never seen the disciples running to the altar. The altar should be for the world to run to not us. We have to many converts and not enough disciples. The ark was still in captivity but the Philistines sent it back with five gold tumors to represent the tumors they received on their bodies . This was a guilt offering .The number five represents the number grace. Half way on the journey the people looked in the ark and seventy died. God's ark is holy. So the ark stayed there twenty years.*

Chapter 7 vs 3 talks about coming back to God wholeheartedly not just in appearance. Then it talks about Astarte. Where easter comes from. That pagan holiday that means nothing. God calls the resurrection firstfruits. You also have those who will argue about the resurrection .Let them have that because it means you die, come to life and die again. Like Lazarus. Then Samuel got old and his sons didn't follow in his footsteps. So the people rejected God and wanted a king like the world. Now the king rules the kingdom which is his government. The U.S was under British rule before we were the U.S. So how did we make God's word religion? They picked Saul as king because he was tall and goodlooking. The Lord was with Saul until he didn't listen. First he did the sacrifice when the priest was suppose to. Next he left the king when God told him not to leave any survivors. God would have them kill everybody so they wouldn't follow their customs. Then I think Saul kept some of the loot when God told him not to. Saul's character wasn't right. He was a immature leader which effected the multitudes. Saul also sacrificed to God but it wasn't the best stuff. God told him he preferred obedience over sacrifice. What does it matter if you give God something but your heart isn't in it and you don't listen to God.

Then God prepares to get a new king for ISRAEL. So Samuel went to Jesse's house. He goes through seven brothers before he gets to David. David's scrawny and, ruddy but he's a kid with a big heart. Jesse was like David's nothing, common compared to his other muscular sons. He didn't think to much of David. God doesn't look at outward appearance. God looks at the heart. The heart also consists of the mind. God looks and sees where your thinking process is. David was musically inclined. God showed me Saul was bipolar. So David soothed Saul with music. When spirits came to his mind. They come to our's all the time but it's what your mind is willing to grab hold to. We have to hold each thought captive and line it up with God's word. So we need to know God's word. We all know the story of David and Goliath. I just want to say one thing. David beat Goliath with the word of God. As he threw the stone one of five (number of grace) he said you uncircumcised giant. Meaning Goliath had no covenant with God. God's faithful and will honor his covenants. David was in covenant with God and God's grace showed up. If we want the power we need to be saying God's word. Another thing about David he was willing to take responsibility for his actions whether good or bad. David became good friends with Johnathan Saul's son. They were like brothers.

Chapter 5 vs 11 stone cutters (masons) They cut the stone for God's temple. This is second Samuel. I just wanted to point out I take people for who they are. Some people won't let masons do anything in church because of the fraternity. We make a issue out of someone being a mason but say nothing about putting a xmas tree next to God's altar. If that's not defiling God's atmosphere what is? David and Johnathan's friendship shows how you can be close in the Lord without being blood. David had victory after victory. Saul grew jealous of David and was always trying to kill him. Even though David was anointed as king it didn't happen till years later. He had to be prepared like Moses. How many of us value our brother? Our brothers have God's Holy spirit in them. So when we see them we should see God. Before Saul dies he goes to see a medium who brings Samuel's dead body up. God no longer talked to Saul. If you talk to God you don't need to talk to the dead. Besides talking to mediums and messing with ouji boards you don't know what kind of spirits you open yourself up to. Then Saul, Johnathan and the armbearer die.

Samuel 2 talks more about David. David becomes king first of Judah then Israel. David captured the fortress of Zion and built the city of Jerusalem. Which they call the city of David. David grew strong and powerful because God was with him. So how can anybody want to take Jerusalem from the Jewish people. David is Jewish and God said one of his descendants will sit on his throne. Yahshuah is Jewish, through his mother. Muslisms don't believe the Messiah came yet. They think Yahshuah was just a prophet. Who better to speak for you then you. I just wonder why they didn't stone him when he said he was God. I guess because Islam didn't come about till a hundred years after Yahshuah's death. David picked Jerusalem because it was easy to defend. David ministered to God. Minister means serve. So how come we don't serve? David pitched a tent for the ark of God. David instituted music in the tabernacle of God. The tabernacle of Moses didn't have music. David was a great warrior. He brought God's ark to Jerusalem.

The ark represents a contract and whoever has the contract will have God honoring it. On his first attempt a man got killed because they put it on a cart and it was falling so he went to catch it. That was a no no so he died. The ark was sacred so they left the ark in front of Obed's house. This man received blessing after blessing. He had God's contract so

God honored his contract. So this teaches us just because it's a good thing doesn't mean it's the right thing. Do the things of God the way he tells us. Seek God on how to do it . When David went back he made sure he had the priests. The ark was suppose to be carried on the shoulders of the priests. So the ark represents Yahshuah and he was a priest to offer himself up.

So when David got back to Jerusalem, he danced so hard ,he danced out of his clothes. Micah his wife watched him praise God and ridiculed him. She was barren until the day she died. So what does this tell us everything in her life is dead where God is concerned. Wonder why you have barren things in your life? People watch in church we made it a spectator event. When Hebrew people are expressive. The Lord is a celebratory God. So we should party before the Lord. We worry how we look in front of people. When you dance you get that spirit moving. Watch some old soul train clips if you have to. I guess it's easy to dance for us because it's something we want to do for us. God wants us to

Unshamingly praise him------------------Saul's daughter

Children of Abraham---------------------look on

Fruitful one----------------------------hinder, thorn, pulldown, reserved worship

Then David loved God so much he wanted to build a house for God. We never think about God but we always think about us. David was a man of war, so God told him he had to much blood on his hands. So Solomon would build God's house. David wanted to do something for the house of Saul. So he found Saul's grandson Mephibosheth who was paralyzed in both feet. He lived in Lodebar. So David went and got him gave him back his land and allowed him to eat at his table everyday. So this tells us no matter how low your life is God will elevate you. David had great victories but he was a lousy father.

One of his son's wanted to kill him. He had one of his wives first husband killed. One of his sons raped his daughter. He could of stood a few parenting classes. He looked out his window one day and seen a beautiful woman. He should of went to war. Kings go to war. Then maybe he would not of gotten in trouble. She got pregnant so he sent her husband off to war and he got killed. So actually David should have been killed by the law, but God supercedes the law and Yahshuah was coming through David's line. So what else is God going to do but protect him? The baby died then she had Solomon .David always repented and took responsibility for his actions. God said David was a man after his on heart. Meaning he was willing to do what God wanted. He was by no means perfect but he loved God. Showing we all fall off and we need to jump back on board. We can't fix anything we need to leave everything in God's hands.

David trained up some great warriors. I think one of the last things David did to displease God was to take a census of the warriors. When numbers mean nothing to God. It's like he was trusting in his men's power and not God's. With God you are always victorious. So God gave him a choice of three punishments. One was going into captivity,one was a plague the other famine. So 70000 died then David cried out for God to solely punish him. So God did. You might say God was harsh but he had to let them know he was God. This was a little tap on the hand compared to what his son got. God put all his wrath on his son. David bought a threshing floor from a man named Aeauah which was in Jerusalem. David built a altar for the lord. David was like if It doesn't cost me anything I'm not placing any value on it. So how can people take the Jewish people's land? This was the same place Abraham was going to offer Issac. Later Solomon built God's temple there. Now there's no temple but the Roc of the dome is there. It erks me that David bought it and us as believers understand nothing. See what's going on. We should be more in tune with Jewish people.

We as believers are the spiritual Israel. George Washington said the same thing king Solomon said over this nation. The only thing standing from the twin towers is that little white church. New York use to be the capital. We are constantly taking God out of everything. They are moving our churches . Getting rid of the crosses. Taking the ten commandments out of certain states. We took God out of our schools and we wonder why our children are a mess. God told me whatever you give your children to that's what you have. So we are busy giving our children to entertainment, sports and the streets. We never give them to God. That hedge is coming down . When it comes down the only thing that will stand is God's church. I'm not talking about the church down the street. I'm talking about the church in

Acts. Look around the church has no power, believers have no rights and the world does what it wants to us. You see where this nation is going. They can make agreements with nations that have believers locked up. American citizens who we don't know will ever be released. Believers are being burned, killed, cut in two and tortured. If they have a N on their homes they take their stuff. The N means they follow that Nazarene. Reminds me when someone uses the N word to refer to black people. So we should think we are all we have and pull out the world's system. We need to help other believers. Take our money and resources and be about us. Don't share God's altar with anything else. Believers shouldn't have to stand by themselves there is power in numbers and the blessing is in unity. The lady who was thrown in jail for not signing a marriage license shouldn't of been standing alone.

It's something gay people are like 2% of the population but we have no voice. So God's talking loud. All the believers have to link together no matter what the race or denomination. Then you will see God's power. God didn't change his people did. I looked at the pattern we have to come out as a unit. Abraham, Eypt, and Babylon came out. They were slaves but they took their captors wealth. Then Peter says save yourself from this perverse generation. Maybe if I keep saying it, it will get down in your spirit. I don't care what the world does I want the church to be respected. We are suppose to be ambassadors for Christ. Meaning we aren't from here but the embassy in heaven. You know diplomats are suppose to be untouchable. Why does the world think they can do whatever they want to believers. Really we need to pull out the world's system and really trust God. We need to make better political choices. We have to many demonic spirits pushing and fueling people. I don't know why we as believers think they went away. The enemy has a well put together army. It pricking us off one by one. So we have to unite. The blessing is in numbers.

Now I come to the book of kings. This book has David dying and Solomon becoming king. David gives his son this advice in 2 vs 2. Fulfill your duty to Yahveh your Elohim. Obey his directions, laws, commands, rules and written instructions as they are recorded in Moses Teachings. What gets me the king runs his kingdom just like the government. We can't understand that. I know, I said that before, but I want you to get this. Solomon married women from countries for political reasons. Basically to united kingdoms and have more power. When he did this his wives eventually pulled him from God cause he would do what his wives did. That's why God didn't want the men to marry foreign women. Even though Solomon knew what was right he did what was wrong. Chapter 3 It talks of Solomon worshiping at these pagan worship sites. Today it would be easter and xmas. We are all responsible for the atmosphere. So how defiled is that placing God next to a xmas tree. Solomon asked God for wisdom to lead the people. When he first sought God. We should humble ourselves before the Lord. Solomon told God he couldn't be a leader unless he led him. We have to approach God with such humility. Solomon's first case two prostitutes. They both had babies . One prostitute's baby died during the night so she took the other prostitute's baby and claimed it as hers. The other prostitute took her before the king. Which was the judge Solomon. Solomon told them to cut the baby in half. The real mother told him to let her keep the baby. Solomon knew she was the baby's mother and gave her the baby. People came all over the world to hear Solomon's wisdom. They came bearing gifts.

Solomon built a elaborate temple for the Lord. Solomon became the richest man ever. He made his money from copper and forced Labor. You can take a rich man's money from him and I bet he will become rich again because of his mindset. The way he thinks. You can give a poor man tons of money and he will become poor again. God never wanted us to think like a poor man. The temple was built. God spoke to Solomon . God told Solomon if you live by my laws , follow my rules and keep my commandments, I will fulfill the promise I made about you to your father David. I will live among the Israelities and never abandon my people. Then Solomon built a palace for him and one for his wife. We better recognize he built God's first. God's presence is in his temple and Solomon talks to his subjects. Solomon is constantly praying to God. Prayer is a setup. So we would communicate with him.

Then in chapter 8 vs 54 Solomon is blessing the people prophetically. This paragraph talks about the cause which is the king and the kingdom. Most believers don't even know there's a cause. The mission is in Luke one, where the angel Gabriel talks to the priest Zachariah. Then you have the command out where Yahshuah tells us to go. He deployed us out just like the military. We are to go make disciples. Which are learned ones, soldiers.

We just have a bunch of converts in church. Solomon starts to commit Idolary because of his wives. Solomon lived in prosperity but God told him he would take his kingdom away from him. It didn't happen during Solomon's time but his sons. Actually he lived in peace because his father whipped all the enemies with God's help. Solomon was worshipping Astarte(easter) because of his foreign wives. He started doing what they did even though it's wrong. I wonder if this has something to do with the church having no power. This is why God said he would take his kingdom from him . We can't serve two Gods.

Solomon died and his son Rehoboam became king. Israel went to the king and asked him if he would lighten the load because they were heavily taxed when Solomon was king. He listened to his friends and instead of his legal counsel and said no. So Israel divided from Judah. They believed they had no inheritance. Then you see how Israel was then divided in a third. Then you see different kings coming on the scene. After that You see Israel going into captivity. Then Judah went into captivity. First by Assyria, Babylon then Persia. You see prophets come on the scene with God's message for his plans. Sometimes the people listen sometimes they didn't. Assyria, Babylon and Persia are modern day Asia, Iran, Iraq etc. Back then they were cruel. They would cut pregnant women open and put cats inside of them and sew them back up. Not to much has changed. Then you have a bunch of bad kings and a couple of good ones. As time goes on Elijah comes on the scene to speak God's plans. God's spirit was on him because the spirit had not yet come back to be in the man. God did a lot through him. You could see spirits over top of people and nations as they are today. Look at Jezebel, Ahab, and all the wicked kings. Kings two basically continues with the fall of Judah. I'm not going to spend anytime in this book.

Chronicles is the next book which talks of the genealogy. I'm just going to point out a few things in this book chapter four speaks of Jabez who asked God to change his life which God did. He was a son of a prostitute. God turned him into a great warrior. Then you have Bilhah. This group followed their own way of thinking . They were covenant people who didn't know their covenant keeping God. Just like some church people who are religious. They don't know God because they have no relationship with God. Then you have chapter six Amrams children's descendants. Who were descedants of Aaron and Moses. This made me think to tell you guys there are black jews. They found some black jews decendants of Aaron in Africa through DNA. Then chronicles goes through telling the stories again. What better way to remember but through repetition.

Now I'm on chapter 14 vs 16. This talks of how God made David great. Where he was feared. My point ,if you are looking for direction consult God.

Chapter 15 vs 1 Basically says walk by faith and carry out the order. God's plan is what he purposed and what he established. We think God's promises are for our pleasure. His promises are for us to bring the kingdom.

Now there's one thing I want to point out in Chronicles 20 vs 20. You got it vision. It's all important in how you see. God said Abraham you can have it as far as you see. God asked Zerubbabel what do you see? He said Lord I don't know what I see so God told him what he saw. God wants us to see how he sees. God says the prophet's prosperity is in God's mouth . So the man or woman of God should be seeking God. The people's prosperity is in the prophet's mouth. So we shouldn't be looking for people to prosper the prophet though the prophet should be paid for what he does. The prophet should expect to receive from God. The people shouldn't think they are responsible for him. Even though the church is the people not the building. The people should tithe to maintain the functions of the church like heat,water,air, cutting the grass etc. We should be united and raise each other up. In God's church there are no have and have nots. The focus should be Yahshuah. The message should be the cross. There shouldn't be any world in God's church. God is like the electric company and the church is sitting with its lights off. We have to plug in to receive the power. God wants a church walking in the spirit and one that has a biblical world view. I'm hoping some of what I said seeps into your spirit.

In Chapter 31 you see where Hezekiel tears down the foreign altars. Asherath being one which is easter. Sisters and brothers we need to pull out of the world's system. It's bankrupt. We see where this nation is heading. This nation doesn't have the believers best interest but everything in this world opposes God. No wonder the earth doesn't know who the sons of God are. In 33 vs 19 God speaks of easter again. I hope you guys are listening.

Let's go on to the book of Ezra. I hope you guys know the bible isn't in chronological order. If God says something over and over it must be important. Ezra means God is help. He was a priest and a scribe. He was in captivity. Ezra devoted himself to study and observance of the law of the Lord. He taught the decrees and laws of the Lord to Israel. When he came out of capitivity he translated the bible(scriptures) from Hebrew to Aramaic. Israel adopted the ways and language of their captors. Ezra translated the scriptures after they came out of exile before the Quran. It's been said that Aramaic should be a Jewish language. The king of Persia allowed them to rebuilt the temple when they returned to Israel. The temple was destroyed during one of their captivities. When the people left to go back they were given wealth (silver, gold etc) to do God's will. God's will is his word.

Now this is what gets me, they say the Quran came from heaven by Gabriel. No one knows what Gabriel looks like . Besides Lucifer masquerades as a angel of light. Like I said before why would God send a book from heaven when he spoke on the mountain in seventy different languages all at the same time.

God goes through the genealogies again. God always wants you to know where you came from so you know where you are going. Among the servants was Hassophereth. I just wanted to point out she was a female scribe. That little note was for those who think women can't do anything in church. Then they started worship again even though the foundation of the temple wasn't set .

I think I heard a tv minister say the word Tisheva means nothing it's just a word. Right it's just God's New Year. God follows his schedule not man's. God's plan is going forth. Besides man is the one that got us in this mess we are in .When they were building the temple they had a axe in one hand and a hammer in the other. So they were fighting as they were building. This shows us we are always going to have opposition when we do the things of God. You see the prophets on the scene. Everybody has a part to play. Then the temple was dedicated. Ezra was a expert in Moses teachings and they say he stood on a podium to talk to the people. Maybe that's where the church got standing on the podium. The king told Ezra to use God's wisdom and appoint judges and administrators. Do we do that? The king told Ezra whoever didn't follow God's teaching would be exiled. There stuff would be taken and they would be imprisoned and sentenced to die. This is the end of chapter 7 around the 8th verse you see a form of government being established with God at the head. When we elect people we should make sure they follow God. No wonder we have what we have. We don't follow God's system. We have taken God out of everything when he should be in everything.

Now the exiles start coming back in three intervals. They fasted, consulted God and followed God's instructions. No self effort. If they listened to self they would of asked the king for a army escort. We have to understand everytime God took someone out they were slaves. Meaning they had nothing. They trusted God and God provided. I thought this was interesting, he knelt down, stretched out his hands to Yahveh and prayed. I never read about a person praying sitting down. There's more than one way to pray. The people who came back were small in number compared to the people who were in the land. They were a remnant. God always has a remnant. Just like when God's people really come out it will be a remnant. A small amount. We like this world to much. So God tells them not to follow the people's ways and not to intermarry. God didn't want anything to pull them away from him.

Now in Chapter 10 around vs 7(prophetically) I see Yahshuah in the grave three days and the world disconnected from him. Then in vs 9 that heavy rain represents the lateral rain. No matter how many people you tell the truth to you still have people doing what they want. It's the same today. If you don't listen to God how do you expect to get what he has for you? God gives us instructions because we have a enemy out there. It's not us earning or trying to qualify. God already qualified us. How can a sinful man ever be good enough to a holy God. So what I say to leadership expect opposition and keep a positive perspective. Fight your battles with prayer and stay close to others. Unity.

My man Nehemiah means God is my consolation. He was helping to build the temple. He had a hammer in one hand and a sword in the other. They said he fought the battle on his knees. How many of us stay in close connection with God? Nehemiah was a cupbearer, commissioned to rebuild the wall of Jerusalem. Nehemiah wore many other hats such as laborer, governor and politician. He saw a need. Became concerned and helped restablish worship to God. How many of us our concerned with the things of God? The enemy gets us focused on us so we get distracted. Everything in this world is a distraction. So we don't see where we are really going. The king allowed him to go help build the wall. If we truly walk in the spirit, people will see the light to bend even though, they don't know what they see. There will always be opposition because the enemy doesn't want the kingdom here. You figure if the kingdom comes the enemy will truly be seen as conquered.

In chapter 5 you see the have and have nots in God's church. Nehemiah put a end to that. There's no have and have nots in God's church. Nehemiah didn't use the funds he received from being governor ,for himself, he used it to help elevate God's people. Nehemiah is constantly getting attacked but those attacks made him stronger. When I am weak I am strong because the power of the Lord rests on me. Besides if I weren't getting attacked I wouldn't think I was doing anything. Then he goes through everything. Ezra and Nehemiah knew each other.

Chapter 8 You see Ezra teaching from the book of Moses. It was God's New Year. A Holy day. The people celebrated. They partied. They observed the Festival of Booths (Tabernacles). Then they Fast, confess, and pray. Then they go through the story. You just keep repeating the story so it can be committed to memory. Like I said it's a complete story. Somewhere down the line the story stopped being told. We made it about us. Then God made a agreement in chapter 10 with the leaders of the people. So it is very important who we choose to represent us. We may not be represented right especially if they are not in agreement with God. That's the problem we have in this country. We are spiritual Israel and we stopped living and dedicating to God. We just accept what they give us and stand for nothing. So if you stand for nothing you will fall for anything. We don't even worship right. We need to give God what he wants.

The last chapter 13 around vs 23 talks about dissolving marriages to foreigners. So what I see in this the believers disengaging from the world.

The book of Esther deals with the people that stayed in Persia. Esther means star. The star is Yahshuah. The star of David is Yahshuah. Everyone of these books point to Yahshuah. Every last prophet is of Hebraic descent, so how do people look at Muhummad?

He's not Hebrew. Esther's story was about saving the Jewish people from genocide. Haman was constantly against Mordacai and the Jews. God turned something bad into something good. Heman's plot backed fired and ended up getting him killed. While Mordacai was elevated. They celebrated the feast of Purim. Which was the purifying of the temple. This was a foreshadow of cleansing our temple Yahshuah. The celebration was Hanukkah. The feast of lights. We see in the New Testament Yahshuah celebrated the feast of dedication which is Hanukkah not xmas. Ephiphanes the king of Syria defiled the temple in Jerusalem by putting a pig on God's altar. Then a group of priests called the Macabees overthrew Epiphanes and cleansed the temple. It's time for us as believers to stand up together. We are always going to draw satan's attention when we look like God. Satan's drawn to the light because he wants to put it out.

Now the book of Job means foe or hostile one (opponent). The book of Job is a illustration of good cop bad cop. Man's obedience (conscience) the way we think invites God in. Job was the most famous man in the east. God will exalt us in his time. God was glorifying and bragging about Job. Satan hated Job. Job came through because he wasn't working with satan. God knew where satan was . God interrogated satan so we would know our enemy and what our enemy thinks of us. The enemy believes you will do anything for your life. Our greatest fear is death. Yahshuah took the sting out of death. The enemy constantly feeds us. So Yahshuah tells you to hate your life. The enemy can use anything in your life against you. The enemy believes you love your life more than anything.

Satan has a entrance up to God. That's approaching the bench. Satan is constantly bringing accusations against man. Satan can approach God's bench whenever he wants. God showed me the difference between a accusation, expose and judgement. Acussation you don't know if its true, Expose you know it's true. You bring It to the light . So it can be expelled. Light expels darkness. Judgement is when you sentence someone saying they are going to heaven or hell. See how God's teachings are so complete.

Job was a man of integrity. He stayed standing even though he had no Torah , no Yahshuah, and no real relationship with God. He just knew there was a God. He knew by the signs in the sky and creation itself. Job is the oldest book in the bible. Moses wrote this book and it was passed down. Chapter one talks about planting and prospering. Everybody talks about Job and his trials I have yet to hear them talk about his finish. It's not where you start but where you finish. Job's first crisis he lost everything . I call that collateral damage.

The bible helps us to live it's not pushing us around. Satan can munipulate our lives, but not God's word. The word Yahshuah. Job had no bible and Yahshuah hadn't went to the cross so he didn't have the Holy spirit. We have the whole bible and Yahshuah came. What's our excuse? At the end God restores everything. The whole story shows Job believing and never cursing God. We read the word so we know whose's talking. We get in the word so we know our father's heart. God's way of thinking. You can't study God. God's revealed. You start to understand and see clear. I can give you the tools but I can't make you do it or believe it. You have to take what I said to God and let the Holy spirit convince you.

The enemy knows us he knows if he does this you will do that. So that's why God says you have to do things on purpose. No matter what Job's still standing. Satan's steady hating him. God's still bragging on Job. What gets me satan has the lease to this earth so he can do whatever he wants to man's body. When Adam sinned he became one with the earth. He just can't harm the man's spirit,the real him. The man's spirit belongs to God. God redeemed man's spirit not his body. The only place this body is going is in the ground. So why do we put so much effort in the body. The spirit was no longer connected to God when man fell so God had to get the spirit back to his man. Man's soul was held captive by satan because it had no other way to think. Job was going by the signs of creation even though he didn't fully understand. Even when we are going through sometimes we need to stop and listen.

Then we see where Job's friends are having a conversation with him. They are trying to figure out God. They wonder why God is so good and Job is in this bad situation. God is good but satan is the god of this world. The only way God can be here legally is if we invite him in. So God didn't do it .His friends are trying to use their natural knowledge to explain the spiritual kingdom. It can't be done. Man can never figure spiritual things. That's the natural man, trying to use his intellect and make it make sense to him. You don't learn God like you do English or math. Like your in college. You go to college for you. God's about unity. God doesn't accuse . Why would he? He already knows the answer. Job keeps going *through and he wants to die. Then you see in chapter 10 Job hates his life. The enemy will use your life against you. You can see his friends don't understand God and misrepresent God.*

Then Job's wife tells him to curse God and die. Job didn't take her advice. You see God silenced her and you hear no more from her. In chapter 14 Job realizes he can't do anything with out God.

When we get down to verse 25 in chapter19 that speaks of the redeemer and then the millenium. The bible is a prophetic form of government. It's not religious. That's why it's food for the spirit.

Chapter 20 shows you how a hardheaded person handles bad news. God gave Job another one hundred and forty years to his life. Then it's a conversation where Job speaks. Then his friends. They are trying to figure out what Job did but we know you don't have to do anything. What we have are the results of a fallen world. So nothing's going to make sense. Job sticks to his story without taking a flea bargain and pleads his innocence. You know I was looking at the inside of a courtroom. I see how we place are hands on the bible and you see in God we trust on the wall. We need to stop, look pay attention. God made us thinking and reasoning. So you can see there are a bunch of adamant spirits. These aggressive spirits are destroying and taking away the things of God. Steady crushing God's people. I talk to believers all the time and wonder why they think the way they do.

In chapter 32 Job's getting beat down still by his friends. That's how we do believers beating down other believers. When we need to stand together.

Then in chapter 40 God speaks and sets them straight. God talks of who he is and what he's done. Then Job takes responsibility for his actions. Job's restored.

Chapter 8
Poetic, Prayers and Psalms (Songs)

Now we get to one of my most loved books in the bible. The psalms starts off the poetic part of the bible. Psalms are prayers poems , hymns(songs) If you sing or recite something you are bound to remember it. Even years later. How do you recite or sing a song you heard twenty years ago? I mean you know all the words you snapped your fingers to. It's the same thing. They had different songs .A chant which means a war song. Praise was for respect, adoration, totally loving on God. What he's done for us. You know we should be living what we sing. We aren't like some R and B artist that sing something but don't have to walk it out. All our songs should have purpose and meaning and take us somewhere. Praise and worship acknowledge our resources. That we share in from God. Religion tells you, you have to measure up. Religion mimics something good like cancer does. Which actually kills the body of Christ. What I hear puts a message in my mind that forms a picture.

Book one of Psalms means songs which sort of sounds like it . Psalms, Songs. This book shows us how to meditate. If you understand ,you can understand your life. God takes a tree through seasons like he takes us through seasons. The first psalm is talking about a tree. So we should change the way we think . We need to think like God. Prosperity is more than money. If you have wisdom you can make a good decision. If we meditate and are constantly fed God's word we will grow. A tree doesn't resist God. The tree cooperates. The tree is willing to go through seasons. The tree doesn't toil. It just goes through the process. It's pretty interesting how God uses everything in the garden, to teach us. Trees, flowers, plants, vines, bushes, fruit etc. He even teaches by showing us government. By believers being clueless it tells me they aren't reading or spending time with God. They aren't getting *understanding. You can't learn God from a man or expect that man to give you one more piece of information. That's going to change your life. Go from Passover to spring you will see a change. See your life in creation. Winter to spring. Death to life. Brown grass to green grass. I might spend sometime in psalms because I love psalms. David wrote a lot of the psalms . He was very musically inclined. I loved the way he ministers through music. People can learn through music. We should all use our gifts because our gifts aren't for us. They are for somebody else. Just like our face is for somebody else. You can't see your face. So why do most believers have a prune face?*

The second psalm talks of God Almighty. Then it talks of God installing his king on his holy mountain which is Yahshuah. Then we get to verse 9 where it talks of purchasing the nations. Nations are considered heathens or this world. The Iron scepter is what Yahshuah will rule with. Then he talks about kissing the son. When you kiss someone you connect to them. It shows intimacy. So we ought to kiss God sometime. The last sentence talks of all that take refuge in him are blessed. That's Yahshuah.

Then in the third psalm David talks to his soul. Sometimes you have to encourage yourself. The last sentence may your blessing rest on your people. Yahshuah . Yahshuah became a curse so we would be blessed.

Psalm four talks of God making us righteous through Yahshuah . God tells us to know the truth and stop living a lie. Then it says we should listen so Yahshuah can impart to us. Yahshuah is the sacrifice of righteousness. Then at the end of that psalm it says Yahshuah is better than anything and more than enough.

Psalm five talks of Yahshuah being king. Verse eleven and twelve talks of the seed and lets you know you can live life on purpose. Rejoicing is based on their trust. Joy comes with a shout. Joy means strength. God is our defense. How can we worry about enemies. Joy is love and trust. It's not fate or humanism. The human point of that says love never gives yourself or anything. It doesn't obey God's commands. It's something how we look to imperfect people to bring us joy. No wonder we are sad. A person can't make you happy. If you are feeling a void. Fill that void with God. God's Holy spirit is suppose to fill that void. God never said people would love us. God loves us. God blesses and empowers us. That's when we have favor which is unmerited grace. This undeserved grace will open doors. In seven we see Yahshuah as righteous, a shield and a judge. In seven verse 14 talks of how evil comes about. First it's a thought like you being pregnant. Then you give birth to it and act on it.

Now psalms eight talks about how we have to have a intimate relationship with God. It's never about performance, we just have to be there. In verse three we see God being mindful of us because he loves us. Yahshuah holds the heavenlies in place. Yahshuah's done everything.

In psalms nine verse 14 you see God giving back the spirit. In psalms fourteen verse 7 speaks of Yahshuah and the end.

Psalms fifthteen shows us how to rightfully stand. I will be skipping around in psalms picking out what God wants me to.

In psalms sixteen from vs 8 down our focus should be Yahshuah. It talks about not being abandoned in a grave because in four days your body starts to decay. That's way Yashuah was up in three days. The path of life made known is Yahshuah.

Now in Psalms seventeen verse 2 Where he talks about making us innocent. God made the way so we could be acquitted. God changed our condition not our behavior. So we need to line up. That's putting our body in line with our spirit. Then in verse 12 That lion crouching is sin looking for a opening to get in . Then when God talks about filling their bellies with the treasures in verse 14 God's talking about the Holy spirit.

Psalms eighteen is God's system. God's instructions.

Psalms nineteen paints a picture for us

Psalms twenty verse 5 God wants to be our desire.

Psalm twenty two David was a New Testament man in The Old Testament. He was speaking prophetically. Yahshuah hadn't done anything yet. This is a Messianic prayer. This psalm speaks of the crucifixion. It shows him lowering himself so we could have the anointing, healing, etc. It's humility before honor. What man can take on everybody's sin. The weight of sin is to heavy for the regular man. You can't clean something dirty with something dirty. Just try to use a dirty rag to clean a dirty surface. You will just spread the dirt around . If you use a clean rag you can pick that dirt up. God said our righteousness is as fifthy rags. So how could we do it. In this psalm it also talks of Yahshuah's feet being pierced. Then the last verse 30 and 31 speaks of the Lord and his finished work.

Psalm twenty three God being our shepherd meaning he takes care of us. Then he protects us no matter what. The table he prepared for us is the life he prepared for us. He prepared it in predestined time. The one Yahshuah gave back to us. So it doesn't matter what darkness we go through he will navigate us to that new life.

Psalm twenty four Is about manifesting God's presence.

Psalm twenty five verse 19 The path is Yahshuah which we should know.

Psalm twenty six. Why do we go to the altar? What are we sacrificing? We need to stop thinking he hasn't done anything. I never seen a disciple running to the altar. When they went to the altar they were sacrificing the best. What are we giving God besides are problems?

Psalms twenty seven .Source of individual light . Salvation, rescuing, protecting, deliverance. How do we approach life? We fear because we know are limitations. God tells us what he tells us because we have a enemy. Verse 10 tells us how to get love even when our families abandon us. We just had to get there. In verse 11 It says we will see the goodness of the Lord in the land of the living. Which means while we are living. Now.

Psalms twenty nine verse 10 talks about Yahveh sitting enthroned. Which means circle. How did God know the earth was round. This was before Christopher Columbus.

Psalms thirty one verse 39 My eyes, my soul, my body, which is spirit, soul and body. You are suppose to see with your spirit.

Psalms thirty two explains if you are holy you can't stand sin. It talks about self will.

Psalm thirty four verse 5 All who look to him will be radiant. That's the spirit on them. So we should look , believe, look through to paradise and it will open up around us. Verse 8 Talks of fear which is respect. Not being intimidated or scared. Freewill now. Verse 16 down talks of Yahshuah delivering us from many troubles verse 20 It talks of none of his bones being broken. When Yahshuah died none of his bones were broken. If you don't die within a certain amount of time they would break your bones. So Yahshuah gave his spirit back which sped up the process after his assignment was complete. Yahshuah did everything in the Old Testament.

In chapter thirty six verses 7 and 9 talks of the fountain of life and light which is Yahshuah.

Psalms thirty seven Saying we should worship based on what's written.

Psalm thirty eight Righteousness will be satisfied in famine never stop speaking your inheritance.

Psalms thirty nine As we trust in God his grace kicks in.

Psalms forty speaks of Yahshuah verse 7 About him being written in the scroll.

Psalms forty one tells of the importance in a name .

Book two of Psalms talks more about meditating, encouraging yourself and thinking like God.

Psalms forty three Just line up verse 3 says send your light and truth which is Yahshuah verse 5 How come when we go to the altar we are always looking to be fixed. If we don't listen maybe we don't really hear.

Psalms forty five verse 7 Speaking of Yahshuah.

Psalms forty eight says we are happy because of God's judgements.

Psalms forty nine Talks of honor carrying out God's word in the community. We need to change our attitude . Have a different mindset. We need to take on the mindset of the king.

In verse 35 it talks about taking us back from the power of hell. If we are defeated how can we have any power without God. Yahshuah got us back.

Psalms fifty verse 1 The earth is summoned. Meaning it's coming to court. Around verse 14 God gives us instructions in giving. When you are in a relationship you give. In verse 16 Says how the world quotes his decrees and promises and his people don't. Then in verse 23 We see that salvation is a person.

Psalms fifty one David wants to be put back into position. So yes you can be out of position. Most people in church are in the wrong position. Verse 5 we are sinners because of Adam verse 12 Spirit of willingness , obedience to the Holy spirit.

Psalms fifty three verse 6 speaks of Yahshuah.

Psalms fifty eight verse 2 How we make up our own rules. Verse 8 How we are separated from God even in the womb.

Psalms sixty verse 31 Says how human effort is worthless.

Then in Sixty two verse 10 speaks how people respect money. It says don't obtain money by force . Says riches come and go. We think money will sustain us until we get a evil report.

Psalms Sixty three verse 11 Talks about people not really with God.

Psalms sixty seven wants us to know that God is happy with us. So we should deal with God like he's a king .

Psalms sixty eight verse 11 Says the women who announce the good news will be a real big army. Meaning it will be more women evangelists. In Joel it says women will speak what is revealed. Meaning more women prophets. God's raising up women. We are all the same in the spirit and there aren't enough men to fight. We are fighting spirits that are evil with intelligence. God's putting Eve back in her rightful position . She's God's secret weapon. The enemy's so busy after the man, God's pulling his ace out. Evil spirits don't care whether you are male or female. You see there are tons of women in church use them. The military utilizes women where do you think they got it from. Verse 30 talks about cattails that's what

Yahshuah was whipped with. The cattail had pieces of glass or metal in it. So when it hit your skin it was bound to pull some of your skin out with it.

Psalms sixty nine verse 28 Says your name will be erased out of the book of life. Showing me that everybody's name was in the book of life before the age of accountability verse 30 and 31 Shows me how there's power in the name.

Psalms seventy two vs 8 speaks of Yahshuah . verse 14 Talks about precious blood in his sight . Which means rare and costly because Yahshuah used his blood to save us. Amen means you agree.

Psalms seventy three No memory in death. If you go to heaven and somebody you know doesn't go to heaven you won't remember them. The principle of the seed is to live life on purpose not let life just happen.

Psalm seventy six verse 2 associates Jerusalem and Melchizedek.

Psalms eighty cycles of instruction 1 Hear 2 Awaken 3 Restore 4 Cryout   verse eight Talks of a vine from Eypt which is Yahshuah. Everything grows from a vine. Verse 16 Talks of Yahshuah being God's son. Verse 17 Talks of Yahshuah's humanity side. Verse 18 Talks about God giving the spirit back to us.

Psalms eighty one Feast of Tabernacles which is us in eternity with the Lord. It says God delivered us from the world. Then it talks about God of self. Around verse 8 then in verse 15 It talks about what's going to happen to the unsaved.

Psalms eighty two verse 6 When he calls us God's of this world, he's talking about his glorious church when we look like him.

Psalms eighty three verse 6 speaks of muslims which are fueled by a adamant spirit.

Psalms eighty seven speaks of every nation born in Zion. Which spiritually they are.

Psalms eighty eight verse 5 Talks about the spiritually dead.

Psalms eighty nine verse 20 Talks of how God anointed David. The spirit would come on people before he put the spirit back in people. Yahshuah through his humanity came from David's line. He had to do everything legally so there would be no mistrial. He had to come through the womb and do everything just like a man or else he would be here illegally and break the law. Adam was suppose to have been a man led by the spirit. Then he fell so Yahshuah came to show us how to walk in the spirit.

Book four Time means nothing to God.

Psalms Ninety speaks of a dwelling place . A refuge. God is it. Believe it. We confuse our lives with the one who gives life. Our by and by verse 11 Talks about understanding Yahshuah and why he does what he does.

Psalms ninety one. Everything we do we were taught by the world. We need to respond to God based on his word. Our thoughts and words have to line up with who he is. Believing lines us up with God's truth. If you don't believe right you won't do right. We have to line up with what he's already done. Thoughts are spiritual. You can talk yourself out of God's refuge.

Psalms ninety two verse 12 Talks about being in right standing with God.

Psalms ninety three God's goodness is a blessing for us. Holiness is God's set apart wholeness.

Psalms ninety five Unmoved. Psalms one hundred and one verse 8 Stand for what's right.

Psalms one hundred and two Why trip over the natural. Intimacy is important. Partaking verse 8 Talks about Yahshuah's life and death. Verse 14 What built us Verse 16 millenium verse 20 defeated enemy verse 23 Explains Earth and everything and the heavenlies. What God made it will fade away. Rule , Government things shaking and perishing verse 28 Things will continue and will be established not because you attend church. Labor not in vain.

Psalm one hundred in three verse 9 because God put his wrath on his son.

Psalm one hundred and four Enlightening the mind. He's greater so be different be better than how we where raised. How God did everything on earth. Moon is for seasons . To show signs and tell time. The sun sets when it's suppose to. Animals see better at night . They are made for the night like we are made for the day. So we need to walk in the light. Just like if you walk in a room that is dark you need to turn on the lights so you can see. Around verse 19. The New moon. We don't function in darkness. That's why we sleep at night. Verse 35 Talks of a new heaven and earth.

Psalms one hundred and six verse 37 Idol of entertainment. Whatever you give your kids to that's what we have a lot of. When we should give our kids to God.

Book five one hundred and seven verse 31 What are we saying what are we teaching our kids?

Psalms one hundred and eight God as the father. God as teacher. Verse 17 human effort

Psalm one hundred and ten It's Messianic, God talking to a resurrected man. Established order. verse 1 What David said about Yahshuah. Who is David talking about Verse four No genealogy . emphasis on Yahshuah. God becoming a man representing us. Took our punishment.

Psalms one hundred and eleven. Application of learning is doing. Verse 10 Understanding by what you do.

Psalms one hundred and eighteen How you purpose in your heart is how you prosper. Verse 25 salvation

Psalms one hundred and nineteen . Who God is. Describes light of God's word. Power of God's word. Executing and carrying out the word. Verse 19 Ambassadors of Christ Meaning we are foreigners who live in the embassy of heaven. We should be diplomats. Where we are respected and represent the kingdom. Verse 25 Yahshuah . Verse 57 Yahshuah's approval.

Verse 89 Yahshuah Verse 99 Discernment Verse one hundred and fifty seven Yahshuah is the promise.

Psalms one hundred and twenty verse 6 Freedom equals Yahshuah.

Psalms one hundred and twenty one verse 5 The right hand represents authority and power.

Psalms one hundred and twenty six If you don't care that dishonors God and he won't be there . We don't have his presence. We just have a meeting . What makes us different from the boy scouts or the red cross. We have to show the name which is God's character. We have to display it in church. We have to know who we are . We have to know who we represent.

Psalms one hundred and twenty seven. If you don't built the way God tells you or you don't have him in it, it's worthless. It means nothing the natural man should be sleep while we do the things of God. Our children should be a reflection of us, while we are a reflection of God. More of us to fight. When you are fighting side by side with people and your in relationship with them you know them. Just take lessons from the military. You know their strengths and weaknesses. You don't want to get hurt.

Psalms one hundred and twenty eight Ways of Yahshuah will produce fruit. Olive trees grafted in from the vine. Which is us grafted in.

Psalms one thirty two Ephrathat is ancient Bethelehem. Ark of the Covenant is what was found in Jaar. Verse 10 Yahshuah will sit on David's throne. David captured Zion which is Jerusalem city of David. Verse 17 Horn that sprouts from David is a king. Yahshuah is the king. You know stuff and it starts coming out.

Psalms one hundred and thirty three. The power to overcome is unity. People are selfish not centered. Blessing is the anointing that allows you to prosper. Unity commands the blessing. Glory is the Messiah. Verse 2 The blessing running down Aaron's beard because Yahshuah is the head and it flows down through out the body. It's a spirit connection. We have to be in the spirit to receive from God. Preach to hear spirit. If spirit is thick on us the shadow will heal.

Psalms one hundred and thirty four pursue peace , look for peace. If you get in a certain realm you will help people. We are blessed to be a blessing.

Psalms one hundred and thirty nine God sees us as complete. How do we see ourselves.? God's thinking is so much higher then ours. Verse 13 The inner being is the spirit. What's motivating us to act. We have to allow room in our hearts. Already in the book until age of accountability. Verse 23 looking in the mirror.

Psalms one hundred and forty one verse 5 Fight

Psalms one hundred and forty three verse 8 Everyday there is a new mercy. Level ground is the spirit.

Psalms one hundred and forty five kingship of God. We are just having events not becoming anything. Verse 9 Yahveh is good to everyone. What else is he going to be? Just because he is good doesn't mean you are blessed Verse 18 Prayer communication with God.

Psalms one hundred and forty six verse nine God gives relief to orphans and widows. Meaning women without husbands and people without fathers. God throws no one away.

Psalm one hundred and forty seven Sing to the one you love. Verse 20 What happens in Israel determines what happens. How we treat Israel.

Psalms one hundred and forty nine. Put laws into action. The laws are only good if they are carried out. Honor and executing judgement is the game plan. This changes lives. The plan is good because it's God's . No human effort. It's good because we didn't come up with the plan. We just have to walk it out. You can only hit the mark in grace. I have confidence for two hours in church. Although Satan is pressing twenty four seven. How I respond under pressure. Natural man is weak and dishonorable. People think sin equals human effort. Holy spirit allows us to hear God's plan. World won't glorify Yahshuah . Why would spirit of God glorify something less then God. Yahveh glorified Yahshuah. We glorify Yahshuah by walking out his finished work and stop acting like God didn't do anything. We need to hear what Yahshuah's showing us through the Holy spirit. Yahshuah's in heaven interceding for us. The Holy spirit's communicating to us everything the father gave Yahshuah. Why aren't we excited and rejoicing. Why aren't we encouraged? We have the spirit of truth. Why do we need a worship leader? To much human effort. We have to learn from the spirit. Seek and search scriptures and see all the things Yahshuah gave us. Yahshuah sent the Holy spirit so he could reach more people.

Psalms one hundred and fifty Praise. What has God done . Am I healed? Redeemed? Are my needs met? How do we respond? Worship raises you. Why so little dancing in the house of the Lord? David went from worship to war. Worship gives you strength to fight. Singers that can fight. Praise will determine how you fight. Everything is done in the spirit. The spirit is the real realm. When you don't move in church you are not moving in the spirit. It's about moving in the spirit. The natural man is defeated.

Chapter 9
Principles To Live By

*P*roverbs is a book of principles. God gave us the thought's of a rich man. God never wanted us to think like a poor man. Solomon was the richest man ever. God wanted us to have the mindset of a rich man. Proverbs are principles to live by. We should be able to live righteously because God's seed is in us. It was nothing we did. Wisdom is Yahshuah. Wisdom is in the mind. So we should think like Yahshuah. When God says Fear ,he means respect.

Chapter one verse 28 Everybody needs God but God comes where he's desired. God told me starving people in Africa need him.

Chapter two verse 1 value God's commandments. Verse 4 Value God more than you value money. Then you will find him. Verse 10 Talks about having Yahshuah in your mind. Verse 11 seeing in head of us. Verse 17 Doing what you understand

Chapter three How to navigate things in life. Wisdom allows you to find favor not only with God but with man also. There's a lot in this one so I'm just going to tell you. It talks about human effort,Self Righteousness, and tithing. How you get in grace. By being gracious people. Wisdom in your finances. There's no mystery in God. We honor God with our substance when we tithe. Honor is heavy weighted. Wow a king. Make gifts so good. God's a king so we should honor him. The Anointing is better than worldly stuff. How costly and rare wisdom is. Wisdom is Yahshuah. First four proverbs speak of wisdom which is Yahshuah. Verse 19 Then it speaks of Christ and God being the same. The ear gate and the eye gate is how we get God's word into our heart. Which is our mind. Sudden terror is that *fish caught in a net. We can't predict what's going to happen. It just happens. Verse 27 Not giving what belongs to someone else. Verse 32 Decent people are upright people. God wants us to be like him. Honor God. God's not interested in fixing our problems. The body was in line with God before man fell. Christ came in the likeness of our sinful nature to pay our debt. You can be a spirit and not be divine. Man yielded to satan.*

In four you begin to understand what God's done in eternity Verse 8 This is a principle First thing say the word and if you stay on the path it gets brighter. Christ is the path. Verse 11 Way of wisdom is Yahshuah. Verse 14 First appearance of light. Verse 20 down Give attention to my words. Ear and eye gate entrance to man's heart. Also reveals light and darkness. What you speak flows from your heart. Thinking process.

Chapter five Beware, to see before hand , power, act of seeing into a situation Verse 10 made me think of child support when your substance is in another house.

Chapter six vs 23 Reproofs of discipline is the way to God's life. Reproof means correction. Verse 26 Cheap. Verse 33 Fornication

Chapter seven verse 1 Value Verse 2 Delicate Verse 10 Trying to get over Verse 14 Being Religious. The rest is how the world wants to suck you in. How you can be easily influenced. Which means anything that pulls you away from God.

Eight Yahsuah .

Nine Yahshuah finished the work and understanding his mind. What he wants. What wisdom will do. Wisdom is the word of God. Why don't we go after wisdom? We need to break through culture. It's amazing how we have our way in church. Verse 17 The world.

Chapter ten The way you know you understand something is when you do it. You should be able to see light in your actions. Ideas ,thought and value mean nothing it depends on what the motive is behind it. Verse 4 Doing nothing verse 5 Does what needs to be done. Verse 11 God made us righteous. Verse 12 Won't think about it because your in love. Verse 14 Know Yahshuah made it personal. Verse 19 Fuel it. Verse 20 How do we value our words. Verse 21 Connect to God. Verse 22 Yahshuah no self effort.

Chapter twelve what Yahshuah gave us.

Chapter thirteen talks about the wise and a fool. Pay attention. My son should listen to me not a fool. Ultimate father God. Foolishness of God wiser then the world. Verse 15 why chase something already there. Verse 22 What was said in Exodus. God wanted to give our children a legacy. What we give them is how to go to church. We show them how to come to a building but they don't know why they are coming. Every aspect, every position of life we need to teach them . If you don't understand God's word you can't do it. For them the ability to attend church will not put a demand on the things of God. It won't teach them how to handle the enemy either. That's not a God problem , God hasn't changed. Verse 25 What they want naturally.

Chapter fourteen Truth of God has falleth in the street meaning no one stands for or with us. Labor gets more difficult. God isn't pleased. No one stands in the gap. Yahshuah came to show us. Verse 24 Talk without doing anything.

Chapter fifteen God sees everything. Verse 14 Yahshuah Verse 29 Disconnect. Verse 30 Yahshuah. Verse 33 Broke and loss equals value how much it's worth.

Chapter sixteen Verse 1 and 2 Thoughts of accuser. Why you did it. Verse 5 Pride Verse 9 everythings done. Verse 10 Words from the Lord. Verse 16. Yahshuah , This world Verse 20 Importance of understanding. Verse 31 Experience Verse 32 Think then react

Chapter seventeen Verse 2 A faithful servant is better than a unfaithful son means dependability Verse 5 made in God's image. Verse 6 Royal live to see Full expression children should grow into us as we grow into Yahshuah. Verse 7 Looking like the devil not God. Verse 9 Keeps going Verse 12 Eventually calms down. Verse 17 Knew we would have a hard time here put us here for one another. A brother is suppose to be able to solve a problem. Verse 22 Strenght, Makes you feel better. Verse 26 Yahshuah Verse 28 Instruction on how to use our words.

Chapter eigthteen We need to use our tongue to speak good things. Taught to speak how we feel and not what we want. Our life should be pleasing to God inspite of what we feel.

Learn to speak on purpose. God's not moved by how we feel but by his word. We use our word for selfish gain not unity. We need to be in Harmony. Verse 12 Submitting to God. Verse 17 What are we saying. Satisfied by words. Your Belly is filled by what you are saying. What you pull out of your heart is your treasure. As you speak it becomes what it is. Eat what you say, reap what you sow. Choose your words carefully, with purpose so they will do something. We learn from this world which is perversed. We are the only one of God's creatures that can talk besides angels. We can choose our words. Satan used the power of words to pull Adam down. He convinced Adam and Eve with the power of suggestion. A question. Satan said did God say that? Power of words didn't recognize warfare was going on. Satisfaction in life comes by what we say. Increase in mouth because hands suppose to follow what you say. Yet we don't like to say anything about God. We get in a bad place it's trouble and we clam up. Where did you learn that? You think that's natural but it's really unnatural.

Chapter nineteen Holding the bible and not reading it. Discipline life so you can be with God.

Chapter twenty Help people with drinking and what goes along with drinking.

Chapter twenty one How we treat self. Who we are in Christ. Obedience. God's will prevails no matter what humans want to do. Verse 2 Why you did it. Verse 3 Mercy Verse 4 Pride,Selfishness. Verse 7 Cleanse yourself, respond to my mercy and truth walk and continue in truth . Gives us his joy. No limit to God. God keeps pulling from himself. Go to the water which is convenient. We are under his finished work. Verse 8 Having little but having peace. Verse 16 God Verse 18 payment for us Verse 19 With nothing verse 21 Yahshuah Verse 23 and 24 How we beat ourselves up and who we are in Christ. Matters of the heart. Verse 26 Dreams Verse 27 What's on our minds. Verse 27 Surface, Integrity. Verse 30 God's plans concerning us brings us peace. Peace being freedom. We have no reason not to do God's plan.

Chapter 22 God's name , What God says is good. Verse 13 Excuses Verse 15 Inexperienced Don't know any better. Verse 16 No God, God is true wealth. Verse 17 Everything God does in our life is for us to trust him. So why don't we do what God says. To have a true relationship you have to have trust. Verse 26 Do what you can do don't over extend yourself. Verse 27 Cosigning. Verse 28 Be honest don't say something is yours and it's not. Verse 29 Be diligent, Know what God's doing

Chapter twenty three Verse 4 Challenge what you learned in the world. Verse 5 As fast as you get it, it's gone. Don't desire things of a evil man. Don't be aroused by what you see. Verse 10 Stealing and taking advantage. Verse 20 What influences you. Verse 21 Lazy Verse 30 Influence and the world. Verse 32 Acting crazy. Verse 33 You chasing after what's not good for you.

Chapter twenty four is another proverb that talks about alcohol. Verse 1 Don't desire to be with evil people. Verse 3 and 4 By God's wisdom, What God has for you, you don't have to chase. Allow Holy spirit to impart to you. Verse 5 Wise counsel. Verse 10 Down out of control. Snatched from fire give a word from the Lord. Means when we save people we should be discipling them. We have a obligation to bring the good news. Verse 15 Plans of the wicked. Verse 16 Plans against righteous. Righteous gets up because plans of the wicked can't stand against them. Verse 23 Can't be a respector of persons Verse 31 To the end ,confess scripture all you want, Ignore, Inactivity,and Idleness. Poor stewardship, sleep in the spirit leads to lack. Learn from mistakes not about feeling bad.

Chapter twenty five verse 1 know they are true, God hid Yahshuah, his plan from the enemy. We search scriptures to show ourselves approved. Verse 5 potter, clay Verse 8 meddling Verse 11 appropriate Verse 12 and 13 Refreshing Verse 14 Bragging produces nothing Verse 15 Fruit of spirit Metaphors are pictures Verse 20 Don't do any good make feel worse. Verse 23 Cause and effect Verse 25 Refreshing , Yahshuah Verse 26 pulls you in gets you thinking dirty Verse 27 Self righteous Verse 28 All over the place. No control over your emotions

Chapter twenty six verse 1 Out of place Verse 2 Has no effect Verse 3 Can't be trained , real discipline Verse 4 feed into it. Verse 7 No good Verse 8 Back fire Verse 9 Can't feel it Verse 10 no reason Verse 11 goes back Verse 12 right in our eyes Verse 13 excuses Verse 14 movement no progress Verse 15 holds bible never reads Verse 16 can't tell anything verse 17 *trouble maker Verse 18 prankster Verse 19 keeps going Verse 23 appearances Verse 24 not saying what he feels Verse 26 light exposes Verse 27 You do evil it falls back on you, fall in own trap*

Chapter twenty seven verse 2 Humility Verse 4 Self praise Verse 5 don't know about us Verse 6 Correction Verse 7 Hunger , meditate verse 8 Lust Verse 9 Friendly suggestions Verse 10 Do not abandon Verse 11 Have common sense Verse 13 Cosigning Verse 14 motive behind it Verse 15 Gets on your nerves. Verse 17 Lifts up Verse 19 Mirror Way we think real us Verse 20 Never learns, see what he wants to see. Verse 21 Condition of heart thinks the same Verse 23 Who is in fellowship? Verse 24 Love Verse 25 Righteousness Verse 26 System, Harvest, God cares for our needs. God first, he is the lamb.

Chapter twenty eight Verse 1 Inspite of what is going on. Verse 2 Morally wrong. To understand and know. Verse 3 Keeps at it until it's destroyed Verse 4 Complain Verse 9 purpose of prayer instruction . If your not going to obey God, why pray? Verse 11 Perfect in what God says Verse 15 Dangerous Verse 20 Inpatient Verse 25 closed fist means your stingy and unwilling to help someone Verse 27 Not God's way Verse 28 Good men go away then they come back

Chapter twenty nine Verse 1 Corrected taught answer but still don't do , unmoved Verse 5 Appearances don't mean it Verse 14 Treat people like family you reflect Yahshuah Verse 18 Know what's coming in spirit Verse 20 Doesn't think Verse 23 Submits to God Verse 26 Want to be seen

Chapter thirty What he affirms to be true Verse 4 Prophecy of God having a son. The name character means is what you represent. You know someone two ways by their name and their face. What about those witnesses who added to God's word. God says they will be reprimanded. Verse 7 to 9 Ask for deliverance from economical extremes. Verse 10 Telling one side of the story. Verse 16 Nothings ever enough except Yahshuah . Whose more than enough. Verse 17 Their peers. Verse 22 Not way suppose to be. Verse 32 and 33 Cause and effect.

Chapter thirty one   Verse 3 Men like sex which drains their strength Verse 4 Influence A woman of noble character Verse 10 Inner beauty Verse 13 Does what's necessary Verse 16 Business Verse 19 Maternal Verse 21 Clothed with God Verse 22 Royal Verse 24 Integrity verse 25 Doesn't worry Verse 27 Doesn't gossip Verse 32 Seen with eyes , physical attraction God doesn't see like that He sees our changed condition . God sees inside out. God gave me a telescopic eye where I see in snapshots.

Chapter 10
God's Wisdom (What's life)

So now we move to Ecclesiastics. This is a book of wisdom. Solomon did everything in life trying to find happiness. What he found out that nothing matters but God. He had the money to do whatever he wanted on this earth. Just like a lot of rich people who believe their money will sustain them until they get a evil report. Anything can happen to anybody at any time. Even though they don't realize it until it happens. Most have a set of rules for us and a set for them. Most rich people won't help anybody. They just learned how to navigate through this world or maybe they landed a really good job. They might of made wise decisions or came from money. We all face the same fate which is death. People may be able to cheat in life but they can't cheat death. I really don't care to much about a person dying. My big concern is where they are going to spend eternity. Read the story about the man and the big barns. He was saving up but he died the next day. Every thing has a time such as to be born and die. These times are specific and only God knows when they will occur. When some believers reap the benefits they forget the focus. Yahshuah should always be the focus. He blesses us so we can bless someone else and bring his kingdom. Now we get to one of my favorite books.

Chapter 11

A Love Song

Song of songs. This book has to be the epitome of love songs. It's Solomon singing to his bride. Covenant love. You could also look at it as Yahveh and his bride Israel or Yahshuah and the church. You know God made a man and a woman so they can enjoy covenant love. God talks a lot about the body especially a woman's breasts . Throughout the bible. The breast is the covering for the seat of emotions. He also tells the man to enjoy his own wife. The world trys to make everything God says perversed. God says we are wonderfully and beautifully made. He says in Psalms we are his masterpiece. God's always thinking about us. So why are we always doing everything for everybody else. In verse 9 and 10 prophetically I saw God change our condition when he put the pearls around her neck .

Chapter two The small things that get in the way. We shouldn't let anything separate us from the love of God.

Chapter three verse 11 That's the rapture. Chapter five verse 11 Yahshuah in his transformation state.

Chapter six How God thinks of us. Verse 9 The Church and Israel. Chapter seven Glorious church. Verse 7 Thoughts produce fruit.

Chapter eight We should be connected to the brothern. We belong to God and we should know that. Verse 7 Raging water can't destroy love. God is love. I had to say that. Verse eight children didn't grow up, How we see self. Verse 9 Do we see ourself as strong or weak. Verse 12 God and God's house. When you wake up in the spirit you will be able to see Yahshuah in every last book of the bible. When Yahshuah was on the cross they didn't see him until the *veil ripped. The veil was high and thick so only God could rip it. Even the Pharisees and the Suducees (the religious people) didn't see him at the time . Yahshuah wasn't religious but legal. He was the way we were reconciled back to God.*

CHAPTER 12
GOD'S SPOKES PEOPLE

The next section consists of the prophets. God's spokes people. All Prophets testify about Yahshuah. They all point to Yahshuah. The Holy spirit was working with them. The prophets took what Moses said, declared it and recited it. All Prophets are of Hebraic decent, Muhummad isn't. The prophets are decendants of the twelve tribes of Jacob. Jacob was Jewish. Even though the name Jewish wasn't coined until Israel divided. Jewish refered to Judah. When the Jewish People start coming back to Israel some won't refer to themselves as Jewish. They found black Jewish people that can be traced to the line of Aaron and Moses. Truth doesn't change . Only facts can change. God is the truth. Prophets explain Yahshuah's coming. Prophets reveal what God already established. God allowed them to see in to eternity. A prophet talks a harsh message. It's not for the weak or faint in spirit. It's a tough call but in the end it's a blessing. The word is controlled by the spirit.

Isaiah's name means Yahveh has saved. Has means he already done it. Everything was done in predestined time. Sin was put on Yahshuah. .Yahshuah was made sin. So righteousness could be put on us. What you do shows if you are in agreement. When you come into agreement you will see it manifest. Heart-Mind-Mouth. When you agree you manifest love and mercy. In this first chapter Isaiah has insights into the nature of God. We See God charging us and the earth is the witness. We influence the lives of others when we stand. The first thirty nine chapters deal with God's judgement. The last twenty seven chapters deal with comfort ,hope , mercy and grace. This talks about Christ. Verse 9 Talks about the remnant. Isaiah was well educated. He was a highly visible minister. He was influential, Dignified and misunderstood. He was a chaplain to the senate and had direct *access to the king of Israel. God took away from Israel not because they had so much but because they cared so little. Kind of sounds like us. Verse 15 Why do people think they can come to God any kind of way? Why do we think we can switch God on like the lights? Why do we think God is our genie? Do this Do that God.*

Chapter two verse 5 Talks of Yahshuah. People look at chariots and horses as being a great army. There's nothing greater or can stand up against God.

Chapter four The branch of Yahveh is Yahshuah. Verse 11,14 and 15 Israel goes into captivity. They have no knowledge and reject God's word. Hell is widening and more people are going for the same reason. We as believers need to get adamant about God.

Chapter six God's handpicking soldiers. Give back God's kingdom.

Chapter seven verse 13 to 16 Talks of Yahshuah coming in the flesh as a man.

Chapter eight verse 14 Yahshuah is the stumbling block for both kingdoms. They don't believe he came yet and they don't believe Yahshuah and God are the same. Verse 19 Talks about mediums and fortunetellers. God says we should go to his word instead. We don't listen that's why we have what we have. In chapter nine the Glory God will bring is Yahshuah. Glory is a full expression of God. God brought that expression in the flesh. Yahshuah broke the hold sin had on us. Sin is the burden and the hold was this world. Like I said verse 6 Talks about government. The government will rest on his shoulders. This earthly government has taken everything from God. No wonder it's a mess. Sar –Shalom. Prince of peace. It's funny how the muslims use this from our bible. His government and peace will have unlimited growth. How did we get religion. In the book of James it says true religion is taking care of widows, orpans, and not polluting our bodies. How many believers do that? When you get to verse 8 Assyria, Babylon and Persia are Iraq, Iran, Bagdad, Saudia Arbia and Syria. Verse 10 Where it talks about bricks falling that's the twin towers. One of our leaders said this over our nation. Best believe It's not a blessing but a judgement.

Chapter ten verse 5 Satan over man. Satan's in people over people over areas and nations. Satan has a well put together army that's constantly fighting our spirits. A third of the angels fell of a infinite number. How much is that? Believers are the only ones who don't know they are fighting. God opened up heaven one day and let me see that demonic activity. Why do you think they are in the ground? They are in the first and second heavenlies.

Chapter 11 verse 1 to 5 Speaks of Yahshuah. We have the same spirit. .It tells of the different aspects of Yahshuah and says he is of Hebraic descent. We know it was through his mother because we know who his father is. Verse 9 speaks of millennial rain. Verse 11 God Almighty the power side of God. This is the Holy spirit. The four corners of the earth are North ,South, East and West. Joseph's descendants will get their stuff back and Yahshuah will take care of Iraq and Iran.

Chapter twelve How we believe? God's not mad at us because he put his wrath on his son. So why aren't we happy? Verse 3 Wells of Salvation that's the promise of the Holy spirit.

Chapter thirteen verse 1 The Roman empire. Verse 11 Tribulation Verse 18 War This verse looks like what's happening here. God's hedge is coming down. People don't realize what that means. You think it's bad now. It's going to get a lot worse. All the demons will be running rampant and the only thing that will be able to stand is God's glorious church. The church in Acts a full grown church. It's on the way. A church full of spirit filled people.

Chapter sixteen verse 5 Yahveh's trusted king Yahshuah.

Chapter eighteen verse 2 smooth skinned people you know that's Ethiopia.

Chapter twenty two Ruler of New Jerusalem. Key of David. The key is Yahshuah that can unlock anything. Key to the kingdom. A key indicates control and authority.

Chapter twenty four verse 4 Fourth bowl judgement. Chapter twenty seven verse 13 Shaphar will be blown . The shaphar being blown means the coronation of a king. It talks of Yahshuah and his millennial rain.

Chapter twenty eight verse 11 and 12 Want to rest gift of tongues. Highest level of tongues is you speaking in another language. So people that don't speak the language can understand you. Then it's our prayer language that only we and God can understand. The enemy can't understand, that's why God gave it to us. We are fighting the enemy and God doesn't want the enemy to know the plans. Just like in the military. The Holy spirit's part of God and you can only fellowship with someone like you. That's why we have God's spirit. The Holy spirit witnessed what God did. That's another reason for the trinity so they could witness what happened. If they didn't witness it, it would be hearsay and thrown out. So how can those other witnesses be witnesses, if they didn't witness anything. We bear witness with God's spirit. Bear means to carry and we carry God's spirit in us.

Chapter twenty nine Saying one thing and doing something else. Verse 7 Rehab evil chaos verse 8 The tablets the bible or scriptures. Saying to the prophets does it take all that. Or come on man I got something to do. Which caused the Holy one not to work. Caught up in our life. which proves what we do for God. We never have time for God but when we are in trouble we cry out to God. God where are you? We have no relationship with the one who calls. We receive the name in vain. We make the name worthless. Simply not doing word doing our way. Verse 12 Is God responding to us. Verse 14 Shaking end of man. God showed me how he closed man's chapter. Isaiah represents the son. I would say we are experiencing some shaking. Jeremiah represents the father. In the Old Testament before the son came God was always covering Israel because the fight wasn't fair until he brought the spirit back. Ezekiel represents the spirit where we are now, God's raising up a lot of people.

God confirmed man's day being over with a story of two little boys one named Jeremiah the other Isaiah. They saved two babies from a fire in Florida. The babies I believe were one month and eight months. Beginning and Eternity. I've seen a lot of signs like crosses in the clouds and red clouds. The four blood moons. Two on Passover and two on Tabernacles. I believe God is saying beginning and end. He said it twice because it is important. Remember when God took them out of Eypt after Passover he told Moses to tell the people it is the beginning of months for them. We need to pay attention.

In chapter thirty verse 15 God tells us to repent. Repent means to turn. We need to turn back to God. No effort from us. He finished the work. Yahshuah spent forty days teaching us how to do it. So all we need to do is do it to change. Israel was a desert but God made it bloom. Russia is much bigger but has a problem producing food. Nothing is impossible for God.

Chapter thirty two verse 15 speaks of Pentecost. Verse 17 What Yahshuah did on the cross. The act of righteousness, that brought about peace. Chapter thirty three verse 14 talks of hades.

Chapter thirty three verse 22 God as judge and king.

Chapter thirty five Grace does what we can't do. We need God's grace so we can do what we can't do. Verse 8 speaks of the millenum. Chapter thirty eight Ahab had a sundial clock. God gave Hezekiel another fifthteen years to his life.

I use this story a lot when I tell my own testimony. A testimony is something that happened. In this life we constantly fight . I've had several attacks to my body. I beat ovarian tumors, breast and lupus. I was on the table and I told God I'm not scared to die but my kids were small and I didn't want to leave them. I remember I was on morphine and I told the doctor I want to go home . I went home and got better. Then with the Lupus I was swollen and wanted to die .I was like God please take me. God sent me manna from heaven and healed me . Then with the breast my breast hurt so bad I went to the doctor .It was coming off. I took it to God I said God either you are going to heal me like Hezekiel or I'm coming to heaven maimed. He healed me. I was on that table and the doctors don't know what happened. Even if they took my breast. I will fight for the cause until I close these eyes. God showed me people praying for me every day years before I had health problems. God told me these people carry a lot of weight with him. You can have people praying who aren't even connected to God. You think God listens to them? God's not a appearance God. If people aren't connected to God it's like shooting empty words into the air. Which mean nothing. The heart's not in it. We should be constantly praying for one another. I pray for everyone I know by name. I'm already in the fight before anything kicks off. What is it when we ask people to pray for our love ones. Is it selfishness? Do we ever pray for anyone? We should strive to be more like Yahshuah.

Chapter forty Get revelation waiting for the Lord expect change don't focus on situation . Waiting ,expecting, strength, and renewal. It's not like waiting on the bus. When God says waiting we are actively doing the things of God. Verse 5 a voice cries out in the desert is John the Baptist. This is when I got hope. Energized. What God said is my focus. You can't say you got it when it happens . We are in manifested time but you can't put time on eternity. We can't change people they have to have a encounter with God. Verse twenty two Talks about the earth being round. Hey that's before Christopher Columbus discovered America.

Chapter forty two verse 1 Speaks of Yahshuah. Verse 4 Millinenial rain. Verse 18 Talks of God bringing Israel home. I think on the news politicians from Denmark are calling Israel home. Verse three Talk of Jacob's name change to Israel. So we know who God's people are.

Chapter forty four It shows us all about us. Self. God's promising what he will give them. Verse twenty Speaks of deception being worse than the actual sin because it goes on. Verse 17 Talks of Israel being saved. Israel became a nation in 1948. Talks about Abraham's decendants coming back. Verse 5 Was Yahshauh . Verse 13 Sinful man can't carry the weight of sin it's to heavy.

Chapter fifty three. It's finished. He paid the price. Who he his and what he's done. Yahshuah settled the debt for his people. He suffered and died for us. He carried sin. It was put on him like righteousness was put on us. The price of flesh was hanging on a tree. He was wounded for our transgressions . For what we done. Standing on what he did. After three hours in church we are tired unless we are doing something we want to do. Don't only go by what you see. John the beloved could only base life on what he saw. He didn't become the revelator until he knew the scriptures. We have a responsibility to pray and study. Why aren't you happy. In tune with the bible. If we are crying we don't see God. Yahshuah's standing there. Everything he has we have . My father is God. No revelation can't see him. Yahshuah's right there. Identifying with us from our aspect. God's always identifying with us. Why don't we identify with him ? God's 100% God and 100% man. God had to come legally as a man. He had to be forsaken to die. If God hadn't forsaken his son he couldn't accept us. We were sinful and unconnected to him. Yahshuah connected us back to God. He had to get in the ground to get the keys and lease from the enemy. Yahshuah had to shed his blood for remission of sin. This was the only way God could accept us. Verse 7 He had a mouth but he didn't speak . He took our judgement. So we be shown mercy .If we don't get anything earthly we don't think he loves us. Verse 11 Judicial Act Verse 12 Name above every name. We declare the name.

Chapter fifty four See things because of disobedience provoke, jealousy. It's like you love somebody and they love somebody else. We make life or a job God. Verse 13 Kingdom and Yahshuah. Ingathering of nations. Verse 17 God takes responsibility of the waster. He can handle him. God's never mad at you put wrath on his son. Came so we would know how we suppose to be. God's word is his image. Words paint pictures.

Chapter fifty five Hear and you get increase. The dollar gets your attention in the natural. Ho trying to get our attention. Hey the number of grace. So hey-ho belongs to God not in the club with a forty. Why are we stressed out ? You have to hear and plug in to God's system. What does hearing have to do with doing stuff. Verse 10 God's word will do what he sent it to do. God's word has a purpose. Verse 12 Creation yielding to us. Then things grow. Strength, freedom and making aloud noise.

Chapter fifty six. Blessed is the one who keeps the day of worship from becoming unholy and his hands from doing anything wrong. Verse 6 Nations look to Israel and scatter tribes came home.

Chapter fithy eight Satisfied in drought, dry places going to encounter, inspite of his finished work. That's why we believe, he continually guides us.

Chapter fifty nine Government of vengeance. Don't box God in. Telling Israel here for you. Sin separated you from me. God wants to be with us . Not going to lower his standard. Verse 20 If redeemer not in covenant we can't be blessed.

Chapter sixty Rise and Shine

Chapter Sixty one verse 1 Willing to receive verse 2 Jubilee Get double blessing double for your trouble. Rejoicing because you have blesseth assurance in midst of defeat your movement not in vain. What you can give and what you like to give. Verse 6 intercessors.

Chapter Sixty three Second coming judgement. Verse 11 Spirit in Yahshuah.

Chapter Sixty five verse 11 Worshipping money verse 25 Millenium verse 26 Earth will be destroyed

Chapter sixty six verse 8 Israel became a nation in 1948 Technology happened fast. Israel became a nation in one day. Isaiah was sawed in half long ways. God said the world was not worthy of his prophets. The world didn't appreciate them. Some of the prophets knew each other and where around the same era. The prophets had dealings with the kings who ruled the government. The bible isn't hard. It's every day life .People just like us. Times moving and you can't redeem it. The only thing that can't be redeemed. The bible's a complete story somewhere the story stopped being told.

Now we come to Jeremiah which means Yahshuah will lift up He represents the father part of the trinity. The father lifted up Yahshuah so his body wouldn't see decay and so he could be our sacrifice. Isaiah represents the son and Ezekiel the spirit. Before you are you,you have a assignment even though most of us never get to do ours. This prophet was sent to a adulterous world. God always exssisted and knew us before we were in our mother's womb. You need to pay attention to their faces. You can't hide your face. Your face tells the story. Your face should look like God. You can't get better until you do better. Verses 6 to 10 Jeremiah saying he's young and can't do it. That's the humanity side of him speaking. He's going by his efforts and abilities to get the job done. God's talking about eternity and his finished work. We have to partake of God's finished work.

Chapter three What we are in life we base it on our knowledge.

Chapter four verse 40 Great tribulation.

Chapter six verse 16 Israel refused correction and ignored ten shimitah years. Verse 17 There is no situation that God hasn't solved. God wants to share his glory with us.

Chapter nine Skill doesn't matter. Why are you allowing that to hinder you. Verse 23 Strength and money don't matter. Why worry about your luck it makes no difference. So why worry about it. God's bigger. Verse 26 Talks about uncircumcised hearts= unsubmitted to God

Chapter ten God says give your heart to me and he will supply. Verse three talks about the Christmas tree. Xmas is cultural you can't find it in the word. Its' not Yahshuah's birthday which I will explain later. The shepherds were at Yahshuah's birth . Shepherds were considered low life and dirty. There were three gifts. Gold, for a king. Myrrh for his death and frankincense because he's a priest. When the wise men came it wasn't at the birth. They came to the house .Yahshuah probably was two and could open the door. We know this because Herold wanted to kill all the boys under two. When the wise men traveled they normally were in a group of twelve or more because of dangerous times. God's the truth .Yahshuah celebrated the feast of dedication. The feast is the feast of lights. God lights us .The light is Yahshuah. The cross is the answer to our mess. If we are working in darkness there's no connection to God . Love has to love you first so you know what love is. Christmas is a pagan holiday. Really what does it mean? Just tell people you like getting and giving gifts. Christ was born around tabernacles. When Constantine decided to make Christianity the state religion he never changed the way he thought. They threw Yahshuah in with all their pagan beliefs. When God told them not to do it. They threw everything Jewish out and kept all those pagan traditions. Traditions of men. The Romans didn't like Jews. Yahshuah's birthday wasn't important because he has no birthday. If it was important why can't we pinpoint the exact day. All the pagan gods had birthdays. They threw Yahshuah in with the sun god's birthday. Which is Tammuz which is Allah. I will explain that later. The birthday had to do with the winter solace. Which marks the on set of winter by the shortest day which is the 21 of December .On December the 25 the sun stops declining. Then the sun starts to rerise. If anything we should remember the feasts. Besides there's no reference in the bible to Yahshuah's birthday. Christ was already here. We get excited over a birthday because it's our first time here. We Should celebrate God's presence. How do we associate xmas with God's presence. Did anyone get saved? It's lustful and selfish. We didn't give God anything. It's something I want. Anything the world embraces it's not of God. All the world does is increase their profits. How morbid. The world constantly mocking God. Look at the color of candy canes. White for righteousness and red for the blood. Then we hang ornaments on a tree . When Yahshuah hung on a tree. He became a curse so we could be blessed. Around this time of year there's, more suicide, depression and high levels of stress. With Tabernacles it's a big party. We are teaching our children to follow diver lusts. They are using our God and savior for their ungodly gain. It's not of God but we embrace it. Christmas is not in the bible. It's all about money. Besides the world took Christ out of xmas. Look at the words happy xmas, happy holidays and holy days. I say us as believers should pull our money and resources out and invest in the kingdom. Yahshuah is so far from our children's minds. Paul references the feasts. How is it of God? We open gifts, eat and sleep. Remember the fig tree. It wasn't walking in the truth. Meaning it was lying, so it was cursed. It was lying about having fruit. We are God's allotment. God can't curse us but we can walk in the curse . Our kids are walking under the curse but we call it mercy. Walk in the truth . God gave us the greatest gift when he lit us up. We need to understand God's light and bear witness to it. There are nine gifts of the spirit. Yahshuah's birth on earth was fleshy and God's not going to let any flesh glorify in his presence. When God tells you to celebrate the name, it means something. Why do we do what we want to do and wonder where the power is? God's not going to share his altar. If not xmas then what? The feast of dedication. Whenever God gives us something he gives it a name. What does xmas mean. Verse 23 talks about preachers that don't seek God. They don't listen are stupid and won't succeed. There's no relationship with God. So how do you get to know somebody if you don't talk to them?

Chapter seventeen verse 5 Talks of human effort. Trusting in man. Why do we only have confidence when we are sitting in church? Satan's constantly attacking. Verse 19 We need to get in God's presence so he can reveal himself to us. The righteous branch is Yahshuah.

Chapter twenty nine I thought I would say more in this book. I guess God doesn't think I need to. God gives you hope and a future. What is God's purpose for our lives. If we execute God's plan how is it ours. We are complete in God. God's over top of everything and gives us gifts to empower us. The gifts he gave us, he gave them to us before predestined time. The gifts are unrevocable meaning he's not going to take them back. God's no Indian giver. Some people say a lot of gay men sing on the choir. God gave them the gift. They are just living from the wrong part of their exsistence. They could sing before they were born. Maybe if we were a bright light they wouldn't be gay anymore. They would be drawn to the light. That's sin we can see but what about the ones you can't see. We need to examine ourselves first. We better take that plank out of our eye first before we start messing with the speck in our brother's eye. Eye represents the way we see . You know you actually see with your mind. Everyone has a part to play to support the ministry. Not to rule over people with our gifts. A man's gifts make room for him. God's gifted us but our gifts are for someone else. Our gifts are for us to serve others. Like a doctor, dentist , hairdresser. We need each other. Iron sharpens Iron. No one person will glorify. God knows us. He wants us to share our gifts not be selfish. We need to give up our life daily and come with humility. Pick up our crosses and be willing to die for the cause. We need to be humble and do good.

Chapter thirty verse 12 Already set what you will get

Chapter thirty one verse 15 Talks of the desendants of Benjamin being slaughtered. Verse 20 Tribe of Joseph being fruitful. Verse 22 Yahveh will create something new on earth .A woman will protect a man. The fight I was talking about goes back to the garden. Verse 31 The New Covenant in the Old Testament. It's not going to be a type and shadow like Passover. Yahshuah took the penalty you break a covenant you would die. Yashuah put the spirit back in us .

Chapter thirty three verse 25 God gives us boundaries.

Chapter Thirty five verse 13 Priviledge and honor.

Chapter forty four verse 10 Allow God to be God which we don't.

Chapter forty seven Six day war. Jeremiah watches the fall of Judah and God's people are cast off.

Lamenations is a book of mourning. Chapter Three talks of Identity and us examining ourselves. God has me breezing through. Whatever God has my eyes focused on that's what I write. Do you guys remember Steve Austin the six million dollar man it's sort of like that.

You guys can read the bible yourself. I wanted to show you guys it's a complete story. I gave you the outline now take it to God. Connect the dots. I am very practical and I talk like every day people. I just want God's people to have understanding. So they can walk in the spirit and be victorious.

My man Ezekiel is very deep and his name means God will strengthen. He represents the spirit in the trinity. In a court all sides of God has to be represented. This is the period we are in on this earth. We are suppose to be moving things in the spirit. You are going to see a lot more women coming on the scene. The spirit is neither male or female. We just have a body to touch this earth. Whatever your nationality that's the color of your suit. I just want all believers to be united. So we can take out the enemy and be who God says we are. The enemy wants us divided because he knows God's system. The believers seem to be the only ones that don't know. Ezekiel was a priest whose wife died. He loved his wife. God told him not to mourn his wife. This was a visual representation of God and his people. God showed examples visually to the people so they would understand. The Holy spirit wasn't in then to teach them. Ezekiel expressed out God's word. He was a prophet who could see. Not all prophets could see. The people were rebelling. They forgot what God did. The hardest people to reach with the gospel are church people. Spiritual fornification was going on. Like us putting things before God. We need to know the Holy spirit gives to us. Chapter one verse 10 Represents the four gospels. Yahshuah as a servant, as a king, his humanity side and his deity. It is also a description of cherubim in the garden. The wheels means the gospel needs to go everywhere. We need ceaseless activity and energy for God.

In chapter one God dealt with suffering with his glory. Ezekiel got to experience God's glory. That happened to me. He was at the throne of God.

Chapter three Shows God putting words in Ezekiel's mouth. We all should be saying God's words. Ezekiel is the watchman meaning he has to see everything. God always lets you know when he's going to do something. There's no mystery in God. God is strictly by his word.

Chapter eight verse 5 That Idol Allah. Tammuz is Allah. So called gods always have more than one name. Then it talks about the men of the east worshipping with their back turned from God's temple and Jerusalem. Muslims are called the men of the east. In the book of Daniel Daniel prays towards Jerusalem. So you can't say they follow the prophets. Tammuz is a sun God and that's who Abraham was worshipping before the true God called him out. God made Abraham a Jew outwardly with the covenant of circumcision. Allah tells you to do but God already finished it. How can you earn your way into heaven . God will not be a debtor to any man. It's like you are working for a pay check. Like God has to pay you. Allah treats you like property. What kind of God would lean to one particular set of people when he made everybody. Now I'm going to say this again there's a ancient paper called The Epic of Atrachasis Coneiform. It tells the story of a great flood. It talks of all the gods fighting for head deity. Now this is older then the scriptures. It speaks of Tammuz and Allah being the same the names aren't covered up. It even says he was a transvestite. Then it talks of a God name Enlil who was the God of breath who took care of this so called Allah. We should know breath means spirit. Which is our God who blew the spirit in the man in Genesis. That spirit being the Holy spirit. Israel knows God as Yahveh also. This epic also speaks of a snake which they link to the beast. The dead sea scrolls has the whole book of Isaiah intact. Which is about the son. Now Muhummad came out of the church in Rome. Rome wanted the land of Jerusalem. They groomed him up, then he went south on them. They taught him the one God theory and also the body was bad and should be silenced. Hebrew people are expressive. God wants us to go deep with him. They believe God's so far away. God wants a relationship with us . God had a relationship with Adam and Eve in the garden. In the book of Deuteronomy, Israel had Gods for everything. The wind ,water, sun,moon,stars etc. That's why God said I'm one God. He's one God because he's in charge of everything. People would have you believe that he three Gods and not the same. Like I said before A man can be a father, son, and a husband. Why can't God Be God as the father God as the son God as the spirit. The Holy spirit represents man's spirit. The Father represents the soul and the Son represents the body. Three in one.

My sister works at a mental hospital and a person that has multiple personalities said to her I didn't do it. He did it. She told him if he did it you all did it. Now you can understand a person which is a perversion of God having multiple personalities, housed in one substance. Believers need to read and think.

A friend of mine who is a muslim said to me that Muhummad had to force the religion on people. Why would God do that if we have freewill? God never wanted robots. He made us thinking and reasoning like him. Besides God gave us a form of government. Religion is man's way to reach God. Man's always trying to pull God down to his level. What I noticed the muslim people took out where God does the talking and turned his word into stories. I tell people they are not just cute little stories. Wake your spirit man up and let the bible define itself.

Chapter 11 God's going to have his people . He's calling them back to Israel. A politician from Denmark made a call to the Jewish people to come home. We need to pay attention to the news. The bible is prophetic meaning it's for the spirit man to comprehend. Now these people who say they are prophets what's the message?

Chapter thirteen verses 17 to 23 Talks of fortunetellers, psychics ,false prophets etc.

Chapter fifthteen Tells how Israel's not fit for anything.

The end of sixteen says how Israel does stuff and gets nothing for it. See God is only revealing himself to who he's in covenant with. God's legal he has to be he's a judge.

Chapter eigthteen God says the life of every person belongs to me. The person who sins will die. Soul means life. Life is your soul which is in your body. The real you. So why do we keep pumping up this natural man. The natural man's defeated and going in the ground.

Chapter twenty verse 13 Talks of people rejecting the kingdom.

Chapter twenty one The sword of the Lord is the word of God.

Verse twenty seven talks of God giving the kingdom to Yahshuah.

Chapter twenty three Russia's the army they are talking about.

Chapter twenty five Ammon Lot's son from incest will be judged. Part of the muslim nation.

Chapter twenty eight verse 11 Speaks of the devil. Tells who Lucifer is. That he wanted to rule and that he had a big ego and was filled with pride.

Chapter thirty talks of end times. God takes care of everybody even if they think they were somebody on earth.

In chapter thirty three God gives Ezekiel his assignment. We all have a assignment. You think God's happy about us sitting in a pew? Hey God I made it. You really think that's why God died? Verse 30 Talks about hearing a good word. Okay you heard, now what you going to do? Are you just going to leave it as a good feeling in church?

Chapter thirty four The new shepherd. Yahshuah. We need to take God's thoughts as ours. In verses 7 and 8 God talks about selfish pastors that don't take care of the sheep. The last part says the sheep won't be food for the pastor meaning pastors shouldn't depend on the congregation for money but God. The church is so out of order you know it's not God's church. The people didn't do God's plan but spend so much time doing worthless things that meant nothing.

Chapter thirty nine verse 4. Israel becomes a nation.

Chapter forty God talks about his new temple. See in the natural, God's temple should be Holy and separate. In eternity it will be perfection, Completion and grace. No sin No enemy. The end.

Chapter forty three. Speaks after the treaty and tribulation period. Israel's going back to doing sacrifices. We will be raptured up. Verse 8 talks of the roc of the dome. They put their doorway by my doorway and their door post by my door posts. Only a wall separated me from them. That wall the one you see hebrew people kissing. The bible's prophetic if the enemy knew that, the bible probably would of not made it.

Chapter forty four Talks of clean and unclean. Verse 30 What value do you put on God? Your condition changes when God puts the blessing on you. You received a name change from sinner to saint. It's up to us to line up . We have to line the way we act with what he did.

Chapter forty seven Talks of the end and the new Jerusalem.

Chapter forty eight the Lord is there.

Daniel's name means God is my judge. How to sing the Lord's song. The Lord's song is his story. Daniel was singing the song in a foreign land. We all know the story of Daniel so I'm just going to pick out a few parts. Daniel was a prophet in captivity

Chapter two verse 43 Ten toes represents kings. War against Yahveh. Verse 45 Roman empire. Daniel prayed three times a day, facing Jerusalem. Look at Ezekiel chapter eight verse 11. Declaration of Independence. The lion is Great Britain . Two feet like a human and was given a human mind was uncle sam .

Chapter seven verse 4 Talks about the wings plucked out standing like a human that's definitely the U.S. I saw the U.S. going into captivity Just like Israel went they were held captive by Eypt and Babylon. This nation doesn't want God and China's buying up the U.S. like hot cakes. You see the U.S in the beginning of Revelation and then they just fade away. The bear is Russia, The leopard is Germany. Verse 18 The horns the Soviet Union. Then it talks of the Anti Christ and Satan forming a union. Verse 9 Brillance Verse 11 Beast, new world order. Then it talks of Yahshuah Verse 19 Great Tribulation. Chapter eight Ram is a grown up sheep Read this chapter this is end time stuff. Daniel wrote the prophecy before the U.S was formed. If we don't obey the word of God we are just like animals . Never manifesting the kingdom of God but the animal kingdom. The best or survival of the fittest ends this chapter. This is a real big book. It speaks of Russia, Asia , Turkey ,Iran and Iraq.

Daniel chapter nine verse 22 Talks of end times. Talks of the Anti Christ covenant. Gensis chapter 15 verse 18 talks of Israel coming home to their promised land. Confirmation of the peace agreement. God's setting the stage. When God showed me muslims praying in a catholic church the stage's being set. Believers better wake up. They don't believe God and Yahshuah are the same. They don't believe in first fruits. I don't care what people believe. I'm just trying to wake up believers. I know it's all about the spirit. If it's a form of government and we are going to court how can it be more than one way? Yahshuah never called himself Christian but of the way. Then it speaks of the sacrifices being stopped halfway through the seven year arrangement. Abomination of desolation is when the antichrist will stand in God's temple saying he's God. Some Jewish People in my area met in the ninties to talk about temple worship. I heard they have the utensils, furniture and may even have the red heifer. It takes nothing now to put a temple together. We are a lot closer then you think. Everything that's happening over here is a distraction to where we are really going. Verse 26 Period of time 400 years. Jerusalem's rebuilt. Ill talk more of end times when I get to Revelations. The Old Testament was a lot of seeing in the natural. A fore shadow. What comes before. The Bible is repetitious. I guess so we eventually get it. This and chapter ten all end time stuff.

Chapter eleven verse 21 Peace treaty. The peace treaty is gueared to hold them back. It's not going to work. It's crazy to me that we agree with people that will blow everybody up. Then in verse thirty two this is like the lukewarm Christian. Who has no intensity or passion for God.

Hosea speaks of deliverance. Hosea was married to a prostitute. The scenario here is us being married to God. We are adulterous, just running around on God. Hosea takes his wife back like God takes us back.

In chapter three verse 3 refers to us working out our salvation.

Chapter four verse 10 Says they will eat and never be full meaning they won't produce anything even though they are working.

Chapter five God condemns leadership. Verse 9 God will make the truth known to Israel. The truth is Yahshuah in the millineum.

Chapter six Verse two Christ resurrected. Verse 3 It's about understanding and knowing God Verse eleven Talks about coming out of captivity. So what believers need to do is come out of the world. The world is holding the believer in captivity. Just like the yoke holds us to sin. We need to be unified. We aren't respected and we are being prosecuted right here. Just cause we aren't being physically killed our spirits are being taken down. Christ our foundation removed rottenness which begins Israel's returning in the last days. Prophetically speaking Verse 9 ministers not preaching word of God. God's word is light everything else is death.

Chapter seven No shame. No morality doing it with out any respect or regards to God. Applauding wickedness. They were influenced by sex and alcohol. Verse seven Israel had no good kings and Judah had some. Verse 11 Looking for help everywhere but God. Verse 12 Speaks of a trap. Verse 13 God had redemption till the people turned away. Verse 14 No remorse didn't realize judgement. Verse 16 talks of rulers falling because of there futile words.

Chapter eight Judgement , famine and enemies taking what they have. Verse 8 All over the world. Verse 11 talks of the atmosphere. God's atmosphere is very important. Verse 12 The people didn't know the law. Law is a written rule for a government. Where did we get religion from?

Chapter ten verse 5 the people were trying to out do each other. Verse 7 Good for nothing.

Chapter eleven What led them to sin. God didn't force people to serve him. That cancels out Muhummad's theory about forcing the people to follow him. Old Testament verse 7 Refused God. Verse 9 They didn't receive what they deserved. Verse 10 God's the intended judge. Verse 11 God's not accountable to anyone. You can fool people but not God.

Chapter twelve Explains what's going to happen to Israel. Verse 2 While in the womb Jacob and Esau's characters were being shaped. The angel brought Jacob to submission and blessed him. You can fight with God all you want but you better surrender because you can't win. Verse 7 Tells of business. Verse 8 How the rich think dishonestly . Thinking money will sustain them . Verse 9 God's not done with Israel Verses 13 Moses Verse 14 Guilt allows you to remain judged.

Chapter thirteen verse 4 Yahshuah verse 14 Conquered death hell and the grave.

Chapter fourteen verse 2 Yahshuah verse 2 Yahshuah's spirit coming back to us. Verse three Horses represent power. Verse four Talks of disobedience.

Joel means Yahveh is God. This book deals with a plague of locusts. The coming day of God. The prediction of the Gospel Age. Fear of locusts, deliverance, and warning. Prediction of Holy spirit age. Need to turn away from sin. Joel said decree a thing and I will do it. God showing this is the day of the spirit. Don't you think we should grow up our spirits. Amazing keys and we don't do any of them. It says by the fruit of the lips you will be satisfied. So it's all about saying something. Even if we are not feeling good we should say something. God's not about feelings. At all times I will praise the Lord. What do I do when I get a evil report? Or if I lose my job? God can't get anything out of us then. Satan closes our mouths. You think your belly which is normal equals life. What you put in your belly sustains your natural life. Then God talks about everything withering away. The first step to prosperity is joy. Joy will propel you into prosperity. What's happening locust famine starvation. Key word nothing. Key words in chapter one hear, wake, mourn. Verse four you can interpret it as a army with bombs and foot soldiers, Verse 5 What influences you should be Yahshuah. Verse 6 Nothing to give. Outpouring of God's spirit on his people. This is fulfilled on day of Pentecost. Verse 11 Instructions for the fall. Hear, Wake, mourn, Cryout. God always gives us Instructions. We aren't speaking the right things. It doesn't cost a thing. Hands fulfill what words say. What seed are you sowing? They were ritually praying. No meaning just doing it. Like they were doing something. Planned. The angels come for our words. They don't come for our emotions or circumstances but words. Most of time we speak death. What are we saying? What are we listening to? World security is based on Israel. Israel as a nation. We need to pray people wake up. Most people don't care. They just want to pay bills. Everything in our nation is opposite the king. Verse 12 Surely the joy of mankind has withered away. Joy is the first step to prosperity. Verse 14 Instruction. Verse 18 No harvest Verse 19 cryout.

Chapter two God speaks warns about judgement .Asurrances. They should want presence of God inspite of their unworthiness. Verse three talks about the terrible day of the Lord. This day is for those that don't know God. Around verses 10 and 11 True worshippers in spirit and truth because the spirit will be put back in the man. The spirit being the truth. The way of escape rend your heart. Turn back to God. Not just appearing to do it like we do but mean it. Then we have to have faith towards God. Doing what we believe. The inner you. Verse 13 tells you who God is. Verse 15 Gives you a Instruction after you repent. Verse 16 They had to gather and leave what they had three times a year. This is a picture of corporate success. Verse 18 end times, prophet to the king New Testament Gospel aged fulfilled. Verse 20 Russia. Verse 21 Instruction . First be glad and rejoice. Already done. Verse 29 Holy spirit. Sons and daughters prophesize. More women prophets. Verse 33 The tribes know he's God now. They know his name and his fame.

Chapter three Yahshuah's reign and judgement . The Lord helps his people and seizes the others. Verse 12 Harvest verse 16 utterance of God's voice , freewill Verse 17 prosperity Verse 19 Esau's descendants Verse 21 Blood shed so they will be punished for what they done.

Amos name means seer and burden bearer. He was a market place prophet meaning he was a street minister. He was the prophet for the poor. God took him from tending sycamore trees to being his man in the streets. Sorta like me.

Chapter one talks of judgement, drought and famine. People in this book were committed to war crimes such as dragging logs with spikes in them over people. Verse 5 The Jewish people were deported and sold into slavery. What I see here is if you don't listen to God you will be placed in bondage. When we were delivered.

Chapter two verse 3 End time. Verse 7 God never meant for women to be passed around. God's word is progressive. Verse 8 talks of a defiled atmosphere. Everything's a cause and a effect. Verse 16 The day of the Lord. That's the day of judgement. It was a lofty justice system. God has a inflexible righteousness which leads him to judge.

Chapter three verse three deals with relationship. Verse 7 There's no mystery in God. He gives the heads up. Verse 10 munipulation. Verse 15 Only thing that's going to stand is God's kingdom.

Chapter four Verse 13 Reveals God's thoughts to humans.

Chapter five verse 20 when the believers are gone. Verse 21 Results in not putting God first. Verse 21 to 23 traditions never coming to reality.

Chapter six stop look and listen. Verse 8 where God swears on himself no-ones higher than God. So it is going to happen. Verse 13 Labor is a low place.

Chapter seven Judgement. A plumb line was used. It was a tool to make sure a wall was standing straight up and down. Amos saw in a vision God using this to measure the people of Israel to see if they were true to him. The people weren't true to God in their worship does that sound familiar.

Chapter eight End of harvest. Verse 3 People pushed the button. Verse 4 God brought them down to poverty level never able to get up. Verse 5 and 6 thinking they are getting over on God. Verse 7 Pride of Jacob is Yahshuah. Yahshuah the Messiah Chapter nine verse 2 God's everywhere doesn't change. Verse 3 there's no escape Verse 4 They go willing but will be judged . Can we escape? Verse 11 Yahshuah Verse 21 Resetting the fallen tent. I saw Kirk franklin in this . Kirk Franklin is musically inclined and loves to dance for the Lord like David. David instituted music in the tabernacle. We should celebrate God. Why didn't God say the tabernacle of Moses. David established praise and he was a man after God's own heart. Verse 14 down speaks of the millennium. This to the end is all end times. The prime minister is calling Israel back home.

Obadiah means servant of Yahveh. This book talks of the fall of Esau's Descendants. They fell because they didn't care and committed violent acts against their brothers. Verse 8 Look at how the weather man can predict the weather. This book tells what's going to happen to them. It's a cause and effect.

Jonah's name means dove. Dove means peace and freedom. This book talks about a prophet who didn't want to do what God wanted him to. He didn't want to prophesize to Ninevah. So he ended up being in the belly of a whale. He was in the belly for three days before the whale spit him out. So he could do his assignment. This was a visual of what Yahshuah would do. Later Yahshuah told the people of his time this would be the only sign they would have. Meaning this would be the only thing they see. A sign shows what time it is and where we are going. Are we paying attention?

Micah means who is like Yahveh? This book talks of the condemnation of the rich because of the way they treat the poor. It speaks of judgement because of moral decline. It predicts the birth of the Messiah. Samaria is the capital of Israel and Jerusalem is the capital of Judah. This is after Israel divided. It actually divided in three. Aram being the other part. You know the writers of the bible had to be led by the spirit because it told the personalities of the prophets. No matter how weird or strange they may have been. A human writer wouldn't of told all that.

Chapter one talks of God testifying against Israel. Then it speaks of the crime being Idols. Chapter two verse 11 talks about the type of preacher the people want and he's not righteous. The preacher is telling people what they want to hear not what God said.

Chapter three where God talks about Israel but you can look at it as being the U.S. The U.S is the spiritual Israel.

Chapter four Prophecy of future glory because of the promise. Yahshuah Verse 6 prime minister calling Israel back home.

Chapter five Bethlehem means house of bread. These people were worshipping the sun. God is to his people like the sun is to the universe. Verse 3 speaks of Yahshuah. Some texts have the sun of righteousness which is a play on words because we all know the sun is bright and the son's way brighter.

Chapter six Pleading , repentance, cause of redemption Verse 9 talks of dishonesty. Verse 16 Tells why God let them go into captivity. Then it talks of pardoning of Integrity. Verse

6 and 7 Because of who God is that's why your family members are against each other. If they don't have the spirit of God and you do they are a opposition to you. Starting at verse 11 Israel starts coming back. Verse 18 examine yourself find the sin so God can pardon you. God doesn't want sin to rule over us. God wants us to put sin under our feet. So don't be ashamed.

Nahum means compassion. Nahum was to prophesize the destruction of Nineveh. I would say most of the prophets did not have a good message. The generation before them didn't pass the knowledge of God. These people did repent and changed their direction after they heard the message. So we need to tell someone. Verse 12 talks of human effort. Verse 15 talks of the gospel of Christ.

Chapter three woe talks of deep suffering, grief trouble and misfortune.

Habakkuh's name means embraced by God. A book of injustice. The just shall live by faith. God allowed someone worse then Judah to use violence and force on them. They were way worse Habukkah was like Judah's not as bad as these guys. The Babylonians weren't covenant people either. To send them into captivity. The Babylonians are the middle east. Habakkuh questioned, Why? God used a pagan nation to chastise his people. The Babylonians were real cruel. Judah didn't listen to God they were about themselves. They were all about self effort when a righteous man trusts God. Then God answers the prophet. God says his people are unfaithful and worship false Gods. Just like us spiritual Israel. This nation is going into captivity. China has a lot of stock in the U.S and I heard they own Walmarts. We don't want God we just appear to want God. A form of Godliness. We share God's altar with everything. God blessed me with the gift when someone says something I know what it is. In verse 3 About God's finished work. What he sees and in closing no matter what, look towards and like God.

Now we get to Zephaniah whose name means the Lord has hidden. God hid Yahshuah in himself because we have a enemy. The enemy hates God's man. God always perserves a remnant. A faithful servant in the world. Things don't seem good. The prophet shows the dark side of love. He prophesizes about the end of the world. He talks about the coming of a pure language. Maybe it's Hebrew or our prayer language. The enemy can't infiltrate our prayer language. It talks of judgement and the day of the Lord.

Chapter one The word is who God is. I don't understand how people trip over God's word. Then in verse 2 Tribulation Verse two is backwards from creation. What God will take away. I will sweep away both men and animals. I will sweep away the birds of the air and the fish in the sea. The wicked, will only have heaps of rubble when I cut off man from the face of the earth declared the Lord. Then God tells Judah what the charges are. Why judgement will be brought on them. The charges worshipping Baal a false god and idolatrous priests meaning they were worldly. They worshipped the starry hosts everything in the sky including angels. Verse 2 Yahshuah is the sacrifice that God prepared for us. Verse 8 and 9 when it says foreign clothes it means turning away from God. We are suppose to put God on like we do our clothes. Then it talks of them being in the middle where they couldn't make up their minds. Like some believers Verse 10 What's going to happen in the business district. Day of destruction is marked to happen. Verse 11 talks about being corrupt and their money's no good. Kind of sounds like the U.S Verse 12 talks about them being lukewarm. Them being undesirable and being sediment. Sediment is the residue that's left. They think God won't do anything. Judah got to comfortable. Just Like the U.S. Verse 14 Describes judgement

Chapter two talks about reforming Verse 8 God talks of judgements around surrounding nations. Verse 7 God talks of place for remnant Verse 8 What's going to happen to Lot's sons. Verse 11 God's going to take care of because he's powerful. Verse 12 Super power coming down place for God's remnant. Verse 15 Talks of how Assyria had it going on. Chapter three Calm after the storm. Future of Jersusalem. The first few verses speaks of the wickeness Verse 6 Judgement for Jerusalem. Verse 9 God bringing back pure Hebrew language correct system of thoughts about God. Judgement of the earth. Verse 12 End times Verse 13 God's remnant Verse 14 restoration Verse 17 God singing over people. Expressing his love for us. Verse 18 God has taken care of everything and there's no more disgrace. Those appointed feasts represent God's seven step redemption plan and the end. God gives us back everything .

Haggai means festive. Where the faithful rebuilt the temple and enjoys God's provisions and hope for the Messiah

Chapter two verse 6 Speaks of shaking which we are experiencing now. God was telling them they should give based on who he is. Giving isn't just money. We have to take care of God's house. So people will come in. If we don't aliange with God's system how do we think that will happen. Money won't work for you. If you are spiritually dead you won't have enough. We aren't suppose to work for money. Money's suppose to be our servant. People respect money but not God. You will run to that job and be early but say heck with God. You have to tap into the system . God has a system for everything in your life. Tithes and offerings which is God's financial system, Communication is prayer, Education system is bible study. This society has a system . I don't know why we would want their system. The world system is bankrupt, so I don't know why we wouldn't want God's system. With God's system we know where we are going.

Zechariah means Yahveh remembers. He was a priest and was in close association with the restoration of the nation of Israel after the captivity. He was in government. He was in association with Zerubbabel the governor and Joshua the high priest. At that time God was in charge of the government. If you don't put Godly people in office how to you expect God to be in the government? Like God said the people run and hide because of the wickness. People get scared to come out. Believers need to step up their game. This book portrays the coming glory of the Messiah. Glory meaning full expression. It has eight references of the Messiah in these fourteen chapters.

Chapter one talks of repenting and rebuilding the temple.

Chapter two Now calling Israel.

Chapter three can't touch God Verse 8 The branch is Yahshuah

Chapter four verse 2 Knew what the manure is. The Jew knew the manure was the only light in the Lord's house. The manure was a candlestick. God had to tell him what he saw with the two olives trees. The two olive trees are the two witnesses. God wants us to see how he sees. Verse 6 No human effort Circumstances, solutions , obstacles Verse 7 Yahshuah is Grace which is divine favor.

Chapter six Belief systems The color represents communion. Verse 9 to 15 Talks of a coronation of a king. That king is Yahshuah . Yahshuah is like Melchizedek.

Chapter seven Talks of hope. Verse 10 True religion Verse 13 Spirit stops.

Chapter eight verse 3 Talks about Yahshuah's reign and what he's going to do about injustice. Verse 6 remnant Verse 7 calling his people back Verse 10 speaks of condition of heart. The way they feel about Yahshuah Verse 12 planting seed in ministry guarantee prosperity of seed Verse 16 and 17 Where it says don't be afraid you must do these things speak the truth to each other. Give correct and fair verdicts for peace in your courts. Don't think of doing evil to each other. Don't enjoy false testimony. I hate all those things declares Yahveh.

Chapter nine verse one Syria and Asia. Damacus Is the capital of Syria. Verse 9 Yahshuah riding on a donkey. This is Palm Sunday. This was 400 years before Matthew chapter twenty one verse 5 Mark chapter eleven verse 7 verse 12 prisoners except change. Hope after cross , double blessing coming because of God fighting for us. Verse 14 promise for new age which is the Messiah. The glorious future of the Messiah coming. Verse 17 We will prosper because of what Yahshuah done. Grain represents the body and wine represents blood.

Chapter ten Talks of Israel's restoration Verse 3 What's going to happen to the preachers and politicians. Verse 6 Yahshuah and Verse 12 Yahshuah.

Chapter eleven verse 6 Going into captivity. Everybody should read seven down. Where God talks of favor and unity. If you don't want God. God's favor won't be on you. That's what's happening to this nation. So I am calling out to the people of God. Let's unite. Let the world have the world. The world's going to be them so why don't we be us. Verse 12 Talks about the thirty pieces of silver which is what Judas did. He betrayed Yahshuah, I wondered if that's what we do when we are chasing behind the dollar. Verse 17 Talks about what's going to happen to the shepherd that abandons the sheep.

Chapter twelve Talks about deliverance. Verse one Talks about when God formed the spirit in the man. God's Holy spirit is his Image. Verse 2 Talks about Jerusalem being a cup of wine that makes the surrounding people stagger. Jerusalem should influence the world. Wine influences people. Yahshuah should be the influence. Verse 10 Yahshuah is the spirit poured out on David's family. Blessing and mercy is what is poured out. Then he says they would look at him whom they have pierced. Remember Yahshuah was stabbed in the side. Everybody will mourn.

Chapter thirteen talks of purification of the Holy city Verse one Talks about unveiling so they can see. Verse 2 Islam being removed from the land. Verse 7 Talks of Yahshuah. Verse 9 Where God says he will bring a third of the people through the fire. 33% priests and believers. God says I will refine them as silver refined. I will test them as gold is tested. They will call on me and I will answer them. I will say ,they are my people , They will reply. Yahshuah is our Elohim. This means the believers will be effective. A third is 33%. The refining is God pruning us

Chapter fourteen Talks of when God extends his rule through out the world. verse 4 Is where Yahshuah was with his disciples. Mark of the beast , War world three. Two billion people will be dead. Verse 6 New Jerusalem and eternity. Like I said they have everything for temple worship. If that cow turns out to be the red heifer. All is needed is the temple, They don't want Issac to be the chosen one. Verse 12 Talks of a nuclear blast. How did Zechariah know? There weren't any nuclear weapons back then. Verse 16 Feast of booths or Tabernacles. Where we will be together with the Lord. This verse talks of the last battle. Verse 13 Is the nuclear blast. Verse 14 Is us fighting against each other. Verse 15 Everything is burnt up. Verse 17 practiced at the end. Once you have rain you can get a harvest. Yahshuah is that rain so we need to get wet. Why shouldn't God express it as rain our bodies are mostly water.

Malachi name means messenger . This book rebukes the people for their shallow worship practices. They were robbing God. Everything is God's. The people weren't taking care of God's house or helping others. They weren't establishing God's covenant. Malachi presents God's case as a debate. God makes a statement of truth. Then God refutes what the people say and proves what he says. Malachi gets on the heads of the church and the people also. God's cleaning up his house. God's setting the stage for his glorious church which is the church in Acts. A full grown church which is the model. That's when God is coming back. The church will have no spot or wrinkle. How can we wonder about God's love? He did all this so we would be ready for him to come back.

Chapter one God's extremes. There's no in between. If you are hot you are passionate , If your cold we know what we have to do and you might need to be saved. If your warm we don't know what you are and God will spit you out. Verse one God says he loved Jacob and hated Esau. God's talking about their behaviors. Jacob loved spiritual things and Esau loved the world. He pointed to natural things when he wanted to feed his belly. This message was to a disobedient people. How are we walking with God? How do we magnify God's presence? God's wisdom? We won't allow God to be God. We are all responsible for the atmosphere. They were trying to give God any old thing. Verse 12 What we give God Almighty. The Almighty meaning power.

Chapter two speaks of the priest teaching God's word incorrectly which results in religion. Verse 5 God promised Levi Life and peace which equals Yahshuah. Verse 7 A priest lips should preserve knowledge meaning to keep safe and protect. Then because he is the messenger of God they will seek instruction from God in his mouth. Then verse 8 Tells why the man of God has no respect. God has said Judah has dishonored the holy place that Yahveh loves and married a foreign woman. God uses the word woman to show physical weakness. Everyone is weaker than God. God refers to the church as his bride. Yahshuah's the bridegroom. Verse 17 Is something how we say stuff and it means the opposite. How we change the meaning of stuff. This verse says everyone who does evil is considered good by Yahveh. He is pleased with them or where is God? This is how man thinks not God.

Chapter three are we robbing the nation of God's presence. If God's house isn't built how can they come? Or if we aren't speaking what God's says or wants? When are we going to seek God and see what he wants? Verse one the messenger who clears the way is John the Baptist. The promise is Yahshuah .We are constantly looking for promises when we should be looking towards Yahshuah who is the promise. God said seek the kingdom and all these things will be added to you. The kingdom is where the king is, his lifestyle. The king is in us the Holy spirit. So we need to learn how to manifest the king. Which we have to walk in the spirit which is walking in the word. So we have to know what God said. So we have to spend time with Yahshuah. We have to have a relationship. Verse 8 and 9 talks about tithes and offerings. Verse 12 God hates pride. I remember God said to me arrogant people think they are blessed. Verse 16 God pays attention to us when we talk. Then it says a book(the bible) was written in his presence to be a reminder to those who fear Yahveh and respect his name. Verse 17 Shows God's heart is with us. Chapter four Talks of the day of the Lord. Verse 2 The sun of righteousness will rise with healing in his wings. For you people that fear my name. It's a play on words because of the winter solace. They threw Yahshuah in with the sun God . The shortest day in winter where there's more darkness. Even though God's birthday isn't in December. I will explain in Luke. Verse 5 Talks about the prophet Elijah coming which is John the Baptist. They have the same spirit. Then verse 6 God talks about bringing into agreement. God wants to turn hearts before he comes back and judges. He wants to give us a chance to do it right. God's to us what the sun is to the sky. It's a source of light, like Yahshuah. God's bringing the turning to the lost and the blessing to the believer. Which is Yahshuah who allows us to see. John's ministry prepared the way for Yahshuah . We have to repent so we can come into agreement. What we have is a picture of something we really don't have. It's deception. God said the deception is worse then the sin because we don't see it.

Section Two

Chapter 13

All About Yahshuah

The New Testament. The New Covenant brought in all the covenants. Rolled them into one. The Abraham Covenant, The Moses Covenant and The New Covenant. It brings all the benefits with out the penalty. Which brings us to Grace. Grace empowers you to go beyond you so you can do God's will. God brings us into the spirit. We left the law to move into the kingdom. Even though some of us still want to live under the law. Trust me God moved from the law. He calls the law the adminstration of death. Under the law you die. The true gospel is you believing in Yahshuah. That you are justified by Grace (what he did) through faith (doing what you believe). Sinners are saved by faith alone. Yahshuah didn't fight so we could stand. Besides he could of called down a legion of angels to fight . It probably took all he had not to snatch up the devil but he had to get in the ground. Another reason he didn't fight he wanted us to know how it felt on the other side. We always want mercy but we don't want to show mercy. When Yahshuah came he came to show us selflessness. He came as a servant. He didn't intimidate anybody and people felt comfortable with him. He wanted to show us servitude so we wouldn't be prideful or into self.

The gospels gives us four different points of view for the same story. We have four people who witnessed the same thing or four different opinions. God leaves no stone unturned. The New Testament is the Old Testament revealed. God gave us mercy but we don't want to show mercy. What do we do in this culture to serve God? The New Testament is hid in The Old Testament. Both books are about Yahshuah.

Matthew means king. Matthew was a tax collector. People didn't like him to much. Just like we feel about the IRS. Yahshuah cared and used people from all walks of life. We see the gospel as being positive commands. Follow Yahshuah and it's the best possible way to live.

In chapter one we see forty two generations from Abraham to the Messiah. God always wants you to know where you came from so you know where you are going. As you can tell God loves us. He put us on the trail to becoming what God made us to be. In the natural our children draw us to love. We should want to be in God's family. God says we are spiritually adopted and become sons. So we should want to be mature believers. A child doesn't receive or know what to do with his inheritance until he grows up. We get our inheritance because Yahshuah died. Our inheritance is the Holy spirit. Which we get from the last will and testament which is God's word. What gets me you see all these people shouting out promises but they aren't mature believers. So what's going to manifest? The anointing grows inward then outwards. Just like you keep pouring water in a cup it eventually overflows. We keep pouring God in. He will eventually flow out of us. When Yahshuah died he left us Salvation and Predestination. He emptied himself out so we could have everything. Under the law we weren't connected to Christ. God went through all these generations so everyone could see including the devil and angels. Yahshuah was a descendant of David on his humanity side. God had to do everything legally if he didn't come through the womb he would be a law breaker. We all know the story of when Yahshuah was born. When Yahshuah was born the shepherds were there. Because of the time of year and the smell of the sheep the wise men weren't there. Let's tell the story right .When the wise men came it was more then three. There were three gifts. The gifts were Frankincense cause he's a priest, Myrrh for his death and Gold because he's a king. The wise men followed a star to get to Yahshuah's house. The star was a sign. A sign shows us something. Yahshuah is a sign to show us back to the father. They took Yahsuah to Eypt so he wouldn't be killed fulfilling the prophesy I have called my son out of Eypt. Hosea chapter eleven verse 1 Yahshuah was called out of Bethelehem, Galilee. And Nazareth , Verse 18 is what Jeremiah said when they were killing the baby boys of Ramah. It says Rachel was crying for her children. Ramah was the land of Benjamin. Son of Jacob. See how the bible is connected.

Chapter three John the baptizer comes on the scene. John's ministry was one of repentance. Repentance means to turn, change direction. Isaiah spoke of John when he said a voice cries in the desert. Isaiah spoke of Yahshuah he called him Immanuel which means God with us. Pharisees and Suducees were the religious sects of that day. One believed in the resurrection the other didn't .Sounds a lot like Christians and Muslims. At different intervals they ran the government. They came to see what John was doing. John called then poisonous snakes because of their teaching. What they taught led to death when Yahshuah is life. Actions speak louder then words .People notice more of what we do then what we say. Then we see John baptizing Yahshuah. The lamb had to be washed. God does everything in decency and order. Everything in the old testament Yahshuah did it. After Yahshuah came up from the water The spirit came on him as a dove. Yahshuah did nothing on earth as God. He did everything as a anointed man of God. Yahshuah was showing us how to walk in the spirit the way God intended us. If Adam didn't fall this earth could have been filled with spirit filled people. The enemy wouldn't of defeated the man there be no sin and God wouldn't of had no need to come as a man. In verse 16 We see the trinity. Suddenly the heavens were open and he saw the spirit of God coming down as a dove. This is the spirit. Then a voice from heaven said this is my son who I love. This is the father speaking and the son is in the person. We see three distict personalities here.

Chapter four we see Yahshuah going into the desert where he is being tempted by satan. Yahshuah's weak. He was tempted so he could show us how to get the victory. The number forty represents a proving time. Remember Moses on the mountain. As you can see satan knows the word he quoted some to Yahshuah. Yahshuah knew how to articulate the word. As you can see the devil can give you things. The devil is the god of this world. We will have victory if we stand on the word. Praying, praise, speaking the word and being united are weapons. How do we know how to use our weapons, if we don't exercise them or know we have them? How do we know what God said if we don't read and find out what he said? If we follow God's instructions we will have access to God. Here's what the enemy offers to us The lust of the eyes meaning what we see we want. The lust of the flesh giving our body what it wants. The pride of life which is self. Verse 12 Talks about the light we have to love and live Yahshuah's life. The devil can't do that. The standard's to high for the devil. The devil doesn't want the light to shine in your mind. That's why he attacks your mind. Maybe that's why there's so much mental illness. It's the same light in the beginning and Yahshuah came to bring the light. We see with our minds that's why the enemy attacks it. The enemy doesn't want us to see correctly. God gave us a treasure which is the Holy spirit so we can work with God not against him. Verse 16 The bright light is Yahshuah. Yahshuah lit the candle in our hearts which is the Holy spirit. This light is for a dark world that's dying. Verse 23 We see Yahshauh curing sickness and diseases. Yahshuah was correcting his finish work because everything was out of order when man fell. Everything was finished by the sixth day and God placed the man over it . The man had to do nothing.

Chapter five The Beatitudes are the morals or values of the king. We should be salty. Salt is a preservative we should be tangy. So people will want a glass of water which is Yahshuah. We should make them want to choke. We should be representing Yahshuah everywhere. Yahshuah came to fulfill the law not do away with Moses teachings. Don't focus on the natural realm we have to do what we believe. There's no way you could do all 613 laws. The law brought death where Yahshuah brings life. Verse 22 Is about fences. If you put up a fence your libel not to cross the line. That's why he says not to call anyone a fool. Because if you don't call him a fool you probably won't take it any farther. Or call him anything worse or actually do anything to the person. Verse 23 Talks about offering a gift but God tells you to forgive so nothing will be between you and God. Verse 25 Says make peace or you will never repay your debt. Peace is freedom. If you don't make peace you won't be forgiven and you will be separated from God. Verse 27 Is what you see , touch and where you go. Verse 32 God is extremes. God talks about divorcing for unfaithfulness. Unfaithfulness covers more than adultery what about abuse mental and physical. God always goes the higher end but there's stuff in between. God wants us to be happy. Verse 36 talks about a eye for a eye. God talks about turning the other cheek because we always want vengence if someone does something to us but if we do something to somebody we want mercy. How do we feel if the shoe is on the other foot? God loves us. God is good even to those who aren't so nice. Everyone receives God's goodness but not the blessing . Yahshuah is the blessing. What else is God going to be but good.

Chapter six we rather have power from men then God. Verse 5 Hypocrites. People doing stuff to be seen and feel big. The show. God says pray in private. Which points to intimacy and relationship. The private place also can refer to the heart. God doesn't want us repetitiously praying like we have to get his attention. God gave us a outline on how to pray. Prayer can't be me begging God when he finished everything. We have everything so we should know it.

Our father--------Us acknowledging God Who he is

Who walked in heaven----------------Where he is

Hallowed be your name-------------------------set apart, recognized

Your kingdom come-------------------------------Heaven on earth, heaven and earth where suppose to mirror each other God's rule and reign

Your will be done----------------------------What God wants ,His word. How come we never ask God what he wants?

Give us this day or daily bread---------------Our needs which is a little over 12% of the prayer so why is that all we want to talk to God about

Forgive our trepasses---------------------------What we do, Our lusts and desires

As we forgive those who trespass against us------------------------Forgiving what people do to us

Lead us not into temptation--------------------Things that bring us to do wrong

Deliver from evil--------------------------------Protection from the devil

For thou is the kingdom power and the glory --------------------WHO God is

Amen------------------Affirm it to be true

Verse 19 Your treasure is where your heart is . What value you place on something. Yahshuah wants to be our treasure. God gives us freewill don't put out the spirit by getting caught up in this life. Satan constantly wants to put our lights out. Verse 23 Talks about the eye . Which really is your mind and how you really see. For us to have clear vision we have to focus. What you see can tempt you to do wrong. Then it says you can't serve two masters. Money answers what calls for money. It doesn't answer salvation. Money's not necessarily bad but it's how you think about it and where you place it in your life. God never wanted us to chase money but wanted money to be our servant. People respect money more than God. People will hit that clock and do anything for their boss and don't even have to like their boss. But we can't even make it to church on time or do anything for God. There's no value on the anointing which will bring the money. Then he tells you to stop worrying which is perversed meditation. We need to respond right to God by acting on what we believe. This life that we think is ours is a distraction . When Yahshuah redeemed us he redeemed our spirit not our body. This body is going in the ground. So why do we waste so much time on it? God talks about seeking his kingdom and everything will be added. We have to carry out God's plan step by step which is his word not quote scripture. That's a parrot. We have to get understanding. Which is seeing what's going on. Most believers don't have any understanding. If you understand something you are libel to do it.

Chapter seven's about judging. God says examine yourself because my behavior is more important to my life then anyone elses. Verse six casting my pearls among the swine. Is me wasting my time. Verse 9 stone is for building so we should give what's necessary if someone is hungry we should give some food not word. Verse 12 The golden rule what's our relationship with people. The narrow gate is Yahshuah the wide gate is the world. A gate is a opening. People will have you believe it's many ways to get to God. God said it's one. Then it talks about false prophets. They may look legit but what fruit are they producing? You can only produce what you are. You know the devil will teach church and so can a minister influenced by the Judas spirit . What are we doing with Yahshuah's ministry? Yahshuah gave us stories so we understand. When God says Lord, Lord and these people didn't enter the kingdom, made me think of the crusades and people who are one way in church and another way outside of church. Also all the other people who think they are doing God's will but missed the mark. Verse 24 Built on a rock. That foundation and rock are Yahshuah. When Yahshuah taught he took possession of the word like it was his. He owned it and had authority over it unlike Moses. Now we come to Yahshuah curing a leper. Leprosy points to corruption and decaying. Doctrines of man is a form of leprosy. Yahshuah restored the leper to his original state. We are spirit so the word says don't stay in the natural. Get understanding and move into the spirit. Natural is where we speak from our prospect and not God's. What your wearing can't be corrupt and has to be examined by the priest. The priest being Yahshuah in the spirit. Yahshuah did everything by the law he told the leper to show himself to the priest. The leper had to show the priest because Yahshuah hadn't died yet. Next we come to the story of the centurion who was a Roman soldier. This soldier wasn't in covenant with God so how much scripture could he know. It was his response to Yahshuah. He understood the principles and knew Yahshuah as one of authority. He acted on what he believed. Why don't we act on what we believe and allow that seed to grow us up? We need to respond quickly to the things of God. Now we get to where Yahshuah healed Peter's mother. She got up and began to serve him. How come when we get saved we don't serve anyone? Come on it's not like us waiting on the bus or train. We have to constantly be moving in the things of God while that door opens. Yahshuah said what the prophet Isaiah said he took up our infirmities(where we fall short) and our diseases. He nailed every one of them to the cross. Verse 14 Talks of Yahshuah not going to any particular place. Verse 22 Yahshuah's referring to the spiritually dead. Then we move to Yahshuah calming the storm. Everything is made to yield to the spirit. Yahshuah had to persuade the fishermen to get in the boat. Fishermen knew the weather. Yahshuah didn't care about the weather he just knew he wanted to get to the other side of the land. Circumstances and situations didn't stop him and it shouldn't stop us. Then Yahshuah cast out two demons. We should be casting out demons on the ordinary. Demons know whether or not we have God's spirit. Where did all those demons go after the fall? We seem to think they went away. They are constantly fighting our spirits. Maybe some are housed in the mentally ill. We just medicate the mentally ill. What do they care, they have a house. Blessed means happy, fortunate and prosperous. When Yahshuah said he knew what the experts in Moses teachings were thinking he was operating in the word of knowledge. They were mad because Yahshuah said he was God. So if he was lying why didn't they stone him? That's what they use to do. Then we come to where Yahshuah chooses Matthew. The tax collector. The IRS . Then Yahshuah fellowshipped at Matthew's house. They said Yahshuah was among sinners. Yahshuah was spreading his light around the undesirable. Like the homeless. We should be out in our communities. The believers should be alright. We need to get out and do what Yahshuah did. Why do some of us think we are better? Verse 16 Is about renewing your mind. Luke warm Christians mix the old and new lives together. Then we come to the woman with the blood issue. She believed in the word. In those days if you had a medical issue you couldn't come out. She pressed through all those people just to get to Yahshuah. Yahshuah knew someone touched him. He felt some of his power leave him. Then he goes to a little girl's house that died. He made everyone leave because they weren't in agreement. We may all be different but we have to have the same focus. We have to be on one accord meaning we speak and think like Yahshuah. The church is divided that's why it has no power. A house divided can not stand. By the church being divided the power is weakened. Like the world separating the believers. When we are together it is harder to penetrate us. Like that three thread chord. The blessing is in unity. How can the church be in agreement with God when they don't understand. We have to have spiritual sight. Verse 35 Few workers not many disciples. Like today we have a bunch of converts in our churches, no one's being discipled. A disciple is a learnth one. A trained soldier. A baby doesn't understand and can't fight. We have some pastors that are converts. That's a problem .You can only make what you are. There are some people who want to hear and know the truth. The truth is what everything is based on. God's word that doesn't change. A fact can change. Why does the church know the truth and live a lie? Or maybe the church doesn't know the truth.

Chapter ten The twelve disciples Yahshuah sent out to the Jewish people. He gave them his ministry. They took no money didn't charge but God made sure they were taken care of. Their needs were met. When God talks about sending them out to grievous wolves, he's talking about a cruel world. Also threats of prosecution. Satan raised up grievous wolves to infiltrate the church. A war tatic to weaken and water down God's church. This is what we see today. Back then believers couldn't be broken by prosecution or by taking their stuff. Satan knows that everything is based on the truth. Truth doesn't change. The truth is God who is unchanging. Verse 26 What God tells us in our private time we should say it out loud. How do we treat witnessing? We will never know more than Yahshuah allows us to *know. People witness so people can become disciples which are soldiers. We make soldiers so we can function in the body a spiritual body to fight the enemy. The enemy are demonic spirits. So how do we think the natural man can fight a spirit. The bible is based on the Holy spirit and everything yields to the Holy spirit, God's spirit. Verse 30 Tells how God created us with detail. No insignificant people. No one is worthless. God says no sparrow falls to the ground without him knowing. God made birds to fly in the air no matter what happens, God cares. Am I being read as a epistle. I should be sowing my life. The soul is eternal. Verse 34 through verse 36 Talks about the way you believe. People will turn against you. He talks about how you can't be his disciple ,if you love your family more than him. That's because the enemy will use anything in this life against you. When God says pick up your cross he means you have to be willing to die. Every one who carried a cross then were going to their deaths. At the close of this chapter God talks how they treated his prophets. The prophet is God's spokes person.*

Next in chapter eleven verse 3 Is where John Baptist was starting to doubt even though he knew the truth. Don't we get like that. He needed some reassurance so God sent the disciples to him. When we get like that we need to pick up the word. Verse 7 Yahshuah talks about appearances so be careful of what you see. Verse 9 John came ahead of Yahshuah to get our hearts ready for redemption. God always lets us know. Verse eleven The least important person in heaven is greater than John because they are in heaven and he's still on earth. John and Elijah have the same kind of spirit. A spirit influences you or drives you. Verse 12 Talks of how heaven has been forcefully advancing and forceful people have been seizing it. We have to take what's ours. The fallen angels are in the first and second heavenlies. They aren't in the ground. They are constantly fighting with us. Satan has a well ranked put together army. Verse 17 Deals with our response. Verse 20 Talks about the natural man seeing and rejecting the spirit. Verse 25 through 27 tells how much we have access to God. We have to believe in God's finished work to access it. You don't learn God like you do English and math. It's not like your in school. For yourself. God has to reveal himself to you. Like pulling up the shades or taking off the covers. The Bible is food for the spirit man. Verse 28 Talks about giving Yahshuah the burden. Burden being sin. The yoke is what holds you to the sin.

The next chapter talks about the Sabbath being meant for man. God rather show mercy. Besides God wants us to share mercy with him over sacrifices. Meaning what's right in God's sight supercedes the law. God made everything. Yahshuah knew the people's thoughts he was constantly operating in the word of knowledge. Yahshuah came to do God's will that's why he came as a servant. So what the prophet Isaiah said was like this part and no one will hear his voice in the streets meaning It's for the spirit. The smoking wick is sin and the hope is Salvation. Verse 25 Talks about dividing the house. If this happens it makes it weaker and it will be no progress. Verse 32 Talks about speaking against God. If it's evil how do we say it's good. So that's what your going to produce. Verse 36 We are going to have to explain our words. The sign of Jonah is a sign of Yahshuah raised from the dead. Then he talks of the evil taking a body. You have a body to touch this earth. Then Yahshuah says whoever does the will of my father is my family. Chapter thirteen To get a Harvest

1. Seed —Word

2. Ground- Heart

3. Hearing ear —How seed is sown

4. Obedient – Increase learning

5. Understanding – Eyes see who God is and what's going on.
*   Ears hear word and do it*

6. Ear and eye gate —Entrance to the Heart

God tells us stories so we will go deeper with him. He explains the story of the seed. The return is the best possible result for you. The kingdom is the life of the king. How you think and act. Thorny you being caught up in your own life. Thorns suck all the moisture out of the seed so it won't bring forth fruit. When the rain comes down the thorn won't allow the seed to break through. The seed coat can't come off but it has to come off so the seed can grow. Actually the seed dies and then comes back to life and grows. Just like the believer. Verse 15 This little passage of Isaiah talks about us not being aware and having no insight . When God's about the mustard seed. Meaning a little Yahshuah goes along way and he's more than enough. Verse 44 Stories about the treasure. The treasure is the Holy spirit. It talks about valuing the anointing. These stories illustrate what going to happen at the end. How we value the anointing and what we do with it. Verse 54 to 58 Shows how we made Yahshuah ordinary and common just like everybody else.

Chapter fourteen Talks about how John was killed. We all know the story. What I saw was how they are always cutting believers from the head. When your in the spirit the spirit is always seeing things. No matter what version of the bible read. God's always correcting his finished work. Verse 17 God's feeding with five loaves and two fishes. Number seven is completion. Verse 20 about God's grace. Verse 22 Talks of Yahshuah walking on water. Meaning rise above everything in life. Beyond your borders. Your self effort. Then Peter walked on the water when he took his eyes off Yahshuah he began to sink. Meaning walk by the word. Keep your focus on Yahshuah. Don't keep your focus on your circumstance. Live in the super natural not by self effort.

Chapter fifteen talks of how the teachers were teaching the word to benefit themselves. They twisted the word to make it fit what they wanted it to say. They taught man made rules. They appeared to be with God but really they weren't. They didn't mean what they said when they supposedly honored God. What they said was worthless and meant nothing. Man made religion. What you see in church ,man's way to reach God. We are always trying to bring God down to our level. God's always trying to lift us up to his level. Then God talks about clean and unclean. It's what comes out of the mouth because what comes out of the mouth comes out of the heart. Verse 13 Everybody that teaches wasn't called by God. God will take care of them. They are spiritually blind. Everything is about the way we think. If you don't believe right you won't do right. The mind. God made us thinking and reasoning like him. Then a caanite woman comes to Yahshuah for her daughter to be healed. Verse 23 Shows how bad she wanted it. They called then dogs because that's what they thought of them. Yahshuah told her he was there for the Jewish people. She was persistant. She acted on what she believed. As you see in this scenario. In the beginning if there was no sin it would have been a world full of spirit filled people. God's going to bring us back to his original intent. Verse 32 God feeding seven loaves , completion natural always wants to quit. The 4000 represents the earth.

Chapter sixteen verse 4 Example Yahshuah. People won't be able to see that Yahshuah is the living word. Who do you say Yahshuah is? The father has to reveal Yahshuah to you. Yahshuah tells them to be careful of what the Pharisees teach. Which they taught religion. Verse 13 Peter unlocked faith. When we have faith we allow the untapped power of God to flow. It doesn't matter who Yahshuah is to people but who he is to us. It's personal. The rock is Yahshuah. The foundation, firm ,unmovable. The church was built on that. Stop looking at the church down the street. God's church is the church in Acts. A full grown church. Yahshuah's not coming back until his church is glorious without a spot or wrinkle. The church should be a organism not a organization. God formed organisms which means they are life breathing. What you see today is the church looking no different then the boy scouts or the red cross. They do good things and feed people. So what's the difference? We should be bringing the power. Moving stuff. Satan can't deal with Yahshuah's life but he can deal with yours. Yahshuah's the head of the church he doesn't care what man made it. God's bringing his church. God showed me how he's making disciples. It's a new day. A new mercy. God cannot and will not deny himself. God is faithful and will always be who he is going to be. Count God faithful. We have to have a personal revelation of who God is. Then we can be the church. Once God tells you, God reveals what's been told to you. From verse 21 to the end of the chapter Yahshuah talks of his plan for redemption and them dying naturally.

Chapter seventeen Talks of God's transformation state. There's no physical appearance of Yahshuah in the bible. So we can't say anything. This was a display of God's glory in his son. Then the disciples seen Yahshuah with Elijah and Moses. The law and the prophets. Yahshuah completed the law. In these first couple of verses it's about recognizing different types of spirits. Yahshuah had to suffer to take on sin. Verse 16 The disciples were getting big heads. Fleshy couldn't heal the boy who had seizures. In self. Yahshuah said the spirits didn't come out because they didn't fast or pray. The fasting represents keeping the flesh down and the prayer represents being connected to God. Verse 26 When God pays his tax. Anytime you can get your tax money from a fish you got it going on. God shows the world's not his family and he made restitution for us not stuff.

Chapter eighteen God always tells us to come like children. Because children love their parents and want to be like them. For the most part their parents are the greatest thing. No self in this equation. If you didn't have great parents you have God. God had to get you here. We couldn't pick our parents but we can choose God. Verse 6 God's extremes .He's talking about what you see what you touch and where you go. Cut it off so you won't be led to hell. Don't do anything to stop someone from believing. Children have just left heaven ,so they still know how to respond to God. The longer we are on earth the farther we have gotten from God. Lost means not saved. Verse 15 About dealing with a believer that's done something wrong. God talks about getting witnesses. DT 19 vs 15 The bible is for believers. Just had to say that again. Somebody asked me why I had so many different versions of the bible. I said I love God's word. The spirit can interpret any version. Then he said I only have one Quran. So I said why do muslims constanly pull from our bible? So why is that?

Chapter nineteen when you get married God makes you one. It's like going back to the beginning when God pulled Eve out of Adam's side. I guess that's why it hurts so much if you divorce. It's like that person is cut from you. Then in verse 16 Yahshuah talking to a man with wealth. The man asks what he needs to get into the kingdom. Yahshuah tells him to give away his wealth. The man was sad. God didn't say you couldn't have wealth he doesn't want you to think your wealth can sustain you or be your master. The enemy will even use your money against you. So if your willing to give it up it hasn't mastered you and God will give you back the best possible return for you. We always worry about what people think of us. We think people will think lowly of us because of what we gave up. Verse 28 Yahshuah tells them you will receive 100 times more what they given up in this life time besides eternal life. You know if Yahshuah gives it to you the enemy can't use it against you. Prosperity is more than money. You drink the cup refers to what you go through.

Chapter twenty one verse 4 Zechariah It talks about Yahshuah riding a donkey and people waving palms. This is where Palm Sunday comes from. Israel knew a king would restore the kingdom back to Israel. All the prophets foretold about Yahshuah . They predicted correctly. If they didn't have accurate predictions ,they would be labeled a false prophet and be stoned. Then the people started praising Yahshuah. Hosanna is the highest praise. Yahshuah overturns the tables. This represents having no respect for God's house. Doing everything but what we are suppose to do in God's house. We should be communicating with God in his house. It should be about him not us. I wonder how God feels about some of the things we do and bring in God's house. We should make God sacred. Then Yahshuah cursed the fig tree. The fig tree was lying about having fruit. It didn't produce. You can say this is a type of redemption. Remember Adam and Eve and the fig leaves. We should have the same authority as Yahshuah. We should be able to overcome any obstacle. Yahshauh pleaded the fifth when he was questioned. Five is the number for grace. Verse 28 People do things because they think it is the right thing to do and have no revelation. The story about two sons. It's all about why and how you do a thing. Not just you doing it any old way. You can't do it like a chore. The more we know, the more God holds us accountable. The stone that the builders rejected is Yahshuah.

Chapter twenty two. Yahshuah. When you see Yahshuah paying his taxes you see him abiding by the government as long as it doesn't interfere with his government. Then in verse 30 Yahshuah explains how we are like angels when we die. Meaning we don't marry or have sex. So that throws out that seventy virgins. Why would God give a man seventy virgins when he believes in covenants. God's legal . He's a judge . I want you guys to think this out. God is the God of the living. That's why he says he is the God of Abraham ,Issac ,and Jacob. Meaning they are in Eternity. God says I am and not I was. God tied all those laws into two. Love the Lord with all your heart, soul and mind. Love your neighbor as yourself. Who is your neighbor? The good Samaritan. When we hear son of David it's speaking of Yahshuah's human side. Then when we see Lord we see the spirit.

Chapter twenty three Yahshuah talks of how the religious people want people to do stuff that they don't even do. They wanted them to do a bunch of rituals and keep all the laws. No way you can do that. The job of the believer is to believe. Yahshuah said don't call anyone father. That's another religion. Then Yahshuah talks about how the leaders are about money. Also how they don't disciple the people they have following them. Meaning grow them into mature believers Verse 23 That one tenth of your mint is a example of a tithe. God showed us how to tithe in the old Testament. So he shouldn't have to say it over and over again. Even though he mentions it in Hebrews. We should live a life of Integrity and do what's important first. Verse 25 Says we should deal with the heart and stop appearing to be something we are not. The heart deals with the mind. The way we think. Verse 27 spiritually dead. Verse 30 to 33 shows how much they are in the world. A lot like religious people of today. Then verse 34 God talks about sending people and how badly religious people treat God's true workers. We rather hear a so called good message. That's not going to help any one. Then doing God's will which will help everyone. Then God talks about his workers being whipped and prosecuted in the synagogue. That's me plenty of my collegues had me in tears. I never let them see me cry. I always had to prove I am a written epistle. Well at least they sharpened me up. Verse 37 God says he just wants to love us. We are the spiritual Jerusalem. Blessed is the name of the one who comes in the name of the Lord.

Chapter twenty four Yahshuah talks of people being deceived. Like I said deception is worse then the actual sin. Verse 6 where God talks of us hearing of wars, rumors of war. Nations fighting against each other. Famines and earthquakes in various places. This is now. These are birth pains. As we get closer to the end the pains will get more intense. Just like birthing a baby. Then it talks about us being handed over, tortured, killed and being hated because of Yahshuah. This is now to. Then it talks of many losing their faith. Getting betrayed and more false prophets. This is also now. Then it talks about more corruption and lawbreaking. People will become cold because of this. Cold being unbelief. This is now. Then God says who endures will be saved. Everybody pulls from our bible but God's people don't know what God says. Listen to those muslims leaders a lot of what they say straight from the bible. Verse 24 That is the anti Christ. Verse 16 When God talks of Judea that is Israel. The church is Yahshuah's bride. He birthed out the church when he died on the cross. To unite all God's people. Jew and Gentile. Meaning Covenant and UnCovenant. Israel is Yahveh's bride. Verse 21 and 22 Talks about how bad it will be. It will be worst then the Holocust. At this time God said false prophets will perform miracles. If you have God's spirit and it is mature you will be able to tell the difference. When Yahshuah comes back ,you will see him come back he won't be hiding. Verse 29 are signs. Verse 31 The rapture.

The rapture is a evacuation. The trumpet will sound in the spirit. If the spirit man is sleep he won't hear the trumpet. If we follow God's seasons we won't be lost. We just don't know which one. The last four blood moons happened on feast days. Two on Passover and two on Tabernacles. When Yahshuah comes back people will be doing the same stuff they are doing now. So we constantly need to put God's word out. How are we handling God's ministry. Will our fate be hell?

Chapter twenty five verse 1 talks of preparation. Verse 14 Stewardship Verse 28 What are we doing with Yahshuah's anointing? Verse 34 How we treat people. We should look at people as having God's spirit. Not less than us.

Chapter twenty six Passover. The Jewish people had to be in the house before the Holy day. A feast day was also called a Sabbath. Meaning the Sabbath could have been another day besides Friday. I had a hard time getting three days out of two. The Sabbath is Friday 6.pm to Saturday 6pm. Then God is sitting at Simon's house and a woman pours expensive perfume on Yahshuah's feet and wiped it with her hair. She kissed and cried at his feet. This woman believed she was forgiven much so she loved much. Verse 26 The meal Yahshuah ate with his disciples was called a sader. The bread and wine communion. Remembering what he did for us. Shedding his blood and lying down his life. The fourth cup Yahshuah didn't drink cause he would become a curse for us. Yahshuah took the pressure. Yahshuah had freewill but he united with God's plan. God had to separate to redeem the spirit of man. The man was defeated and lower now then a fallen angel. God had to get the spirit back to the man. So we can defeat the enemy until he can legally be here. Yahshuah had to get in the ground to dismantle the enemy. He went to enemy territory. The shadow of this is when David paraded Goliath's head around after he cut it off. Yahshuah paraded the devil around so the principalities could see. If God didn't do it we would be immortality corrupt forever. We would of never been able to be reconciled back to God. We are suppose to yield to the spirit and allow it to guide us. No human effort. Verse 39 Shows Yahshuah identifying with us. Yahshuah talks about Peter falling asleep. This represents the natural man whose weak . Prayer is a setup so we will communicate with God. Now we get to the part where Judas brings them to take Yahshuah. The people who came to arrest Yahshuah fell out. His spirit was to strong so he allowed them to take him. In the midst of that Peter cut off one of the people ears who came to take Yahshuah. Yahshuah picked it up and put it back on the man. Yahshuah said the plan must go forth and I could of called a legion of angels to take care of this. They took Yahshuah to Cephanias. The disciples stayed back because of fear. All that's natural man. Then in verse 64 Where Yahshuah says I am, he is saying he is God. Verse 65 said Yahshuah committed blasphemy which means disrespect by saying he was God. Everything Yahshuah said happened.

Chapter twenty seven Many believed Judas wanted to turn Yahshuah's hand and make him use his power. Verse 9 Talks of what Jeremiah said about the thirty pieces of silver. The priests didn't want the money back so they bought Potter's field. Which they buried poor people there. Showing us that you can't take something bad and make it good. Verse 27 we get to them putting a crown of thorns on Yahshuah's head. This crown of thorns redeemed the ground. Remember Adam had to work the ground and the ground yielded thorns and thistles. The ground was made to yield to the spirit. The ground doesn't know who the sons of God are. The sons of God are believers walking in the spirit. Verse 30 after they had spit on him, they struck him and kept hitting him on the head. Moses striking the rock was a type and shadow of this. Yahshuah carrying his cross means he is going to his death. When Yahshuah died the sun was at it's hottest point. Three o clock. God forsook Yahsuah so he could accept us. Meaning if Yahshuah did not die and get in the ground and disarm the enemy we would not of been reconciled to God. We would not of been able to have the Holy spirit back. We can thank the sin issue for that. Verse 20 the thief on the cross, Yahshuah took to paradise. That was like a jail house confession. He didn't speak in tongues and wasn't baptized but we know he went to heaven. Yahshuah laid down his life because they couldn't take life from the one who gives life. Yahshuah was in the ground three days . God promised to get him up before his body saw decay. Your body starts decaying the fourth day. When they took Yahshuah off the cross none of his bones were broken. Isaiah prophesied that. Yahshuah was already dead. Why can't we accept the real gift that hung on a tree? Why can't we open up the gift he gave us? The gift he gave us is for every day. Now I told you a feast day is also called a Holy Sabbath meaning that Passover did not have to be a Friday. Yahshuah was hung on the cross at twelve, died at three and was taken off the cross between three and five.

The people were in the house by six. They put Yahshuah in a near by tomb that was never used cause he would not be in it long. Sabbath is Friday 6pm to Saturday 6pm Yahshuah rose after the Sabbath. Here is how you get the three days Wednesday 6pm till 6pm Thurday is day one. Yahshuah was on the cross 12 noon in between on Thursday. He was on the cross at the hottest point being 300pm. He laid down his life. Thursday 6pm-Friday 6pm was preparation day two. Friday 6pm till Saturday 6pm was the Sabbath and day three. Yahshuah rose sometime after the Sabbath. A feast day is also called a Sabbath and can fall on any day of the week. No matter how we calculate Friday to Sunday doesn't makes three days. So I was glad to find out God has a calendar. The world's doctrine consists of easter, good Friday, santa clause. To you our lives we raise. When you leave out of church live your life to his excellence. Know the meaning of what you are saying or singing. Easter is a pagan holiday that started with the fertility goddess Astarte. That's where you get the eggs and rabbit from. All this pagan stuff infiltrated the church. We need to promote the kingdom. The flesh is always trying to work and masquerade as the truth. God gives us twelve hours to work our Dad's business. When man does it his way the church is not free and there's no power. We need to pray and find out what God's instructions are for our life. Prayer is not based on God moving, God already moved. God moved based on covenant. His word. Praying is a priviledge. God will not deny himself. These man made holidays move us away from God's cycles. The feasts allow us to know exactly where God is. We can't make a proper connection with God without Judaism. We have to see Christ in Moses writings. God was not trying to start a religion.

Holynist- praise if your not holy you will never see God and not be sacred

Baptism- Believe in baptisms

Catholic- Universal church

Methodist- Believe in righteousness of God and Sanctification

Synagogue- circumcision

Pentecost- The power

Yahshuah is for everyone and wants to be all things for all people. God is bible based and wants all to be saved. Easter means to spring not resurrect. It has to do with the sun not the son. All these man made holidays have something to do with the sun. When Yahshuah died on the cross the wealth transfer occurred. The power of the blood. We should forget the easter clothes and chocolate rabbits and invest in the kingdom. If you have a revelation from the father he will elevate you. Judas had no revelation. When Yahshuah was in the tomb he folded up his garments he took his time. He showed us he was in no hurry but he got up. The first one to see him was a woman. She went to touch him. Yahshuah told her not to . God had to get him first. He had to show his assignment was done. That the evidence wasn't tampered with. He had to show he was a perfect sacrifice. Yahshuah blew on his disciples giving them the spirit back like when God blew in Adam. Yahshuah taught his disciples forty days then Yahshuah told them to wait. They were waiting for Pentecost. The power. It was a two step operation. Tongues was the evidence that something happened. When Thomas felt Yahshuah's side he knew it was Yahshuah. That's like you have to see it to believe it. Yahshuah had healing properties in him to heal his body .You knew it was the same body because of the pierced side that Thomas felt. When he was on that tree he was just flesh hanging on that tree. He was unrecognizable. His mother watched her baby die. Yahshuah entrusted his mother with John. Yahshuah's brothers weren't believers yet. Yahshuah's brothers thought he was crazy. John called himself the beloved because he knew Yahshuah loved him. Do we know Yahshuah loves us? Yahshuah tells us to do stuff but we don't. When you love someone you trust and do what they say.

Mark means servant. A servant was what Yahshuah was he showed us selflessness. Yahshuah used people from all walks of life that he could develop. People felt comfortable with him. You see Yahshuah around sinners which are the undesirables. People that people did not want to be bothered with. Like the elderly in the nursing home or the homeless. Everybody needs to hear the message. Maybe believers don't know the message. God said the workers are few. Yahshuah doesn't look at people as being second class. He's not like us. We tend to think we are better then others. Why because we have more money, a bigger house or car? Mark was a regular associate of Peter's. They would come together at his mother's house I wonder if they considered her a pastor? They use to go house to house. God wants his church to be like a family. So why is there so much strife and division? I basically said a lot in Matthew

Chapter two verse 2 talks about John the Baptist Who is the forerunner of Yahshuah. John had a ministry of repentance. Verse 12 when Yahshuah was being tempted that was a proving and pruning period. Verse 14 Yahshuah's ministry. We should see with new eyes and do what we believe because the Holy spirit carries out the will of the father. Yahshuah backed up everything he said. Like he owned it. Verse 40 where Yahshuah restored the leper to his original state. Yahshuah was correcting his finished work which he completed on the sixth day. Yahshuah has authority he has the power to influence thoughts and behavior. What religion can do that?

In chapter two it shows where they lowered a cot. It had a paralyzed man on it. This shows desire. We have to desire Yahshuah. Everyone needs him. Hungry people in the world need Yahshuah. He comes where he is desired. Most want God for what he can do for them. What is our response to God? What will we do to get it? Glory to God. Get God's wisdom. Value God's anointing. Go grace to grace with God. Allow God's finish work to lead us. Sabbath was made for man . Sabbath means rest. Now we get to verse 18 Where they ask Yahshuah why his disciples aren't fasting. God shows us that you can fast but it was out of order at this time. We should be showing Yahshuah in our every day life. Religion and tradition can be a terrible yoke of bondage. When you follow Yahshuah you experience peace and rest. Yahshuah should be our standard since he sets the standard. Righteousness supercedes the law.

Chapter three verse 18 God lists the disciples. Simon the Zealot was into politics. Verse 20 They think Yahshuah was crazy and not the Messiah. Verse 29 Says whoever curses the Holy spirit will not be forgiven because that's cursing God because the Holy spirit is God. Whoever does God's will is related to Yahshuah. Yahshuah came as a man so what he did would raise up man. God is always trying to raise us up and we are always trying to pull him down. Sin gives death the right to hold the body. That's why the body is going in the ground. Death came by Adam a man. The resurrection came by a man Yahshuah.

Chapter four Yahshuah shows a lot of comparisons. Might of fact he is sitting so why is the reverend always standing? The set up we have in church is from the Roman pagan churches that they threw Yahshuah in. They use to go house to house to show the family relationship. Yahshuah was obedient and conquered death. What God did in Yahshuah is greater than what satan did in man. We made church a spectator event. When the church use to pray, praise. eat and everyone had a word. We can't be fruitful with weeds in our life. No harvest if we leave the seed or word behind. Life circumstances choke the word and produce nothing. Circumstances can be good or bad. Thorns stick and suck the life out of you. Our lusts, what we want distract us. A Sower, sows the word. The enemy snatches which equals no understanding. A stony heart is happy when it first hears the word but there is no root so there's no growth. We need to be patient. We need to tie our harvest to the word. God tied his feasts to his people's harvest in the Old Testament. The Harvest now is the manifestation of the promise. Yahshuah wants us to have a harvest. So we need to hear the word and do it. We will get the best possible return for us. Verse 11 Talks about the kingdom that's where the king lives. The kingdom is the way God thinks and acts. Verse 12 The natural man can't see anything and won't understand. Everything is revealed through the Holy spirit. Verse 21 God reveals to us what he wants us to know the other stuff we can ask him when we get to heaven. We should listen with the intend to do. How's are attitude? Why do we always want something for nothing? What's the value we put on what we hear? Verse 30 The mustard seed is small at first. A little Yahshuah goes along way. Grow in God, study the word. We have to grow up the spirit. A baby in the word won't know what to do with his inheritance. Just like you feed and exercise your natural body you need to do that with your spirit man. Verse 35 Yahshuah calms the storm. Fishermen knew the weather. Verse 46 They were scared what is that about? All Yahshuah knew was that he was going to the other side. He did not care about the advasary. Yahshuah can handle him. God did not say we would not have trials and tribulations. The storm was out of order so he spoke to it. Yahshuah had authority over it. Everything yields to the Holy spirit. What action are you taking through the spirit?

Chapter five verse 5 That man was cutting. Nothing new under the sun.

Chapter six talks of a prophet not having honor in their own home town. They gave Yahshuah no authority and made him common like everyone else. What's are response to God? Are we mature? We should respect God more then we respect money. Verse 13 using oil as a contact point. Verse 34 Hungry and thirsty for the word. Verse 52 closed mind is the natural man. It's not what you know but who you know.

Chapter seven Traditions of man and man made doctrines Verse 6 Is all about appearance God's not about clicks, phoniness and foolishness. Verse 8 We see them doing what they want. Instead of what God wants. They twist the truth. Verse 11 Here you have a son who does not want to help or support his parents. We should keep our focus on God. God told me his people reap the benefits and forget the focus. Verse 27 Jew first then Gentile Verse 29 Shows persistence and humility.

Chapter eight verse 15 yeast refers to teaching. Verse 19 bread of life number twelve his disciples. Verse 30 Who is Christ to you? Verse 33 We see Yahshuah rebuking Peter so you can correct believers. Peter was being selfish like save yourself and let the world worry about it self. Peter was about being thought of as important. Satan always get you to think of you.

Chapter nine. Testimony from heaven testifies about faith and whose in the disciples. The Holy spirit is in the disciples. The power came on Pentecost. Verse 4 The law Moses represented and the prophets Elijah represented. The transformation. Verse 23 response. Verse 29 fasting and praying means keeping the flesh down and being connected to God. Understand what's going to happen to Yahshuah. Verse 37 a child imitates who he wants to be like. Verse 39 everything done for Christ is a reward. Verse 40 we have to conduct ourselves so none will be lost on our account. Be careful of what we see, touch or where we go. Verse 48 torture Verse 49 person knowing the word of God in us. Yahshuah is very passionate about the word.

Chapter ten verse 29 Whatever you give up for God, God will repay you in this life time. Show what you believe. The world doesn't think very much of us.

Chapter eleven verse 9 Palm Sunday means Triumph. Hosanna means Yahshuah saves prosperity come now. Verse 12 Yahshuah approaches the fig tree. It showed leaves which meant it should have been some fruit on this tree. The tree was lying. What are we producing are we lying? The fig tree was sentenced and judged so it died. God covered everything from the Old Testament. God is always with us. We shouldn't let situations and circumstances stand in the way of what we need to do for God.

Chapter twelve talking about self. Verse 17 Christ's obedient to government. The natural government wants to keep church and state separate. Christians should be obedient to the government as long as it doesn't interfere with God's government. We are suppose to be ambassadors for Christ meaning we are foreign diplomats here. The world does not treat us like that it doe not respect us. We should have amnesty they shouldn't treat us like they do. Verse 29 We should love the Lord because the enemy can't do that . The Lord first loved us. Obedience is better than sacrifice. The woman with the two mites. She put in all she had. What value or how much does it mean to you what you give God? The people who pulled from their wealth should have been her bridge. They should of made sure she was alright until she could do better. Also her being a widow shows she has no husband. Which means they should of cared for her. God wants orphans and widows cared for. No father no husband that's the natural but God is father and husband to us in the spirit. If we don't do things naturally how will we understand spiritual things. Verse 14 man of pertition the man in temple who says he is God. Verse 18 Satan through out great tribulation period. Verse 20 Israel God's chosen 144,000 From the twelve tribes. Verse 24 The heavenly bodies telling what time it is. Verse 26 The trumpet Be alert follow God's time line his feasts. We just don't know which Tabernacle?

Chapter fourteen Verse three Yahshuah was reclining showing he was relaxed and free. A woman poured perfume on Yahshuah preparing him for his death. She felt she was forgiven much so she loved him much and expressed it. God said her story would always be told. It's like she poured out her life and God gave her a new one. Her being at his feet showed she was doing the necessary thing and being intimate with him. When you are intimate something is imparted to you. When a man and woman are intimate the man imparts his sperm and they produce a life. Yahshuah imparts his word and we get life. The lord's supper was a sader the same thing Moses had before they left Eypt. Verse 24 Yahshuah became a curse. So we have the blessing. The four cups are sanctification, wrath, redemption and the fourth one we will drink together in heaven because he became a curse so we would be blessed. Verse 27 Yahshuah is the shepherd. He is obedient on the cross. Verse 36 Abba a Hebrew word that was left in the bible. Which means source. It also means deepest affection. Why did God leave that in? Verse 44 Enemy multiplies kisses meaning they really don't like you. God's words go hand and hand. Verse 51 Are we willing to die for the cause? Verse 61 Yahshuah saying he is God and equal to God. Then it goes on about Peter's denial of Yahshuah. How many times do we deny Yahshuah?

Chapter fifhteen verse 2 You see Yahshuah in court. Verse 16 The purple represents royalty. The thorn and thistle crown Yahshuah redeemed the ground. I explained his death earlier. In verse 38 the curtain in the temple ripped. This curtain was high and made of heavy material. God ripped the curtain so they could see who he was. It's like us having him revealed to us. When he places his feet on the ground everyone will be able to see. The natural man can't see in the spirit. Yahshah made the way he never called himself a Christian. He said he was the way. He made the way back to God. When he died on the cross. The word Christian came about a hundred years after he died. When God put Adam and Eve out of the garden he had to make away back to him. In Leviticus he talks of the way not being made. Every other belief changes the book so the spirit man won't be fed or grow up. If you meditate on the bible the spirit will see something in there one day that will wake it up. When the other beliefs tell the stories that's how they tell them as stories taking out what God says .If that's not a trick of the enemy what is? The power is in what God says.

Chapter sixteen when Mary went to the tomb she recognized Yahshuah's voice. Sheep recognize their shepherds voice. Do you? In the Old Testament God said there are many voices in the land. Do you know which one is talking to you? There are a lot of voices calling us. Verse 17 We have to act like Yahshuah is right there with us. Tap into God's untapped power. When God talks of them picking up snakes or drinking deadly poison and it won't hurt them. Means they will complete their assignment before they die. That's if it's unintentionally done. Yahshuah was the minority but he convinced the majority. You can't do that with a lie. Maybe that is why the churches are empty. God said walk in the truth so we need to stop lying.

Now we get to the book of Luke that represents Yahshuah as the son of man. Luke was not Jewish or Gentile. Meaning he was not circumcised or not uncovenant. Yahshuah died so he did not have to be circumcised. Luke was a doctor who traveled with Paul. He also wrote the book of Acts. Peter and John were the closest to Yahshuah. Peter started the church and John wrote the book of Revelations. They were ordinary people The Pharisees knew they had no book knowledge or seminary training. They knew they spent a lot of time with Yahshuah. They got to see up close how his character was. We got Yahshuah the same way Paul did through revelation. We didn't see Yahshuah face to face. Or his natural appearance. Might of fact Paul was the top Pharisee and he gave it all up when he had a encounter with God. All that book knowledge meant nothing. It is all about the fight are we willing to die for the cause. These people were accountable witnesses. They just kept passing down the story. With the infiltration of the church the story stopped being told.

Now we get to meet Zachariah John's father. He was chosen to do the sacrifice. So he was in the temple in the holy of holies. This was during atonement. We know this because they went in the holy of holies once a year. After he came down from doing the sacrifice his wife Elizabeth became pregnant at sixty. Now we know John is six months older than Yahshuah so that would make John born around Passover and Yahshuah born around Tabernacles, not xmas. Why is it hard to pinpoint the exact date. Because his death is important not his birthday. All the false gods have birthdays and he always exsisted. That was just a incantation period while in the womb. The real us is the spirit.

Chapter one of Luke is a mission statement .This Basically brings John in as the forerunner of Yahshuah. John and Elijah have the same kind of spirit. Meaning spirits have influence. The Cain spirit, The Jezebel spirit, The Koran spirit and the Balaam spirit which most have which is the spirit of compromise. John's assignment was to go ahead of the Lord with the spirit and power Elijah had. Some people say that's me. He will change attitudes. People will be closer with their kids and more will accept God's wisdom. They will listen to those that have God's approval. In this way he will prepare the people for God's coming.

Remember we had the cause in kings. The king and the kingdom. The mission statement in Luke verse 68 and Yahshuah gave the command out. Now if Gabriel comes he will agree with God. Now we get to Mary being pregnant. God asked Mary. He told her she found favor. All God needed was a womb so he could come legally. Verse 31 You will become pregnant , give birth to a son and you will name him Yahshuah. Son of Most High God. God had to show us how to walk in the spirit since Adam lost the spirit. Mary was a virgin so how did the baby get in there? By the Holy spirit God's power. Now if God can blow his spirit in Adam ,why can't he blow his spirit in Mary. It is all the same spirit. Verse 51 God does not like prideful people. Verse 54 John being circumcised. Verse 68 the mission statement . Praise the Lord God of Israel. He has come to take care and set his people free. He has raised up a mighty servant from the house of David. Verse 70 He made this promise from his prophets along time ago. He promised to save us from our enemies and all those who hate us. He has shown his mercy to our ancestors and remembered his holy promise. The oath that he swore to our ancestor Abraham. He promised to rescue us from our enemies power so we could serve, him without fear by being holy and honorable as long as we live. Your child will be called a prophet of the God Most High. You will go ahead of the Lord to prepare his way. You will make his people know that they can be saved by the forgiveness of their sins. A new day will dawn on us from above because our God is loving and merciful. He will give light to those that live in the dark and in death's shadow which is the law. He will guide us into the way of peace. The child John grew and became spiritually strong. He lived in the desert until he appeared to the people of Israel. You can have the son and not know the way of life and suffer.

Chapter two verse 12 Yahshuah wrapped in strips of cloth, when he died and rose. So we could see. Verse 14 Angels introduce God from eternity to earthly realm. Yahshuah was God's gift to the world but the Holy spirit is God's gift to his children. He brought peace, good will, towards men coming from heaven to earth. When you ponder on something you think about it over and over again. Glory to God .Glory being God's full expression . God's in the third heaven. The fallen angels are in one and two. There are three levels of heaven. God brought his peace which is freedom and his good will which is his grace. When we do God's will he gives us grace for grace. So we have the ability to do what we need to do in the Lord. Only the shepherds were at the birth. Verse 22 Mary following the law to be clean after child birth. Verse 23 Did exactly what was said in the teachings about setting the first male apart. Verse 24 They did a sacrifice. Before Yahshuah died the spirit would come upon people now the spirit comes in people. Verse 25 Simeon prophesied about Yahshuah. Verse 34 This child is the reason many in Israel will be condemned or made guilty and many others will be saved. He will be a sign that exposes. Verse 36 We see Anna a female prophet that God allowed to see in heaven and earth. Like me. Verse 49 Yahshuah went to the synagogue to stay connected to his Hebraic roots even though he could speak Aramaic. Most believers have been cut from the roots meaning they will die. Verse 50 what you value status quality or status given.

Chapter three John doing his assignment baptism of repentance. We all have a assignment how many of us know our assignment? Let alone doing our assignment. Verse 11 talks about sharing what we have. How many of us do that? Verse 13 about being honest. Verse 14 being satisfied with what you have. Verse 16 Yahshuah to baptize us with the Holy spirit and fire. Meaning power and passion. Verse 23 Yahshuah was baptized and the lamb had to be washed. Now Yahshuah starts his ministry. In verse 24 God goes through Yahshuah's ancestry. So we would know where we came from. It helps you to see if you know where you came from.

Chapter four the devil's system Lust of the flesh, the lust of the eyes and the pride of life. Verse 3 The devil knows scripture. Remember he spent a lot of time with God before he was kicked out of heaven. He doesn't want us to know God. Verse 5 the enemy can give you stuff. Yahshuah showing us to walk his way even though life happens. Yahshuah did nothing as God but a anointed man from God. Verse 8 Yahshuah reads Isaiah verse 18 Salvation Don't let the devil influence the person in the mirror. We should mirror Yahshuah. Verse 19 God gives us his favor to act. We don't have to wait for the prophecy. What God speaks right now. Rehearse. Verse 27 This passage came true today. When you heard me read it. Scripture made history. Verse 24 A prophet is not accepted in there own home town. Like me. Verse 28 The people were mad at Yahshuah and wanted to kill him. He walked right by them. They may kill our body but they can't kill the real us the spirit. God redeemed our spirit we are all the same in the spirit. Verse 40 we have twelve hours of day light we should be working. We are children of light.

Chapter five God calling his disciples. He came across two fishermen who allowed him to use his boat. If we allow God to use our life we will be better. Verse 8 Peter recognized he was a sinful man. We have to recognize the sin so Yahshuah can deal with it. Verse 13 God healing a man with a skin disease. God wants to touch you. Are you willing for him to touch you? Verse 17 there is no power in religion. Verse 21 What's are response to God? Do we disrespect God? God's rounding up his disciples. God said follow me. Are we willing to follow God? God did not say sit. Verse 33 there is a time and a place Verse 39 Talks about your old life and your old way. Your predestination is beyond the law. Everything was done in predestined time. Chapter six verse six God doesn't need anything. Worship is for man. We should want the presence of the king. God wants a New Testament church. The normal complains church is to long .If we were going to the club we would get there around ten looking good, smelling good getting your drinks on and leave the club when the sun comes up. That's because it's for us. God is a celebratory God. Where did you learn church? Yahshuah stayed in connection with God everytime he prayed. We don't even want to pray even though prayer is a weapon. Verse 18 tormented by evil spirits. Doesn't that sound like schizenphrenia? Verse 20 Yahshuah teaching his disciples. Verse 21 down. We have to have a sensitive heart. We have to want and desire God Verse 22 Talks of us being hated excluded and insulted because of what happened to Yahshuah. Verse 24 people think money will sustain them. Verse 25 talks about earthly stuff. God tells us to love our enemies. God says love, help, lend without expecting nothing. Our stuff is not for us. The enemy will just use it against us. Verse 36 what else is God going to be but love. He is a fair judge. When you judge people you are sentencing them. It's a difference between judging , accusing and exposing. Accusing you don't know if its true , exposing you know its true. Verse 38 talks about giving. The standard we use for others will be applied to us. So why don't we use Yahshuah's standard. Verse 41 wrong teaching. My behavior is more important to my life than my brother's behavior to my life. We can't make something we aren't. If we don't build on the rock Yahshuah we are movable and can't stand.

Chapter seven is about a Roman soldier that wants his servant healed. How much scripture could he know he wasn't in covenant but he understood Yahshuah had authority and he responded appropriately. Verse 9 When he talks about not having great faith in Israel he is talking about our response. Verse 13 We see God's mercy verse 18 we see John doubting even though he seen Yahshuah. Everybody has disciples. How many are we making? Verse 26 to 27 Your performance shows who you are. Verse 32 The response. Verse 34 What you think you see. Verse 35 proof in the pudding Verse 37 Shows if you are forgiven much , you love much and give much. Verse 44 Affection.

Chapter eight Mary Magalene possessed by seven demons sounds like multiple personalities to me. Verse 9 pressure and care of the world given to the disciples. They are like soldiers that occupy until Yahshuah comes back. We have to spiritually occupy and hold back the enemy that's a spirit. God talks about being blind because they have no understanding. God continues to correct his finished work. Satan attacks your mind because he knows that's how you see. The sick woman with the issue of blood knew she had to press. She wanted God to touch her. She wasn't even suppose to come out but her respond got her her healing. God always sends out more than one disciple because he doesn't want his soldiers pricked off. No believer should be by their self.

Chapter nine people starting to get curious. Who do we think and say Yahshuah is? You are a soul that possesses a spirit that lives in a body. You only have a body to touch this earth. At the time of Yahshuah's transformation Peter, John and James were scared. Peter was the teacher ,John was the revelator and James was willing to die for the cause. They were also witnesses. Verse 51 Sons of thunder meaning they had tempers. They wanted to call fire down from heaven. Be careful of what spirit you are operating in. We should be walking in love and truth. Verse 58 Yahshuah had no permanent place he was going where he needed to go Verse 60 spiritually dead. Kingdom is where the king lives. Verse 62 If we are working for the Lord,we are not going back to the world.

Chapter ten talks about workers being few because nobody is being discipled. Verse 5 The muslims use this phrase about peace out of our bible. Verse 18 talks about him seeing satan fall. So he had to be there. So if he was there he just couldn't be a prophet. Verse 21 spiritual discernment. Verse 25 Good Samaritan which is your neighbor and your brother. So why do so many of us act like the priest that represents religious leaders that walked across the street or the levite who represents the believer who walked across the street. They cared nothing about their brother like most believers. So how can we claim to love God? A Samaritan is a mixed person. The woman at the well was Samaritan. Yahshuah was mixed with God and man. Verse 30 represents God. How do we represent God? By the way we treat other people. People that don't even consider themselves believers treat people better then believers do. Verse 32 Tells us to follow the good Samaritan's lead. He was kind .He was also a mixed breed for all of you who push being racist. I already discussed Mary doing the right thing and broke down the Lord's prayer. Mary was busy tending to her life and not spending time with Yahshuah. A lot of us do that. We get mad at the person for having a unmovable relationship with God. A believer should have TBA Have trust, believe and have accountability.

Agent	element	purpose
Yahshuah	Holy spirit	witness
Yahshuah	fire	Intense pressure

Yahshuah gives us stuff so we can do stuff

We should be turning the flame up. Verse 9 we should be persistent. Verse 11 Gives whats needed not what you think. Most of us might know our brother is hungry but we want to give him some word instead of giving him some food. If he is hungry that word does not mean much. We have to show are brother we care. Verse 13 Holy spirit is a gift so why do many churches think you have to tarry to get it? It's all about the relationship. What are we claiming to be? Verse 24 Once we clean the house means if the person doe not stay clean or stay connected to God and the believers, spirits come back. Make them mature believers. We need to grow them up. The enemy brings more spirits and goes back to it's so called house. So why do we think unclean spirits just went away? We need to be obedient to the word. The sign of Jonah is Yahshuah. A sign is so you can see. Verse 33 The lamp of the body or candle of the Lord is the Holy spirit. Your eye shows you what's in your body. What you value so *don't have evil or jealousy in your heart. Verse 39 Is all about appearance. Don't appear to be something that you are not. You have to have it in you. You see on the out side what is in you. We have to do our part. Yahshuah's way. Verse 43 don't be for show. Verse 44 Spiritually dead. Verse 46 want people to do what they won't do. Verse 50 left the faith. They did what their ancestors did by killing the prophets. So they will be held accountable. Verse 52 Blind leading the blind.*

Chapter twelve teaching of Yahshuah . How to value ourselves and the kingdom. Yahshuah is Grace and Truth. Yeast of the Pharisees is what they are teaching. Everything will be exposed. Verse 6 God cares about everything. When a person dishonors the Holy spirit he will not be forgiven because the Holy spirit is God. It is coming down to the court case. So I have to present the evidence. Invest in God instead of the world. Verse 14 Yahshuah came to bring Salvation. Verse 16 think wealth will sustain them until they get a evil report. Verse 22 Worrying is perverse meditation. Eternity is more important. It is forever. The natural is temporary and wears out. Verse 25 We can't do anything anyway Verse 28 God takes care of everything and cares more about us being in his image. Verse 31 Stop worrying about the world. Verse 33 What you love and desire. Verse 35 We need to be ready. Verse 39 It is all about preparation. What we did with his ministry? Verse 46 How are we treating the flock. Verse 47 much given much required. Verse 52 Talks about division based on belief. How we believe about Yahshuah. Verse 54 Tells us to know what time it is. Beware of what's happening around us. If we follow God's time line and seasons it helps us to be aware and stay awake.

Chapter thirteen talks about all these things happening to people and it boils down to sin. Sin equals death no matter how you add it up. We have to respect God and change the way we think and act. Why we still have time to do it. Verse 6 how we live our lives. Believers that don't make disciples are fruitless. Verse 10 Righteousness supercedes the law. Verse 18 The mustard seed grows big from a small seed. That's how the word responds when we implant it in our heart. When you study and feed it, it produces fruit. The narrow door is Yahshuah. Verse 26 The eating and drinking. No relationship , most church people. Verse 30 talks about last and first positions in the world. Lowly and humble. Verse 32 A fox means clever and deceitful. That's the enemy. Verse 34 Jerusalem was his chosen who also rejected him.

Chapter 14 mercy over the law. Verse 2 A man whose body was swollen with fluid sounds like edema to me. Which is something Luke is a doctor so he's telling the story from a physician's point of view. Verse 12 We should not expect anything from people and respect people from all walks of life. Verse 18 Do we give excuses when it is time to move for God. Verse 19 Business. Verse 20 relationship Verse 23 us going out Verse 25 the cost of us being disciples. Enemy can use anything in our life against us. So we have to be willing to die. Hate your life Instruct show, manifest, show oneness. Life continues. Verse 28 to verse 33 talks about planning and counsel. Salt is what we should be. Salt speaks of our character it can qualify or disqualify us. Salt is also a preservative so we should be preserving. We should be real salty and tangy so the people will want a glass of Yahshuah. Salt makes you thirsty. If we aren't like this what good are we for the kingdom?

Chapter fifthteen The lost sheep and the lost coin are about winning a soul. The lost son means your dead to me not living in the right principles you sleep with the pigs until you come to your senses. It's all about reconciling the soul back to God.

Chapter sixteen the spirit gives us rest. The object of money should be for the master's purpose not our pleasure. The World uses God's principles. How can you change without a plan? Verse 6 Have to give a account. Verse 7 advocate Verse 8 Learn to be wise to people which will bring you to your future destiny . Stewardship made it possible to hear gospel and get to heaven. Money is unrighteous and is suppose to serve us. God made us sons but we can't get the benefits if we act like guests. Lazarous was a homeless man. It all comes back to how we treat people. Heaven use to be in the ground. It was called Abraham's bosom. It use to be long side hell but you could not cross over. That's how the rich man seen Lazarous. The people were unconnected to God so their souls were down below until Yahshuah rescued them and gave us back the spirit. When Yahshuah ascended to heaven he took heaven which was below and put it in the third heaven. There's a scripture that says they seen the dead walking around on earth before they ascended to heaven. Just don't serve People because you have something in common with them. Yahshuah washed Judas's feet even though he betrayed him. Believers have homeless tendacies in the spirit . They hang on to stuff like someone's going to take it from them. They don't know if they have enough to survive. So are we really trusting? Man looks on outer appearance God looks at the heart. So how are we seeing like God if we don't see the way he does? We have homeless spirits. We don't know what we have. God says give yourself away. God poured it out so we know how to pour it out . God already broke us through. We are released. As you do that more stuff comes to you. We have to have God's mindset. We need to be in agreement, so we will have power and advance God's kingdom. We have to think of ourselves as sons or relatives not just attending a service. Our participation is needed.

Chapter seventeen God should always be our desire. Things are always going to come up. We should always be forgiving. Look how we treat God and he always forgives us. Leprosy represents any flesh problem and it's a sign of corruption or break down in our life. We should go right to Yahshuah who sees all and can take care of any problem or situation. We have to identify our sin, confess, look to God and allow Yahshuah to make us clean. We have to get to where Yahshuah is. We think we are alright and tend to stay away. We think we don't need God's help or are we afraid of what people might say? Or we might think we can fix ourselves. How Can we fix anything? Besides God wants to give us a brand new life. God doesn't care about your failures. He carried our infirmities that's what it means. He wants to restore us. The way we think isn't God's thoughts, that's why he tells us to meditate. When we pray it's like a weapon but our words have to get through all that demonic activity. Daniel's prayer got hindered twenty one days by the king of Persia which was a demon over the territory of Persia. Angels ascend and descend for our words. They are fighting as they go back and forth. They come for our words to take up to God. We have to work the system until Yahshuah comes back. Verse 9 Us thinking we are right . Self righteousness. How we think of ourselves before God made us righteous. Imitate God and believe how God does. Verse 24 About a camel going through the eye of a needle before a rich man goes to heaven. It's how the rich man thinks about his money .The rich man makes his riches his master. Money is not necessarily bad but it is how we think about it. Money can't be all bad. God made Abraham and Solomon super rich. We have to put God first. We punch a clock for money so we better do more for God. Verse 29 to 30 Talks of how you leave everything to follow Yahshuah and how you will receive in this life time. More than you give up.

Chapter nineteen talks about a short man trying to see Yahshuah. So he climbed a tree to see Yahshuah. What are we willing to do to see Yahshuah? The people at Zachaeous house disapproved of Yahshuah being there for dinner. The closer you get to God the bigger the devils will be. God will give you more grace. Which is the ability to handle it. I see so called believers can be the hardest on believers when we should be proving ourselves to the world not other believers. It's all about the press. We need to press through that natural man. Verse 23 Palm Sunday represents victory. Triumph. They knew someone in David's line would restore the kingdom to Israel. Verse 48 talks if the people were silent the rocks would cry out. Silence isn't golden when you should be talking. Now we get to where Yahshuah throws out the money changers. They had no respect for God's house and where conducting there private business in God's house. They were doing things to benefit themselves. The widow gave all she had . I discussed her earlier. God became her bridge. People give out of their excess when they should give from their heart. Hopefully their heart is in the right place. The people should of been her bridge. We should not be talking about these people we should be helping them. Maybe we don't believe God's system.

Chapter twenty one verse 15 talks of God giving words of wisdom Verse 24 Talks of man's day and man's judgement. Verse 25 Talks of the shaking. God's not holding it together anymore. The hedge is coming down. Do people realize what that means? It's going to be more of the dark forces over here. The only thing that will be able to stand is the New Testament church . Not the church down the street. A church full of believers walking in the spirit. Filled with the Holy spirit. It's happening in the spirit, so you know it's going to push out of the spirit.

Chapter twenty two verse 1 communion , part of the sader. Verse 18 didn't drink cup of blessing because Yahshuah would become a curse. Verse 42 Humanity side of Yahshuah. God forsook him to accept us. He was a stone's throw away. Why didn't they stone him if he was a false prophet. He said he was God. Verse 44 Yahshauh sweating blood on the ground redeemed the ground back for us. Remember the ground was cursed in Genesis.

Chapter twenty three verse 38 End times. The green tree represents the tree of life. Verse 43 A jail house confession did not speak in tongues. He was saved. Verse 44 The sun that Yahshuah caused to shine was unfriendly .It was extremely hot while he was on the cross. Verse 46 Yahshuah laid down his life and made the way. Yahshuah had to release his spirit.

Chapter twenty four is the same as Acts one to eight Women were always first with the things of Yahshuah. God's secret weapon is the woman. Verse 12 Yahshuah took his time folding up the linen. It was not about him being in a hurry to get out but them to get in. So they can see. His disciples didn't recognize, Yahshuah because he had healing properties in him. They remember he was unrecognizable when he was on the cross. We know it was the same body because Thomas felt his pierced side. Everything that is done in the spirit has to be pushed out to the natural. Yahshuah's constantly called a prophet but who better to speak about you, then you. I can tell you a lot better about me then someone else. God said his spoken word out rides a vision. Moses got God's spoken word so that would over ride whatever a prophet saw or heard. The prophet would have to match up with what Moses said. Men chase skirts so if you elevate the woman the man is bound to follow. Verse 23 Bible was called scriptures. It was translated from Graphic. Which means it is written. Sacred writings. Yahshuah is a real person they could touch him. Verse 44 They taught the Old Testament, psalms and the prophets the New Testament was not wrote yet. When the New Testament was wrote they just took from the Old Testament. Verse 49 Holy spirit. Acts 1-8 Verse 50 Yahshuah was taken to heaven in a cloud. He defied the laws of gravity. Gravity keeps you to the ground. Yahshuah supercedes every law including gravity. Yahshuah was our first fruit but he made the way so more can come. He told them to wait for the power. The power is the Holy spirit. Little note-The son always exsisted but had to put on flesh so he could be son of man. Adam the last man came from dust and Yahshuah was the word that became flesh. Yahshuah had to do his assignment legally so he came from a womb.

John the Apostle wrote the book of John. This book shows the diety side of Yahshuah. John was probably the closest to Yahshuah he called himself the beloved. He knew he was loved. Do we? John was the one who had his head on Yahshuah's heart at the last supper. Showing he wanted to know his father's heart. This book was invoked by Genesis.

The first chapter of this book shows no beginning and no end. It picks up where Genesis leaves off. It allows you to see that God and his word are the same. Yahshauah took on carnality. Yahshuah had to put on flesh. The son is the essence of the father meaning he came out of the same substance. Just like we came out of our parents that came out of God. God is also power and grace. The grace and power gave him the ability to complete his assignment. The grace and power are the Holy spirit. His body represents Tabernacles. God dwelling with us because he is in us. We know everything God spoke came to be . So God asked Mary to Borrow her womb . God spoke his word into Mary's womb . Remember God has power in his words. Which his power is the Holy spirit. Just like you say something terrible to somebody and it hurts their feelings. The words you said had power to cut in the spirit. John chapter one starts off in the beginning. Just think of your words being with you and you release your words as you talk. Verse 5 The world does not understand Yahshuah like the world does not understand us. Light dispels darkness. Verse 6 John came to prepare the way. Verse 11 No human effort. It was a God effort. Verse 14 The word became flesh. Yahshuah became flesh to identify with us. We saw his glory which was a full expression of God. Showing us how to live. Verse 16 John's a witness. A witness is one who gives evidence. Truth never changes, Facts change. The world doesn't understand because it is not connected to God. We received grace which is undeserved favor. Yahshuah is the blessing. God calls Yahshuah the only begotten son because he only had one son. That's for those that think Yahshuah and the devil are brothers. God is the father of everything because everything originated and was created by God. Begotten means placed in a womb. We were spiritually adopted. God wanted to show us relationship. He wanted more sons not fathers. Father and son is the greatest relationship in eternity. All other relationships follow that one. The father and son reveal each other to us because they are one and the same. No one can get to heaven by following the law or works. God said it is one way through the son. In a court case there in not a whole lot of ways. John was a advocate on behalf of Yahshuah. Verse 24 baptism of repentance. Verse 29 the lamb was a foreshadow of Yahshuah. Verse 32 anointing Verse 33 John's spirit recognized God's voice. The Holy spirit is God so it will recognize all those false spirits in end times. You always see at least two people with Yahshuah. Meaning two or more witnesses. You have to have more than one witness. Verse 42 Yahshuah operating in the word of knowledge. Verse 45 prophets and Moses pointed to Yahshuah. Verse 46 Is like saying if someone from low income can make something of themselves. Verse 48 word of wisdom and knowledge. Telling something about self. I will say it again it does not matter where you start but where you end. Verse 51 God's angels hearken to God's words.

Chapter two Yahshuah did not do any miracles until God ascended on him. When he tells his mother it's not time, It's not time for him to die and take on sin. Only something clean can wash away dirt. Dirt can't clean dirt it will only smear it around. Where a clean rag will wipe it away. Verse 13 respect of God's house. Doing everything in God's house but what we suppose to do. Sharing God's altar. Not making God sacred. God's house should be used for what God said. A house of prayer for all men. Prayer meaning being connected and communicating with God. I don't know about us conducting our private stuff in God's sanctuary. Seems like a Idol to me . I seen a office sign that had a sign way bigger then the sanctuary sign. Why do we make God real small? Verse 16 A market place for everything but God's word. God's house should be the priority. Verse 19 Yahshuah is the temple. Yahshuah proved out everything he said in the Old Testament Verse 24 and 25 Yahshuah had a gift of discernment.

Chapter three verse 3 Have the spirit. Verse 7 and 8 Man can only produce human life but the Holy spirit can produce a new life from heaven. You know the wind is there even though you don't know where it came from or where it is going. Verse 10 Nicodemus was a religious teacher but he didn't understand what Yahshuah said. Showing us that the natural man can't understand spiritual things. The word has to be revealed to you. Verse 14 Moses lifting up the snake on a pole. Remember the snakes were biting the people in the old testament because of disobedience. God told Moses to put a replica of a snake on a pole and have then look to it and be healed. Now we look towards the cross. People stand condemned because of fallen man. Fallen angels won't be redeemed. So they want to take as many people with them as they can. The first heaven is the air and atmosphere , the second heaven is the sun and stars, the third heaven is where God dwells. The fallen angels are in the first and second. Don't be double minded while dealing with God. Yahshuah was afflicted so we can be whole. Verse 18 Job of believer is to believe. Verse 19 liking the world. Verse 20 don't want people to see them doing wrong ,come to the light prove what God's done. Verse 22 Shows us how to submit to another ministry. We should be linking together. Unity is the key. Verse 31 Holy spirit what everything is based on. God's constant anger is hell because It's never going to stop.

Chapter four Samaritan woman was mixed breed and one of the first evangelists. She professed who Yahshuah was and what he did. Samaritan people came out of Jacob's son Joseph. Verse 6 Yahshuah had to charge self up. We have to stay in the word so we can stay charged up. This gave Yahshuah a opportunity to witness to the woman at the well. Verse 9 Jews did not associate with Samaritans I guess they thought they were better. Yahshuah associated with everyone. Living water equals eternal life. Eternal life equals salvation, deliverance, protection and redemption. Verse 14 What Yahshuah gives will grow quickly because he is the source. The water is the Holy spirit and we see the woman desiring it. Verse 16 Yahshuah operating in all the spiritual gifts. Word of knowledge when he knew the woman at the well had no husband. The woman was truthful when we are truthful God can deal with us. Verse 19 The woman was able to see who Yahshauh was. Can you see who Yahshuah is? Verse 21 refers to the spirit that will be in us after Yahshuah dies. And we believe we receive the spirit which is God. We don't have to go to the mountain or Jerusalem because the spirit is in us. Our spirit identifies with God's spirit. The woman at the well did not realize what she had. Yahshuah is spirit and truth. He is the Holy spirit and what everything is based on. Verse 26 She knew when Yahshuah came it would not be in the physical. Verse 27 witnessing Verse 32 about feeding the spirit. The people did not believe her because she's a woman. They came to see but they stayed because of Yahshuah. Verse 46 They believed what he did. Verse 35 four represents earth. Harvest means people are ready to hear and be saved. Verse 43 prophet not honored in their own home town. The festival they are at is one of the feasts. Verse 46 How we respond to Yahshuah. Verse 50 Do we honor, respect or value Yahshuah? Number seven in verse 52 represents completion. Verse 53 It takes you to show your family what a believer looks like.

Chapter five be made whole. Verse 3 when I think of people up under these porches I think of homeless people undersireables as society says. Verse seven stirring up the gifts. We stir up the gifts by joy, praying and thanksgiving Verse 14 Attacks, line your behavior with your changed condition. Verse 16 Sabbath made for man. Yahshuah correcting finished work. One and the same with God. Verse 24 Believers not being judged with the world. Meaning being sentenced. Be woke in the spirit. Verse 22 to 30 Evacuation . Which judgement? judgement seat of Christ or white throne judgement. What will you choose? Verse 36 to 40 Yahshuah has to be revealed. It's all about the spirit. Verse 43 How we accept a preacher and not Yahshuah. Verse 46 and 47 the Torah speaks of Yahshuah and Moses wrote the Torah.

Chapter six We have the right to touch things that God presents to us. Righteousness established by Yahshuah accepted by father. Verse 15 understood when Messiah came would set up millineal rain. Verse 19 Walking on the word. Yahshuah had authority over everything. Everything can hear. Everything was made to yield to the Holy spirit. The believer needs to know what he's working towards. When we had sandy- The earth was groaning but as we get closer to the end the earth will groan more and more. It will increase just like labor pains. Everything knows the creator. Do we bow to other Gods? Other Gods like self, fornification, or greed etc. Here's one God of entertainment. God says the agressive will occupy until he comes back. I will talk about this at the end of the book. If you look like the devil how are you going to deliver the oppressed? God loves us but he won't compromise for us. Yahshuah gave us the tools a mouth and wisdom, to use against the advasary. Are we laboring for the things Yahshuah has for us? We always want to know what he will do for us. What we want naturally. Just like Esau wanting his belly full. We shouldn't let our job or anything else drive us. We never seem to do our part. The natural man has no value for the truth or spiritual things. We need to do everything Yahshuah says. Jewish people embrace the feasts. Yahshuah is the bread of God that gave life. Verse 34 we have to receive him and not make him ordinary. Verse 39 reconciling people back to Yahshuah. Everything Yahshuah said was spiritual remember he said his words were spirit filled. Verse 60 Natural man doesn't accept the things of God. Even though it's not the real you. Verse 65 father provides the way which is Yahshuah. Verse 66 going back to old man letting old life get in the way. Verse 70 Yahshuah operating in word of wisdom.

Chapter seven feast of booths. Which is Tabernacles. When Yahshauh said he was the bread of life he was that manna in the old Testament that God sent from heaven. For the Israelites to eat while they were in the wilderness. God knows whether or not you believe even if we don't. You have to purposely push pass the old man. We all have freewill to choose how we want to live. Verse 15 Didn't go to seminary. Verse 16 Learn from relationship with God. Verse 17 know truth by relationship and revealing it to us. Verse 30 not going anywhere until it's your time verse 37 Yahshuah was at a water ceremony. This is where they poured water on the alter. It was celebrated as a party. It was a foreshadow of lateral rain. Explained what rain was and it represented the Holy spirit. It was a foreshadow of no drought or a dry life. To have a good life and eat well. So we need to line up and get the real thing with God. Have to trust in God. Verse 42 Every verse that Yahshuah says he came from he came from. We need to tell the story truefully. The scriptures have to be revealed. The bible is coded for the Holy spirit. The bible was wrote in dangerous times. The natural man will never see. The Jehovah witnesses omit chapter eight. We knew Yahshuah could write he was writing in the sand. The woman who was caught in adultery was brought to Yahshuah. Where was the man? The religious sect was always trying to trip Yahshuah up. Yahshuah wrote the law so he knew it and he never condemned a man. Verse 12 says he's the light of the world. Light dispels darkness. Yahshuah tells us to follow him. Why are we still sitting? Verse 24 Says they will die because of their sins. Wages of sin is death in the law. Verse 30 true disciples live by what Yahshuah says Verse 42 If you have Yahshuah's name you are your father's children. Hashem means name. Which is Shem's name Noah's son the line Abraham and Yahshuah came out of. Names are important. We are children of wrath and disobedience in the natural but by choice we become children of God. The devil is the father of lies. Yahshuah is a mix breed half God and human. Verse 51 won't see death will have eternal life. Verse 58 saying he's God this the Jehovah witnesses omitted. I guess they are witnesses to him providing since Jehovah means provider.

Chapter nine They thought people caused things like blindness to happen. Sometimes you will stay in a circumstance so God can show his power through you. While living in the natural. Will hold you up. God's word on display. Verse 16 Traditions of man Verse 20 parents scared to say what happened scared they will be put out of synagogue. Now we just say we are leaving church. Verse 28 everybody had disciples. Disciples are learnth ones, soldiers. Verse 41 spiritually blind don't see him. Yahshuah's the door. God's people know his voice. Verse 10 The thief is the devil who comes to kill, steal and destroy. Verse 11 Christ gave his life when he was crucified. Verse 15 God's people all over the world. Verse 22 The feast of dedication which is Hanukkah. This dedication was because Anthony Epiphanes sacrificed a pig on God's altar and defiled the temple. A group of priest the Macabees overthrew Epiphanes and cleansed the temple. They only had eight hours of oil to light the temple but God kept it lit until they could purify the temple. The manure was the candlestick which was the only light in the temple. If you put forth some effort to the things of God, God will pull it the rest of the way. Verse 32 If Yahshuah was lying about being God why didn't he get stoned. Verse 35 Called people of God because the Holy spirit is in them.

Chapter eleven Lazarous, Mary and Martha's brother was sick and died. Yahshuah raised him after four days just to die again. Yahshuah took his time getting to his place of death so they couldn't say anything and have faith. At four days you start to decay. Yahshuah working his ministry. Verse 44 Lazarous was wrapped up like a mummy. Romans ruled. Verse 50 Yahshuah died for the cause. Different kingdoms ruled at different times. I guess you could say it was the survival of the fittest. Caiaphas was high priest and said Yahshuah would not only die for the cause but would bring God's scattered children back and make them one.

Chapter twelve verse 12 Yahshuah presents himself as a king. Hosanna is the highest praise. Meaning Yahshuah saves. This is where Palm Sunday comes from. Triumph, Victory. Yahshuah rode on a donkey's colt and the people were waving palm branches. Verse 23 principle of the seed. When the seed is in the ground it is dead. You can't see it. The seed coat protects it while it's in the ground. Moisture comes, the seed coat comes off and dies and the seed grows and sprouts. Just like Yahshuah is the vine that everything grows from. Verse 28 Did Yahshuah really want to go? He yielded to the father's will. Verse 32 Yahshuah prophesied, how he would die. Verse 30 when spirit left couldn't see word. Has to be revealed only revealed by coming to him. Verse 43 Cared about what people thought. Appearance Scared of what people thought verse 47 Came to bring salvation.

Chapter thirteen Yahshuah had a unconditional love for his disciples. Verse 5 Washing the disciples feet. Showing servitude. How to be selfless and not intimidate anyone Verse 8 Prideful people won't be Yahshuah disciples. Verse 14 wanted them to live a life of serving others. Verse 23 John the disciple who Yahshuah loved. His heart was close to Yahshuah's. Verse 26 Word of wisdom. Verse 34 Love, The Holy spirit is the spirit of God in man. Yahshuah told them to wait because he was going back to the father. Yahshuah is the truth and the life. No one goes through the father except through the son . They are one and the same. So how can there be more than one way when Yahshuah says there is one way him. Verse 12 walking in the gifts. Verse 16 The helper is the Holy spirit. Which is the spirit of truth which everything is based on. The Holy spirit is our counselor. Our D.A Verse 14 Beware of the tactics of the enemy. We can straticize and plan and be on one accord. God chose ordinary people that he saw greatness in. To call men back to returning to the father. They left their current lives to follow Yahshuah and he showed them the cost of ministry. That it came with a price. They learned as they went along . The Holy spirit lives in the believer permanently. Verse 14 and 15 If you trust Yahshuah follow his instructions. Trying to get something to you not you earning something. God puts us in position so we will never be deceived. God does not need anything when he asks us to do something it is for our benefit. Verse 22 Relationship, Yahshuah starts showing us stuff. What a cold glass of water does for a thirsty person is what the Holy spirit does for us.

Chapter fifthteen To minister before the Lord. Yahshuah is the vine that everything grows from. When you prune back more grows. A Renewed mind makes, more fruit, the seed is in us. We got all of God we are going to get when we believe. We just have to grow the seed. When we prune our minds it cuts worldly stuff away from us. What's our approach? Kings had to clean themselves as a daily ritual Yahshuah already cleansed us. The branch has to stay connected to the vine so it can produce fruit. So we have to stay connected to Yahshuah. Confession will keep us connected to Yahshuah because a confession leads to repentance. When we acknowledge and come into agreement with God we change our mind and change our direction. Repentance changes our minds and brings a change of behavior. Work this thing out. If you don't aim for anything you won't hit anything. What's your purpose? Yahshuah gave us his character to rule and reign. Be a influence over those who make decisions. Verse 9 Yahshuah loved us before we loved him. So why do we think we have to earn something? Joy is the first step to prosperity. Joy carried Yahshuah to the cross because he knew what it meant. The man being reconciled back to him. Verse 15 We don't earn friendship Yahshuah chose us and allowed us to know what he's doing. Verse 18 We shouldn't have anything in common with the world. That's why the world hates us because of the spirit we have in us. I see how the world puts all these other beliefs and lifestyles above Yahshuah. A natural man is not greater then a spirit man. God says the natural man is a opposition to him and receives nothing from him. The natural man is constantly fighting against God. Verse 20 and 21 We are suppose to be just like Yahshuah walking in the spirit. Verse 26 Yahshuah gave us the Holy spirit as our helper and it will declare the truth about life. Meaning it will make it known what the truth is. When we look like Yahshuah. Then we will understand because we will know what's going on.

Chapter sixteen verse 2 like Isis verse 7 Spirit coming back to earth the spirit will convict the world of sin, Judgement and righteousness. The sin is not believing, not breaking the commandments. Righteousness, we need to go to the father and see if we are in right standing. Judgement means sentenced and the prince of this world is already sentenced. Yahshuah knew we would be tempted to be offended. Believers killed kicked out of the synagogue, Job loss etc. When Yahshuah was with them in the physical he took the heat. Now he is in us so we have to take the heat. We have to be willing to die. The Holy spirit advocates on our behalf. The spirit helps us and guides us. So we don't need human effort. I'm not saying we don't have any activity we do as long as we do the things of God. It's a God effort. God's plan. Add Yahshuah subtract you and you have the Fullnest of God. The blood connects us to God. So we shouldn't let anything interfere with the king or the kingdom. Me being black stands down where the kingdom is concerned. Color is the natural man while the spirit is in the kingdom. We are ambassadors meaning we are from a foreign land . The embassy in heaven. So we live by the government in heaven. We should be highly respected and have diplomatic amnesty. We go out as a righteous person and reconcile a unrighteous person to a righteous person Yahshuah. Yahshuah's humanity wasn't referenced to God but us. Everything refers to the spirit .The spirit shows us how to witness and preach who he is and what he has done. What man can judge living or dead? Judge means sentence you to hell. Not expose. We need to come to Yahshuah. He knows where you are so don't lean to your own understanding. Verse 24 Act like Yahshauh is there. Verse 33 Yahshuah speaking a eternal reality. Son always exsisted.

Chapter seventeen Prayed for disciples because they were left here. Verse 6 Yahshuah manifested his name never ran around saying his name. You have to see it. Verse 12 Judas Verse 17 Yahshuah is past, present, and future all at the same time Verse 21 unity Verse 24 Always with God Verse 25 Yahshuah's mission. Our focus should be into Yahshuah's assignment. God took sting out of death. First we may mourn but we shouldn't let it turn to grief because we know are fate.

Chapter eighteen verse 4 word of wisdom Verse 6 Yahshuah had so much power in him they could not take him. Yahshuah had to let them take him. Verse 10 You see Peter acting naturally when he cut the servants ear off. Verse 11 Have to do God's will. Verse 15 Peter wasn't known. Got in because of John. John was known. You know how it goes when you are boys. The chief priest found no fault in Yahshuah. What father says in secret, we say in public. Like Yahshuah did with the high priest. Verse 26 They wanted to get Yahshuah because they said he said he was better then Ceasar the king. That was what he was accused of.

Chapter nineteen verse 5 a crown of thorns and thistles to redeem the ground. Feast day also called a high Sabbath. Verse 16 Judgement of sin at calvary. Examine yourself. God put the same glory on us that he put on Yahshuah. God made us one with him like Yahshuah is one with him. Yahshuah's mother Mary saw him die on the cross imagine the pain and suffering. He bled just like we do. This relates to a mother losing a child. Nobody else can save. Yahshuah entrusted his mother to John. Yahshuah lived to fulfill scripture. The sun didn't shine when he died. It was the creator the son's hour to shine and be made sin. It was finished. His assignment is complete. Yahshuah layed down his life to settle divine justice. Which would only come by dying. Isaiah chapter fifty three verse 26 John knew he was loved and saved. Mary lived with him. Verse 30 Yahshuah drank the cup. He became a curse so we would be blessed. Cup means he did what he had to do. Man's redemption was done and it made the gentiles heirs also. Gentile means uncovenant people. Covenant is another word for contract. Doctrines of men waters down Yahshuah. There was nothing weak about Yahshuah. A eye witness saw what happened. Yahshuah took all the ordinances against the man and nailed them to the cross. Ordinances meaning charges.

Chapter twenty Yahshuah took his time and folded up the linen which showed order and respect. The stone was rolled away so you could see he got up not that he was stolen. Verse 11 Mary was the first to the tomb. She was also the last to leave. What that shows being early and staying late when it comes to the things of Yahshuah. Verse 17 Yahshuah had to be the perfect sacrifice. He was the firstfruit so he couldn't be tampered with. That's why he told Mary not to touch him. Yahshuah provided for our redemption. Verse 27 Yahshuah breathed on his disciples the breath of life. They received the Holy spirit. Genesis chapter two verse 7 God breathing into Adam. They did not realize what they had until the day of Pentecost. When you go to a funeral the body is not moving because the spirit is gone. If we don't have the Holy spirit we are lifeless. Verse 24 Doubting Thomas. Thomas had to see it to believe it like most of us. So Yahshuah let him see the nail marks and pierced side. Yahshuah had healing properties in himself so he healed himself. Verse 29 If you have spiritual faith you are blessed. Yahshuah spent forty days teaching and they spent ten days waitng for the power. Yahshuah spent forty days and forty nights going over scripture and making sure they have understanding. You don't get Yahshuah's way of life by doing nothing.

Chapter twenty one verse 13 Yahshuah made himself known by breaking bread. Showing you about relationship not knowing tons of scripture. Verse 14 About God knowing what you have if you don't see it. Verse 15 Yahshuah asked Peter three times if he loved him to cancel out the three times he denied him. Everything is Yahshuah and everything is ours through Yahshuah. So we should speak like Yahshuah. Verse 23 Yahshuah was showing don't worry about what I'm doing with John you just worry about yourself and what's the next move in the plans. That was the final instruction before Yahshuah departed. When the Holy spirit comes upon us it empowers us to be witnesses. The church should be empowered like the son. We need to manifest who Yahshuah is and the only way we will find out who he is, is if we meet with the father. We need to identify with the Lord. What happened spiritually placed us in the family. Through the spirit of adoption. Everything he did we should do. Yahshuah finished the finish work and his finish work points to rest. We don't have to do anything we should just witness. A witness is one who testifies and gives evidence. Has personal knowledge of.

Chapter 14
The Model Church

The church in Acts was the picture of a full grown church. God always gives us a model so we should know what we are suppose to have or look like. This church that Yahshuah is coming back for without spot or wrinkle. The glorious New Testament Church. The stage is being set for it. The way this soceity does us it probably will push the church into unifying and believing we are all we have. This church shows us how we should act as believers. God gives us the blueprint and we don't carry it out. The church is suppose to be the pillar of the truth and represent God's name. So why is the church lying? We should receive light and understanding. What we have is a Roman Greco mindset. The greek influence over the way we think. We made church like a spectator event. We sit in church on Sunday hear a message hope it's good and hope it's something in that message that will change my life. Penecost birthed the church so we would be prompted and led by the Holy spirit. Then we get fed the word . The combination allows us to know what's going on in the spirit. People think if they pray real hard the hand of God will move when God's hand already moved. We just need to move by what he has already done, his word. If you are born again we need to understand how God operates. The church is suppose to be a group of believers coming together operating as one. A church filled with spirit filled people. Mature believers. The church of today doesn't know God's mind or breath was breathed and his anointing empowering us for service. We pray in the spirit because we don't know how to pray. Yahshuah is the gift to the world. The Holy spirit is God's gift to his children. What is my responsibility to God? What does God require of me? That's what we should be asking ourselves. Not what does he look like and why did he let this happen to me. We need to understand how to be a obedient servant, not how to figure God out. The church won a majority with a minority. You could not do that *with a lie. Yahshuah birthed the church out so the world would get a revelation of who he is. If they see a full grown church they will. This book shows us how to function as a church a living organism. If we are a church filled with the spirit that's what we are . The Holy spirit gives us life. A matyrd is a person willing to die for the cause. No amen in this book because we are suppose to continue what the disciples did and be the church in Acts. This book gives us acess to God's plan. It's God's direction not a ritual. Most believers have no understanding and are just wasting God's time.*

Chapter one verse one is Luke chapter twenty four. When Yahshuah ascended in a cloud he defied gravity. Gravity holds you to the ground. Yahshuah defied the laws of nature. The spirit supercedes the law. Yahshuah just kept ascending as the people watched. The people were probably saying I don't believe it. The day of Pentecost the believers received power and the teaching came right from the Holy spirit. Peter realized what he had at Pentecost. Yahshuah transferred the power. The Holy spirit is the same spirit Adam and Eve had before the fall. How much warring are we doing for are brothers since we have the power to do it? Know what God did through you. Go to war. Our lives may be reflecting Eypt. Maybe that's why we are not going to war we are to busy maintaining us. We should have integrity. What God says to you regardless of what people say to you. Our pursuit should be in glorifying God. It has to be done on purpose. They want to separate church from state. God says come out from among them. We need to pull our money and resources out of this world's system. We need to utilize Christian businesses. Support each other like family. All we have the creator gave to us. Let the world do what they do. We should not have to bend for what we believe. We need to get adamant for the king's government. The spirit of the world is very aggressive and adamant against the people of God. Only 10% of God's people have a biblical world view. God's word is a mirror showing us who we are. Babies don't try to be human they just walk it out. You meet the truth through the word. So are we reflecting the word or the world? The enemy gets us distracted so we never look in the mirror. We always live in what you did to me never in who I am. People not being who they are believed to be. Who are you following? Are we walking in agreement? What do we think prayer is? You shouting promises like you have to convince God. Believe God has graced us. God's grace is enough. A capstone is the top of the building and it is finished. The cornerstone holds the building together. We are spiritual stones in the body of Christ. Everything is done in the spirit . No control over grace. Grace works just like the heart pumps blood. Continually. From the time you are conceived even if you feel you're a bad person. God still works his grace. God gave sinners gifts and talent in the natural which are irrevocable. Meaning he's not going to take away what he's given you . God's no Indian giver. So just how much do you think he gives us in the spirit? If we spend time in the book with God, he will take us grace for grace. Grace to be saved. Grace for this life. Love of God is poured out on man. You don't need God's grace to sit in a location which is the church. The church makes up the body. Yahshuah's the head and the church is the body. So Yahshuah works through the fellowship. Everybody does their part so the body works perfect. The bone marrow is the essence of life if we don't have that we die. If our kidneys shut down we have no blood filter. We all have a part in the body we have to find out which one. Verse 3 Yahshuah talks about his kingdom which represents his way and millennium rain. Verse 5 manifestation of the Holy spirit. Verse 6 God didn't restore the natural kingdom but he graced us with the promise, power and anointing. The millenial rain in us. Verse 9 Yahshuah walked on water and elevated in the air. Verse 12 When you love someone you will go the extra mile. Verse 15 disciples are soldiers trained learneth ones. Everything is done for our benefit. Pentecost brought Yahshuah's spirit so we should see how he sees. This was the introduction of the Christ like mind to believers. Limitless ministry means service so we should be meeting a need. We should know and understand Pentecost. God wrote his laws on our hearts. Jeremiah chapter thirty one verse 31. Spirit has come. God's about corporate success. The church tries to do the opposite. Just take this as a example. I live where the casino use to be booming. They were the corporation . Then they closed and trickled down to the small businesses where they started to shut down. Like the place that use to do casino laundry and the businesses that made the slot machines even nail salons started closing up. Then the little individual was put out of work.

Chapter two verse 1 God came to give us power not a denomination. A spirit filled church is what God wants. The New Testament church. Verse 4 Gift of tongues. Which is evidence of the spirit. Holy spirit made another entrance. Holy spirit was put back in the man. Born again .The spirit comes in us so we can move. Put us back to original intent as in Genesis. The fire was on the people so they were passionate for the cause. Everything's in place for a thousand years. We are getting this place ready to entertain the king.

Man's perpective-------------------woman has power

Man's the head

Carries the seed

Based on creation

Satan is hung up on rights

Not God's order, God's order supercedes law

When we violate order in creation, creation doesn't yield. God watches over word. God's spirit supercedes everything. God moved in wind showed up as fire at Pentecost. Verse 3 Highest level of the gift of tongues where the people heard and understood in their native languages. Verse 7 and 9 People from all over came to God's feast. The feast of Pentecost and experienced the first church. This was before any other belief system. Partians was Rome, Medes was Iranian people, Mesopatamia was where Abraham was originally from, Elamites were pre Iraq, Judea was Judah, Cappdocia is Turkey, Pontus was turkey, province of Asia, Phrygia is Turkey, Eypt and cyrene Libya which is south Africa. Let the bible define it self. They did DNA and found a tribe of black Jewish people linked to Aaron. Verse 12 Spirit went from mountain onto man. Holy spirit made another entrance. Verse 16 They thought the disciples were drunk. Peter told them it was to early to drink. Not in spirit won't see. We are God's masterpiece. The spirit came in so we could move in our original intent. We shouldn't be intoxitated with a unknown substance but with God's spirit. It's something, how they call drinks spirits. When you get drunk you take in those spirits and you prouduce fruit from that spirit. The fruits could be misery , imprisonment, mean, no self control etc. When they say drunk they mean what influences you. In the book of Joel God talks about a out pouring of his spirit we see the outpour in Acts. There was no chapters in the scriptures they were put in by the translators. God talks about his sons and daughters prophesying in these last days. Look for more women prophets. Verse 19 signs the blood moons could be a sign. What is God saying? The terrifying day of the Lord, Tribulation. Verse 21 Says who ever calls on the name of the Lord will be saved meaning you have to know the Lord. You know someone by their name and their face. So I figured I better know God's name because I probably won't see his face until I get to heaven. So we should know God's character and what his name represents. Yahshuah is the Lord not just a prophet. Who better to talk about you then you. God told me he used his Holy spirit power to create the universe. He also used power behind his words what he spoke to create. That's where you get power in words. Power pushes. So how can you not believe in Holy spirit power. Verse 27 Yahshuah redeeming our spirit and God not allowing Yahshuah's body to see decay. Your body starts decaying on the fourth day. Verse 26 know Yahshuah. David spoke of this which was fulfilled. Yahshuah's at the right hand of God interceding for us. He took our place. Tell the truth give God what he wants. The economy of God is about hearing. You hear the word to do not qualify. It's so we can access. It's not possible to qualify for something that is given to you. Verse 40 Peter telling them to come out of the world. Then Peter baptized 3000 which were saved. Baptism doesn't save you but it allows you to recognize what Yahshuah did and shows the principalities who and what you stand for. This might of redeemed the 3000 that were killed on the mountain. In the Old Testament when Balaam got the men to be disobedient and sleep with foreign women. Verse 42 Acts is a full grown church. God would show you what you are suppose to have so you can grow into it. The believers were happy in every day life. They didn't need a big house or car. The believers were devoted to the word, fellowship meaning they shared what they had, they ate and prayed together. This was church. A church full of disciples meaning they were willing to give up their stuff for the cause. There were no have and have nots. They believed they were all they had. They looked out for one another. They respected God and the anointing more so then money. God's not into events or appearance he is about helping your brother. The single purpose they shared was the king and the kingdom. This system brings increase to the church. God says he brings increase.

Chapter three verse 4 Peter and John gave God a voice. They valued the anointing over worldly stuff. If you seek the anointing the stuff will follow. We need to hunger and thirst for the anointing. We don't know how many times they walked around and saw that paralyzed man before God gave them the instruction to raise him up. That's like us going out *and evangelizing which is reconciling lost man back to God. Verse 13 You see them telling the story of Yahshuah. Somewhere we stopped telling the story. We should be conducits for Yahshuah so he can touch this earth. Verse 20 those refreshing times is tongues. It revives our spirit the real us. Verse 22 Dt 18 the prophet like Moses will be Hebrew. Yahshuah through Mary is Hebrew. Verse 23 those who don't listen to Yahshuah will be excluded. God explains everything so we can be witnesses. God changed Jacob's name from Jacob to Israel. So you know his people came from Jacob. When we tell the story God increases the believers.*

Chapter four verse 10 Important people in the world ran Israel. Peter had the Holy spirit boldness. God did a miracle he glorified his son. What does the name Yahshuah mean if no one is healed? Verse 12 one way to be saved. He was called a stone because people kept tripping over him because they had no understanding. Verse 13 people will know you spent time with Yahshuah when you speak even if you are uneducated and ordinary. They wanted to stop them from speaking about Yahshuah. So the power could be denied. The church today has stopped talking about Yahshuah. Verse 21 Yahshuah broke all generational curses by becoming a curse. The word is revealed in layers. Peter and John were happy to be whipped so they could identify with Christ. Verse 24 They praised God and there were a lot of spirit filled people. So evil had a harder time penetrating. Now there's less people walking in the spirit. Even when people talk about the bible it is never about the spirit. Verse 26 the enemy is why people act the way they do. The enemy is in people over people, nations and places. For the script to flip it has to start with the church. We have to get back to the word. The focus needs to be Yashuah. The message the cross and the world needs to be outside the church not in it. First he took Abraham out, took them out of Eypt, took them out of Babylon and Peter told them to save themselves from this corrupt generation. When they were in Eypt and Babylon, they were slaves and they came out with all their stuff. There is power in numbers and the blessing in unity. It's hard to penetrate when it's more people in the race. By ourselves we are sitting ducks. Verse 32 The believers share their stuff. When we share God brings his so why is there so much lack? Could it be we are not sharing? Selfishness that's, that homeless mentality.

Chapter five When we are in church we should be representing the Holy spirit. A man named Anania and his wife tried to cheat God. They sold a piece of property for a set price when actually they held back some of the proceeds and lied to the Holy spirit that was in Peter. They were about appearances. Trying to make themselves look good. In a full grown church any spirit that's not suppose to be there the Holy spirit is going to kill it. God said he can't have that kind of spirit in my church. Peter full of the spirit represented God. They both died and their bodies were taken out. It was so much power in that church and the anointing was high. The churches around here are no where near full grown. God's going backwards right now we have the church in Corinth where there's a little power in some churches. God says he's not coming back until his church is glorious with out spot or wrinkle. The church in Acts was a full grown church back then either you were willing to be a part or you know you couldn't go in there wasting time or playing around. The church was respected. Verse 12 You see the Apostles doing not sitting being fruitful. The believers were kingdom minded and met on a king's porch. Peter had a high anointing where people would put the sick around him in hopes of his shadow falling on them. The anointing grows up in the inside then it flows out. Just like you pouring water in a glass non stop eventually it's going to pour out the glass. God's inside out. The chief Priests were jealous of the disciple's popularity and anointing. Every chance they got they messed with the disciples. Verse 17 The disciples were constantly being put in jail for the word. The guards were scared of the people so they had to get the disciples to go peacefully. The disciples wouldn't stop discipling. So you see it can't be about you. They discussed it and let them go the first time the angel released them. The priest felt if they were doing God's will they would be fighting God if they stopped the disciples but if it weren't, God the disciple's cause would fail. They always went in two so the enemy couldn't prick them off. I was furious when they placed the lady in jail for not signing a marriage license for a gay couple. I don't care what the world does but why make her go against her beliefs. The church should have been right along side of her. All the believers in the U.S should of stood with her and prayed together in unity for her. The believer has no voice. The Homosexual population is about 2% but it's a adamant spirit pushing it. Really I don't care what the world does. I just don't like them messing with the believers. Why are we always prosecuted? We should honestly pull out of this world's bankrupt system. I bet most believers don't even care, we are losing more and more of our rights. We have a believer in Iran named Saheed who is a American citizen who they aren't even thinking about releasing. So how can our politicians be negotiating about giving these people nuclear weapons. They are prosecuting , killing, cutting people in half taking their stuff and we are siding with them. We as believers better get uncomfortable and see what's going on around the world. It's crazy to me what's happening to believers and no one cares. It's all because of the spirit in us. The world wants to stomp out the Holy spirit. Look at how they mock God on tv and in every day walks of life.

Chapter seven says some priests accepted the faith. Remember when Peter and John were in jail these were the priests that prosecuted them. So we need to be throwing more seeds. You see the believers were in harmony meaning they believed the same. If we are in harmony that blessing can bring what we need. Satan taught us how to act and not be in harmony. Stephen was the first one to die for the cause. All he was doing was telling the story. I look at people as individuals because masons were stone cutters in the Old Testament. They helped build God's temple. Stephen had virtue. What do we have? He told them how the God of glory met Abraham. Stephen told them which God so why do we act like we are scared to talk about God? We need to speak up and stand up for God as believers. The slaves were to comfortable in Eypt so they did not leave when they were suppose to. So a Pharoah came who did not know Joseph said there were to many of them and made them slaves. The people were just like the people who killed the prophets disobedient.

Chapter eight after Stephen's death wide spread prosecution broke out against the church. Believers were scattered. So some believers started to evangelize where they were scattered. People are happy when everything's in order like God intended it to be. Phillip the evangelist was a evangelist in his every day life. He started out in hospitality as a deacon, which is a servant. He was part of the seven under Paul and filled with the spirit. At the prompting of the Holy spirit he came across a Ethiopian eunuch. The eunuch worked for Queen Candice of Ethiopia. Phillip explained the book of Isaiah to him and baptized him. This eunuch was a high ranking official and knowing he was from Ethiopia, I'm going to say he was African American. He left Phillip rejoicing. So you know he took the gospel back to Ethiopia before Islam.

Chapter nine Christians called of the way not Christian. I'm not going to go through the story of Saul but Saul got Yahshuah the same way we did by revelation. Saul had a encounter with God and it changed his life. He had no physical description of Yahshuah. Verse 12 Peter heals Aeneas who was paralyzed and confined to a cot for eight years. You can say this verse represents the lost in eternity. We should be healing the lost. The next story Peter healed Tabitha so she could finish her assignment. We all have a assignment whether we find out what it is or not .I asked myself why did they go get Peter if they were believers to raise Tabitha up? Peter was a mature believer telling me if you aren't grown up you won't know what to do with your inheritance and you are not moving anything no matter what you are speaking. A baby can't fight. Then Peter goes to Cornelius's house because Paul wasn't ready yet. You can't receive the spirit unless you hear and believe. It's a set up we learn, go and make disciples. Verse 46 Evidence of gift of spirit doesn't matter if you speak tongues first or baptized first. It's a two step operation .

Chapter eleven Anyone can be saved without being physically circumcised because Yahshuah gave us circumcision of the heart. He changed our condition now it's time for us to line up our behavior. Believers were called Christians about a hundred years after Yahshuah was dead in Antioch because they were acting like Christ. We should commit ourselves to the Lord.

Chapter twelve Cornelius was the first uncovenant man to be saved. Peter was in jail. The believers prayed and a angel released him. Maybe we should pray more collectively as believers. We act like we don't want to pray. The angels hearken to God's words. We have to be connected to God or our words mean nothing. They are empty and produce nothing. When Rhonda opened the door for Peter that represented a usher for all you guys who say women can't be ushers. Verse 25 They thought it was Peter's angel which means spirit at the door. Now it talks about Herold's death .He dropped dead on God's feast day because he thought he was God. It was said he dropped dead at a appointed time. Appointed time means feast day when we meet with God.

Chapter thirteen You see there were black prophets and teachers. Verse 15 Taught from law and prophets no New Testament. Now Paul's telling the story. Must be important. Some believed some didn't signs and wonders followed the believers. The greeks thought Paul and Barnabas were Gods so they had to show them their stuff to prove they were men like them. They tried to kill Paul but God was with him until his assignment was over. They fasted and prayed before they chose leaders. They went around making disciples not converts. Paul was Hebrew but not Jewish. The term Jew was coined after Israel split in half. It was ten tribes and a two tribes break. Jew was a nickname for the tribe of Judah. Paul came from the tribe of Benjamin and was a Roman citizen. So he could explain why new believers did not have to be circumcised. Circumcision sealed a covenant with God. Now it's done with the heart.

Chapter fifteen verse 16 God will set up the tent of David. David instituted music and heavy duty praise. This made me think of Kirk Frankin when he first came out. He really praised God. I love Kirk Frankin. The spirit led them .So where ever the spirit led them they went. They were jailed several times but they knew God was with them even in the midnight hour. God knows us and has mercy on us. They were even scrutinized by other believers. If it happened then you know it will happen now. Verse 16 Paul seen all the statues and false Gods. Which upset him. Reminds me of some of the religions that still have statues today. Wonder what God thinks of the statue of Mary? And some of the saints? Paul was in Athens and the greeks were philosophers and all about intellect. The Romans allowed that greek way of thinking to still have influence. That's why we have the bibles translated from the greek bibles even though the Hebrew bible goes back to the millennium. It doesn't matter which translation you have if the spirit man is woke. The Greeks were about the body pumping it up. They started the Olympics. The Olympics use to be nude. They put so much into the natural man. Paul's still telling the story. When you tell the story and go out God will give you grace but if you don't ever go anywhere you don't need grace. Verse 29 made me think about the Greek Orthodox. Verse 31 Yahshuah.

Chapter eighteen Paul working with other believers. He held a regular job making tents. Shake the dust off that natural man who came from dirt and is going back to dirt.

Constantly telling the story which is the testimony and giving a line of defense Verse 6 We should accept correction and be able to correct.

Chapter nineteen verse 6 Speaking in tongues and prophesying verse 11 using hankerchiefs as points of contact Verse 14 Seven sons of Sceva were the sons of a Priest who had no connection or relationship with Yahshuah. They tried to cast out demons but got beat up instead. The sons of the Priest tried to know Yahshuah through Paul. You can't learn Yahshuah through somebody else. You have to have a personal relationship. So we can grow more and more like Yahshuah. Evil spirits know Yahshuah and yield to Yahshuah. They know if you know Yahshuah. Verse 18 were in a occult and they gave it up for Yahshuah. The Lord can take a circumstance that looks like a obstacle and turn it into a opportunity. Verse 23 Not Christian or of the way. Talking about how they were making Idols. Paul let them know there was only one God. They were talking about handling the matter in court. So a riot would not break out. The bible is a form of government. You see a lot of going to court. The problem with God's people they have no understanding. They are just fooling around in church wasting time.

Chapter twenty verse 4 We see men from other areas traveling with Paul. Verse 6 See him celebrating feast of unleven bread. Verse 16 Paul going to celebrate feast of Pentecost. How can we say they are Jewish Feasts when we see them in the New Testament? You miss God when you are religious. Verse 23 Paul kept on his mission following the seasons not having fun. Still on mission for Christ. Don't let things move you. Satan can handle anything in this life. Verse 24 God in life directs you. Holy spirit puts leaders in place verse 28 Where did God get blood when he became a man? Verse 29 Grievious wolves deliver false doctrine and feed the church of God. Also you have the devil teaching at some churches. Some pastors may have the Judas spirit. They want to distort the truth. Verse 31 takes three years to disciple Verse 33 Paul supported himself while doing ministry. I like this verse 35 I have given you a example By working hard like this we should help the weak. We should remember the words Yahshuah said it is better to give then to receive. Verse 37 to 39 shows love, They loved Paul

Chapter twenty one verse 4 the love the disciples had for each other. Verse 8 Paul hooks up with Phillip the evangelist. Verse 9 Phillip had four prophesying daughters meaning they could see in the earth. The bible is in code for the spirit man the natural man will never get it. Verse 10 God spoke about Agabus. God can speak to anybody not just the pastor. Verse 13 willing to die for the cause. Verse 14 The Lord's will is the Lord's word. Verse 18 Paul was anxious to bring unity to the Jews and the Gentiles at all costs. Paul's locked up. Verse 39 like Jim Jones

Chapter twenty two Paul telling his side in court. He would have been top of the top Pharisees but he gave it all up for Yahshuah. So he knew the word. Verse 5 Told about his experience with Yahshuah the bright light. Verse 20 to 29 Paul explains he is a Roman citizen so he didn't get whipped . The soldier who guarded him said ,he paid a lot of money to be a Roman citizen. Sounds like immigrants that become citizens. Paul's in jail the Lord came to him. Verse 11 given encouragement so he can keep telling the story. In the process there was a plot to kill Paul but God will always have you protected to complete your assignment.

Chapter twenty four verse 1 Five represents grace. Paul went to court where God's grace showed up. Verse 5 Nazarene sect Verse 14 Of the way Paul pleads his case Paul's defense his life, his faith his service Verse 23 Paul on house arrest Paul would talk to Felix the governor but the governor could only handle a little word at a time. Like most believers Verse 26 Felix wanted a bribe Paul files a appeal when a new governor comes to office. Paul's case is going to be sent to a higher court. Verse 18 Paul's assignment Verse 24 Featus thought Paul was crazy. Agrippa said he was almost convinced in being a Christian. In the original bible Christian was mentioned three times the other two times when believers were acting like Christ in Antioch and when Peter says suffering like a Christian. Paul sent to Rome. All Paul's needs were met even thought he was in prison.

Chapter twenty seven verse 14 speaks of a Northeastern. Nothing new

Chapter twenty eight Paul bit by a poisonous snake . God protected Paul so he could do his assignment. He didn't die when he was bit by the snake because it wasn't intentional.

No matter what attacks are thrown at you keep going. Verse 20 willing to die for the cause. Verse 27 Believers not seeing. The bible is for the spirit man. You see with your mind so if your mind is closed you can't see anything.

Chapter 15
Letters to Live By

Now we get to the next section which is the letters. The letters show us how to walk out our new life. Paul was sent to Rome. The government was ran by Rome at this time. They still left the influence of the Greek. Romans started paganism in the church. This opened the door for Greek ideas. If it didn't make sense to them or they didn't agree with it, it was out. They had all these ideas of worship and none were Hebrew except for Yahshuah. They even changed his name to Greek even though there is no J in Hebrew. Romans believed that the natural was evil and had to be silenced. Greeks believe you ascend to God with the mind. They taught the body was evil. That your body should not be expressed. That does not agree with the book of Acts. They thought all physical things were bad. No movement or intimacy towards God is the spirit of paganism. This infiltrated the church. Hebrew people are expressive. The Enemy was put in church to cut power and tone down worship. They could prosecute, beat, kill, and take their stuff and believers wouldn't break the faith. They kept growing. The only way they could stop the move was to infiltrate in. Mess up the doctrine. Just think of the military. Romans did not like Jewish people. The Romans fed Jews to the lions. Nero had believers dipped in tar set on fire and hung them around as lights at his garden parties. When Constantine made Christianity the state religion he never changed the way he thought. So you had all these people who said they were believers but they did not want to believe. The church format that you see in church is based on the pagan churches in Rome. There's nothing new under the sun Nero's boyfriend was wearing a dress. Christians were the minority but they convinced the majority. Hebrews taught about Yahshuah for over 2000 years. We were cut from the roots. The enemy really did not want me to finish this book.

Chapter one verse 1 Paul separated for service. Verse 3 Kings come from David. Messiah comes from house of David. Melchizedek supercedes the law. He made Yahshuah king and priest. When you first see something in the bible it sets the order. Melchezedek stepped in time for the first time with Abraham. He was king and priest of God Most High. He had no genealogy. Paul is a thankful servant whose heart is operating through Yahshuah. When Yahshuah died on the cross he emptied himself out. He became poor so we could have. He strengthened us by giving us the Holy spirit back. Verse 15 Yahshuah is the good news. Verse 16 makes us ready for heaven and right with God. Tells from start to finish how you find life through trusting God. It's what he's done we did not do anything. Verse 18 talks about the truth being suppressed that means everybody knows the truth and it's way down buried deep inside of us. Verse 19 We can see all around what God has done if we pay attention. Verse 21 No respect for God. Verse 23 What we put in place of God. Verse 24 It kills me how they change a law because of the way a person wants to have sex. God told us how to have sex a man and woman in covenant. Homosexual sex is just like adultery or fornification. We kind of say the other two are okay because it deals with a man and a woman. God doesn't like any of it we might as well have sex with animals. That spirit is aggressive. I really don't care what the world does. I just hate when they make the believer bend. God will judge the nations. Why do we just keep adapting to the culture. When men in the bible didn't. We are hypocrites. Verse 30 wicked man going nonstop. Verse 32 people know what's going to happen but they don't care.

Chapter two we say wicked people should be punished but we do the same things. God is kind so he can lead us to repentance. You make the decision of what's going to happen to you on the day of the Lord. Verse 7 When you choose to follow the wrong and you know it's wrong God will judge you. God does not play favorites. We have to go by what God says is good not what we think is good. On the tree of good and evil there was some good on that tree but God did not want us to eat of it. If we don't do what God says it does not do us any good. We know right from wrong. Verse 21 We are one way in church and another way outside of church. Verse 24 Says God's name is cursed because of us because of the way we live. Verse 29 Just because you say your saved. It's inward then outward.

Chapter three God trusted the Jewish people with the law. So they know and do God's will even though they broke their promise. God is still faithful. If God did not do what he said he would he would have to destroy himself. God stays the same. God chose the Jewish people because they were weak and he could show his power through them. Verse 4 God's word will prove true and right. We can't tell one side. God does not choose sides. It's his side. God is just and fair. Judgement Dt 31 God is a judge we need to know we need a savior. Verse 9 Question, accusation, being under the power of sin. Yahshuah took care of all of it. Scripture says why he gave us righteousness. Verse 10 He gave us a gift so we can't look at ourselves from a human point of view. God says this. Verse 14 No Godliness or Mercy, Haven't received the gift Verse 19 think it's about works. Verse 21 talks of God changing our position. We went from sinner to righteousness. God did a judicial act that got us acquitted. Verse 27 people aren't made righteous by anything we do. We do what we believe Verse 29 God is the God of everybody Verse 31 the law justs rolls into Yahshuah

Chapter four All Abraham had to do was believe. Everything from God is a gift. All we have to do is receive. If we have to think we earn something it's like God has to pay us. Like us getting a check. God's not going to owe any man. If you have no joy you don't believe the message. People were counted righteous because they believed Yahshuah finished everything. It's about believing. I believe, so I do. Faith is action. How we live our life. Abraham believed first before he did anything. Then later he responded Verse 22 Grace is a Yahshuah effort. Speak God's word and he will rejoice. God is a real being that has feelings Verse 25 Yahshuah was forsaken so we could be accepted

Chapter five Made away so we could come in God's presence. When God looks at us he sees the blood on the mercy seat and the Holy spirit in us. Atonement allowed us to be reconciled back to God. Verse 4 Grace allows us to endure. Verse 6 Yahshuah died for the cause. Verse 11 God gave us the ministry of reconciliation. Us reconciling people back to God through the spirit. How do we do that? The same way Yahshuah did it. By casting out demons, healing the sick, raising the dead and preaching the gospel. We see Yahshuah pray, teach and witness, not all this other stuff we do in church. Yahshuah was the blue print that Adam came off. Just like you make a picture off a negative. That's how Adam came off of Yahshuah. Yahshuah always exsisted and did everything before the foundation of the world. So he was not under the curse. Verse 15 What God did in Yahshuah is greater then what satan did in Adam. The ten commandments were given so we could see the extent of our failures. So we could obey God's laws. The ten commandments were called the Administration of death. The wages of sin is death. So if there are no more sacrifices more people should be dead. If they follow the law. God provided the way so the verdict would not come up guilty. A God effort.

Chapter six We should not sin because Yahshuah gave us a new life. So we should have a changed mindset. Verse 14 The spirit should control the natural man because we have God's undeserved favor. Our flesh is against our new created spirit.

Chapter seven verse 1 There is no law against a dead man. That man died with Yahshuah. Verse 5 allowing our body to rule. Verse 6 Yahshuah fulfilled the law. God moved from the law when he changed our condition. Verse 14 Paul talks about his corrupt nature. He's talking about his body. Even though it is dead we still have to carry it around. We won't get rid of our body until we get to heaven and get a new one. So sometimes we do what we shouldn't when our flesh rises up. We just need to get back on track. We should not look like the world. Verse 22 We should be serving God with our mind because that is how we see. Verse 24 Your body is going in the ground and it is not the real you. So why do we constantly pump it up? We should be walking in the spirit.

Chapter eight God gave us a higher law ,his son who is the heart of God. Verse 2 Yahshuah is the standard our body is condemned. We are suppose to see spiritually or else we are the walking dead. The natural man has to always feel something. Verse 8 The natural man can't please God. Whoever doesn't have the spirit of Christ doesn't belong to him. Yahshuah says we are sinless because he is looking at our changed condition. Living from the body is also from the spirit of disobedience. Verse 14 Sons of God are those walking in the spirit and led by God. Sonship is where we are spiritually adopted into the family of God. We inherited everything Yahshuah had when he died. We have to be mature believers to receive and enjoy it. Verse 15 Abba father .God allowed the translators to leave this Hebrew word in the bible. Abba is not a English word. English can't grasp the meaning. It means source and dearest affection. Daddy. You know the bible is true. Somebody asked me why I have so many versions of the bible. I said because of the different periods in history and how we changed the way we talk. Like English, Greek, Hebrew. God wants to reach all people. If the Quran was around before how come it was not written in Old English or Hebrew? God's getting ready to flip the script with his remnant. Verse 19 creation waiting to see us walking in the spirit. Everything yields to the spirit. Creation was subject to frustration from the fall. The earth is groaning and the pains are getting more intense as the time gets closer to the end. Verse 23 We are groaning until we are released from these bodies and receive our new bodies. Which will be sinless. Verse 24 We have to expect and be patient. Verse 26 praying in the spirit. The spirit intercedes for us because it is God's spirit and knows God. And we know that all that happens is working for our good. If we love God. God is fitting us into his plan. Tribulation comes to knock us off the mark and separate us from the love of God. Verse 27 God's manifested love towards us. God's love knew before in eternity. Verse 29 already done suppose to look like Yahshuah. Verse 30 Yahshuah the first born means it is going to be more. God gave us freely all things by his son. Yahshuah decided to shape the lives of those who love him. To be like him. The son stands first. The son restores and predestines us. Our walk is important . God is shaping us to be like him. We have to understand. Christianity means we are in pursuit of something we already have. If we don't live the way Yahshuah did we take his name in vain. Passover moved us into the realm of the spirit. Verse 33 What can separate us from the love of God? If we are walking in the spirit nothing. We can be harmed or even killed in the natural but that is not the real us. Verse 36 Things are always going to happen to us. This stuff wants to disconnect us from God. What do we think we are. We are not in heaven yet? As long as we are in the anointed Yahshuah we should not be concerned with anything else. What is our response?

Chapter nine Yahshuah is the reference point. When somebody cares about you they care about the little things. Verse 58 talks about spiritual birth. Everything's based on God's call and not what people do. Scripture said God loved Jacob and hated Esau. God is extremes. God loved Jacob because of his response and he valued the things of God. Verse 15 Where God says he will be kind to anyone he wants to. He is referring to being kind to the saved, the believer. Verse 17 God divinely selected Pharoah because he thought he was

God. Pharoah chose to disobey God. So God used him to benefit his people. God put Moses in Pharoah's house. So he would be trained in the mindset of a prince. Moses could go head to toe with Pharoah. If Moses had the mentality of a slave he would of not been able to stand up against Pharoah and deliver the Israelites. Verse 18 Saved Verse 19 Says that God finds fault with people because they are not like him. Verse 20 refers to Yahshuah. Verse 25 We were suppose to provoke Israel to jealousy. Verse 28 we should be doing God's will. Verse 29 If God hadn't left a remnant we would have been wiped out. Verse 30 Not believing in Christ, think you are saved by keeping the law which is impossible. Verse 33 men stumble over Christ. Yahshuah the foundation. Speech has to be about spirit and wisdom of God.

Chapter ten verse 2 Don't understand Yahshuah so they are misguided. Verse 6 We are not saved by what we do. We shouldn't be self righteous or speak against the word of God. The message is near us if you declare Yahshuah and believe that God brought Yahshuah back to life and they are one and the same. You will be saved. Don't doubt or try to reason. Until it is spoken it can't be. God is no respector of persons. What does Yahshuah mean to us? Verse 14 Getting the message out so people can hear and believe. Verse 15 Have to be sent. Verse 16 we have to speak the same message Christ spoke. Some people still won't yield or believe even though they hear the message. Verse 21 Everyone else found Yahshuah because Israel rejected him.

Chapter eleven verse 1 When the church age is over God will go back to dealing with Israel. We will all be grafted in. Verse 4 people not of the world. Verse 6 God's remnant Verse 7 closed minded natural man. Verse 8 don't see Yahshuah. Yahshuah is the vine source of everything. Verse nine the table David talks about is your life. Verse 11 God's chosen breaking the law. Verse 16 We are holy because the giver is holy. We are the lump sanctified. We are holy because the first fruit which is Yahshuah is holy. Yahshuah is the substance we live from. He made us righteous. We are the olive branches. When we believe we are placed in the family. When we don't believe we are cut off. God grafted us in. God doesn't spare anybody if they don't believe. God's not going to have any sin in his new heaven and earth. If the spirit doesn't look like Yahshuah it won't be in heaven. It will be immortally corrupt and disobedient and not in God's presence. Verse 25 Church age. God will remove

Godlessness from the line of Jacob when they believe. When God takes away Israel's sins it will be the end. Verse 28 They are enemies because of the way they think of Yahshuah but God loves Israel because of where they came from. They came from Jacob. Verse 29 God never changes his mind when he gives gifts or when he calls someone. God's no Indian giver. We all have gifts which are irrecovocable. God is merciful. Verse 33 God's to much for finite brains to comprehend or understand all of him. If we did not have any sin we would not have to repent. We need to know what God said and what moves him. The heathen shouldn't move us. We should give effort to Yahshuah's name. God does not take sides so we should take God's side.

Chapter twelve Give ourselves to God for his will. Don't be like the world. Being like the world is worse than us being prosecuted. It is more dangerous. No power in the church today. Verse 3 We shouldn't think we are better then other people. Verse 4 We need to function as a body. Most believers don't know we are suppose to be for each other. We have to connect like a natural body. Yahshuah is the head and we are the parts. So if one part is out of sequence the body malfunctions. We have to be a spiritual body so we can take out the enemy. The spirit man is that one new man holding back the enemy. Disciples are soldiers who fight in the spirit as a unit. Verse 4 The gifts you use in the body are these speaking what is revealed, encouragement, mercy, serving, teaching, sharing, leadership, helping those in need. If you find out the dominate one and plug it into the body it will turn. This is what unlocks your prosperity. It's your body part in the body. You will go to your wealthy place. Wealth is not just money. Just start serving and God will reveal it to you. You may have more then one but you need to function in the prominent one. I just want to reveal the one true living God. I want to show others how to be in a Relationship with God and the brothern. Also I want to show each believer that our lives should be committed to service. Ministry is not the glamorous job people think. Ministry means service. We should be sincere, respect and love each other. We should not be lazy when it comes to God. We should be happy, patient ,humble,friendly and not prideful. We should pray always. We should be there for people and be there for our brother. God made us so we could solve a problem for our brother. We should treat people better than we treat ourselves. We should think about what we do and people should see the kingdom in us. Be about it. We need to constantly feed ourselves with God's word. So we can overcome our flesh. If I know my flesh is sinful why do I constantly feed it? We need to focus on Yahshuah. We have a preacher so we can hear in the spirit. Angels don't preach the gospel because they can't relate. We should produce fruit meaning people should see fruit in our lives. Here are the fruits we should be producing. Joy, peace, patience, kindness, goodness, gentleness, faithfulness, selfcontrol, perseverance, long suffering. So why do most believers look nothing like this? Really what's are attitude about church? It is like we are shopping at the thrift store or cheap burger joint. We want it our way not God's way. We want a king size meal but not the king.

Chapter thirteen talks of government. God made his government. First. The earth's government was suppose to mirror God's government. The world's government is so far away from God. So we follow the natural government until it conflicts with God. Then God's government supercedes this earthly government. So we have to be willing to die. We have to take off that old man and put on Yahshuah. Then we won't satisfy the flesh. We have to put on Yahshuah like we put on our clothes. Live the way we are suppose to. Be law abiding citizens. Verse 8 Love Verse 11 Time to wake up Verse 12 pretty soon we will be able to see . Get rid of worldly things. Shouldn't look like world. Verse 14 Be like Yahshuah. What do we want?

Chapter fourteen Not making someone weak in faith lose their faith. We need to hold them up. Verse 4 Who am I to judge another man's servant? God will judge. Either at the judgement seat of Christ where believers go. God will show them if they get a reward or the white throne judgement where non believers go. What are we doing with the ministry, Yahshuah gave us? Verse 5 We should honor God in all we do. How do we believe? Verse 12 All of us will have a chance to explain. We should not hinder someone's walk or belief in Yahshuah. God's kingdom consists of God's approval. Us being reconciled back to God. Part of the kingdom Joy which is strength, Peace which is freedom and righteousness which is right standing with God. We should do things based on what we believe. We make ourselves guilty if we don't believe or don't act the way we believe. We should help our brother grow into being a mature believer.

Chapter fifteen verse 3 Yahsuah put everything on himself. He gave us what we need so we can give others what they need. Verse 4 everything is written to teach us. Verse 5 God's grace allows us to endure and stay encouraged. It also allows us to live this life and look like Yahshuah. Grace and Salvation are Yahshuah. Because of his grace and loving kindness we should give grace. Verse 12 The root Yahshuah. Root means you come and grow from. Verse 13 The Holy spirit power produces us to expect and fills us with peace and joy. Verse 16 Paul got Yahshuah like we did through a revelation. The revelation was of who he is. God gave Paul as a gift to give the people understanding so they could be reconciled back to God. Paul was a yielded vessel for the Lord. Verse 20 Paul didn't want to undercut his brothers in Christ that had started discipling on Yahshuah. Each worker has his own style or maybe a different twist on the same thing. He didn't want to get anyone confused. Verse 21 will have a revelation of Yahshuah. Verse 24 We should support other believers that do God's will. So the message can get out. Verse 27 spiritually fed so they should help out financially people that have more than enough should help those that don't. Verse 30 Paul asks the believers to pray. Prayer is a weapon and we all should be praying because we are in it together. Amen means we come into agreement.

Chapter 16 Pheobe is a woman deacon. Deacon means servant. There were several women working in ministry. Verse 16 says greet each other with a holy kiss. When you kiss someone you connect to them. Verse 11 I think this is important brothers and sisters. I urge you to watch out for those people that cause divisions and make others fall away from the Christian faith. By teaching false doctrine. Stay away from them. People like these are not serving God. They are serving their own desires. By their smooth talk and flattering words they deceive unsuspecting people. Everything is disclosed in The New Testament. The New Testament took from the Torah and The prophets.

First Corinthians is in Greece. Ephesus is Asia Minor. Here's a little food for thought. Grace ensures the promise not works. Sees you get what you act on. When is a gift hard? How do you want God to get promises to you? If you get it based on your goodness your saying Yahshuah's goodness isn't good enough. Christ removed human effort. Faith is accepting God's grace which is Yahshuah. Trust. There's a resurrected man in heaven speak in his name. *Yahshuah's name carries so much weight like he's doing it. If our spirit testifies with Yahshuah's spirit it comes into agreement with it. Everyone is made the same.*

Corinthians was a letter wrote in Corinth which is ancient Greece. Paul used his own personal life as a example. Sosthenes was the ruler of the synagogue. God knows everything that's going on before we put it on paper. God wants us to walk out sonship and function as a body. We are sinless because of Christ, who supplied righteousness.

Chapter one verse 1 As we work God's effort God gives us grace. Grace is unmerited favor. Like when you get a grace period on your car insurance. They give you something extra for nothing, you did nothing so you can still drive. God gives us grace so we can still do his will. As we go forth in him. We will never know all pertaining to God. We can't allow what's in our mind to effect our response to God. Forget all you been taught. God's given us a picture of all he's done so we can know Yahshuah. God's answer for the fall, which picks you up. Our message the cross. Verse 7 Yahshuah has to be revealed. Verse 8 Holy spirit is the strength . If we live from the spirit we won't be judged with the world. Verse 9 Yahshuah is faithful, sonship. Verse 10 Be likeminded there is one cause Yahshuah. Verse 12 It's like the different denominations. One follows Apollos another Cephas. When it's all about Christ. Think and speak as one mind. We have to see the same thing. Our focus should be Yahshuah. The message should be the cross and we need to get the world out of our church. They were not grounded and rooted in Christ. They were church hopping. We need to base our relationship on what Yahshuah did not on our emotions. If we base our relationship on how we feel we will get hurt. Verse 13 who did it Verse 18 the message of the cross there is no other way to be saved. There was no work effort from us. Gentiles can't get pass the natural mind. We would still be in sin if Yahshuah is not God. How can we qualify to remove our sin? Yahshuah is our advocate. The church of Corinth was the first church established by Paul. Spiritual gifts from God were used to elevate the church and build up the Christian community. The outside world started to influence the church and the miracles started dying down. The more unrighteousness in church the less God you will see. God is everywhere but he won't be anywhere. Then finally you won't see any God. If someone's dying or sick and needs prayer that's not faithfulness that's desperation. Faith is us doing what we believe all the time. Not just when we are in need. When nothing is wrong God is the last thing on my mind. When the person is in need he is the objective not God. God shows all this love but few people understand. Verse 19 Meaning they don't see Verse 20 people who think they know so much. Verse 24 The called are saved. The cross offends some people and makes no sense to others. Verse 25 humans have no strength and greeks are big on knowledge. Yahshuah's thinking is so much higher than ours. Mind of Christ equals a mature believer. Knowledge puffs up meaning you are all about God and don't know him personally. It's just like the wind we can't see it but the effects are enormous. The wind can be mighty, gentle are rushing. By the holy spirit God's thoughts were revealed to Paul. Each of us gets are own anointing. All of us are responsible for the atmosphere or are we to busy with the natural man? What or who were we in the world before Yahshuah? Verse 30 What Yahshuah became in us. We did nothing so we can't brag unless it is about Yahshuah.

Chapter two shows us how to do the word. It's not us earning anything. It's us receiving, partaking from God's finished work. Everything God gives us is a gift. When someone gives you a gift you get a instruction manual, so you will know how to use the gift. You get a car or a dvd player there is a manual. Our bible is our manual. Who better to talk about us then the one who made us. The bible is our mirror so we should look in it to see how we are suppose to look. It should be our reflection. God desires us to trust in his power. God's power has a lot to do with living. Everything yields to the Holy spirit. If we don't do the word we have man's wisdom. Man's wisdom is humanism. If you trust your job you are trusting man's wisdom. Where do you find yourself? When we don't tend to the things of God we are trusting in man's wisdom. Verse 9 speaks of world's wisdom. God wants to reveal things prepared for you. It was already ordained for you. If you are feeling a void. The Holy spirit is suppose to be there. Everything is in Yahshuah because we have a enemy. The world hasn't received God's spirit because it is hidden in Christ. Spiritual people evaluate everything but are subject to no one's evaluation. Because they go by a higher law. We have to press and spend more time with God. Instead of doing church stuff. If you can't understand you look like God. How can you ask God for forgiveness when you separate everything from him. Really what is it based on when you separate God from his power? We make God so small. Nobody would of thought a man dying on a cross would save us from sin.

Chapter three carnally minded. Influenced by natural man, the body part of our exsistent. Living by world standards or worldy. All of us have a part in making disciples. Yahshuah's the foundation . The foundation was tested and the only foundation that will stand. Our work will be tested at the judgement seat of Christ. To see if we receive a reward or if we barely made it in. The bible is the mirror for the soul. The bible is for the believer. So why do nonbelievers want to pull from our bible? We are God's temple because we house God's spirit. God's spirit is the Holy spirit. God is centered around the Holy spirit which is Yahshuah. God is what he does not his name. Yahveh is his name. The world is a disillusion of the spirit realm. The wise people of this world mean nothing to God. The world's wisdom amounts to nothing. When a person is carnal he's in that natural man and can't grasp Christ. What do you think Yahshuah thinks about the church? Everything we do should reflect Yahshuah and his mininstry.

Chapter four teach Yahshuah, become a servant. Verse 2 man's day man's opinion. God showed me man's day is over. When you judge something you sentence it. It could be good or bad. God will reveal why people do what they do. Don't add to the word just go by what it says. Wisdom is the proper knowledge of words. People don't know what they have but the higher the anointing the more you get attacked. You get attacked because of whose spirit you have in you. Some of the worst attacks come from so called believers. Some of them have become self righteous and believe their way is right. Disregarding God. It should never be about us. The world disregards and disrespects believers. We should be a family whose focus is Yahshuah. We should show we believe by the way we live. The Lord's will is God's word. There is always a chance to repent as long as we have breath in our body. Verse 20 Man has no power. God's about action. Power is just not talking. What's father's day?

Chapter five speaks of a man who is in church and he is sleeping with his father's wife. Why did Paul wait five chapters to tell us. Because it was more important to talk of how the believers should be then dealing with the problem. Paul says put the man out so he can come to himself. I think the man had a prideful disposition. I think he was arrogant and thought nothing was wrong with his behavior. It was a big thing to be put out of church. Now we say we are leaving church. I believe if we come knowing we need a savior and seek God, God will deal with us in his house. God said his house is a house of prayer for all men. I notice we bend in this country where sexual immortality is concerned. It's running rapid. I don't care what the world does but the world shouldn't, pull the church through the mud. That's a polluted stream. I am tired of luke warm believers. If you let one person do something other people think they can do it to. We have to understand what the cross has done in our life and live it out. Or are we saying there's no cross in our life? The believers we hang around with what are they like? We should associate with believers who are walking in the truth so we can keep walking. It's easier to follow the wrong then pull someone over to the right. We should be models for the unsaved. We see a lot of wickness in the hearts of some believers. God is coming back for his spirit filled church. Believers walking in the truth .

Chapter six there are various church disorders. We are suppose to settle are disputes among believers. Why do we involve the world in our disputes? Unbelievers form all kinds of opinions when we air our dirty laundry. Why give them a reason to talk about us? Verse 20 The kingdom is the life of the king. Do we have to really come against other believers? Can we work it out? God told us to stay away from sexual sin because we are one with him. When we have sex with someone we connect with them and whatever spirits they have. God is suppose to make us one with him in covenant. Verse 12 You can do whatever you want but should you do it? You should fully express God.

Chapter seven The husband and wife belong to each other. Don't give satan room to come between the two of you. Paul wasn't married. Everybody is different. God called us to live in peace. We should marry someone evenly yoked. If we were unsaved when we were married we shouldn't divorce our mate not unless they want to leave. Verse 28 Says some married people will have trouble because they will be bouncing back and forth from the natural to the spirit man for their mate. We should walk like Yahshuah did. There is sorrow because of this fallen world. It's getting worse. Everything in this world can be a distraction. People always learning, and never coming to the knowledge of the truth. Truth is what everything is based on. Which is God. One God . The next few verses talk about the way people think. Who does this verse sound like can eat certain foods because of the false God *they worship? Watch what you do. Don't want to hinder someone's growth or give them a false belief.*

Chapter nine Says that the workers should be compensated for what they do. Verse 17 How you do it and why you do it. Paul was talking about how you bring the good news which is Yahshuah. Paul went to great lengths to get people saved. Eternity is at stake. We need to keep the flesh down and run the race. So we can get to heaven and predestination. We aren't beating the air because we have a purpose.

Chapter ten This is a example for us, so we don't make the same mistakes. God's talking about when they made the golden calf. God wants us to be fulfilled and escape all the stuff they went through. Verse 16 communion, bread which represents Christ's body. The blood gave us the blessing. We are united with Christ. We shouldn't mix the new life with the world. Verse 23 It may be legal but is it in our best interest? We don't want to make someone fall by what we are doing. Maybe if I don't do this they will be saved. We aren't judged by what some one else does. Verse 33 placing others above ourselves. Imitate means I imitate Christ.

Chapter eleven verse 11 Decide for yourself about the woman. Whether you want them teaching or whether you want to work with them. The man or the woman could not exsist with out the other one. They came from each other. Verse 16 no customs in church. Verse 18 opposing groups, when we should be on one accord. Verse 19 divisions shows who the true believers are. Verse 20 love feasts, Succoth. We should care about our brother, family and reflect God. Verse 22 How you treat other people. It doesn't matter about stuff but how we do God's work. Verse 24 We should remember what Yahshuah did. Verse 25 Yahshuah is the promise. Verse 30 Have to examine self. We need to examine what we see, touch, and say. We don't eat pork but we curse. We are judged by Christ's righteousness. You know what you eat will come out your body and means nothing what comes out of your mouth comes out of the heart . What's worse? Christ is the standard. How can a sinful man become righteous? We have two ears so we should listen and hear twice as much. Or are we talking more even though we only have one mouth?

Chapter twelve speaks of spiritual gifts. We have the same quality of faith Peter had which is Yahshuah. The best gift is the one that's needed at the time. Spiritual abilities are all from the same spirit. They may have different services to God. It's the same God. The gifts are to benefit the fellowship. We ought to value spiritual gifts. The gifts are through the Holy spirit. Which is God's power. The gifts are Word of wisdom-which is present to future, word of knowledge-which is past to present, discernment-which is seeing spirits, Healing- which consists of healing,deliverance,restoration and grace. Then there's faith,signs ,wonders and miracles which are manifestations of the spirit. Tongues —Highest level when you speak in a foreign language and the people from that country understand you. Then you speak in tongues and interpret it that's two nickels compare to prophecy's dime which is speaking what God revealed then you have tongues which is our prayer language and is a gift to all that ask. Our gifts aren't for us but for somebody else. God wants us to be a body and function like a body . These are gifts to edify God's kingdom. It doesn't matter the denomination or your race. We are made one in the Lord. God gave us a example by using a natural body. If we start functioning as a body, God will place us where we need to go. God doesn't get any honor when we come for ourselves. You can't care for somebody else if you are thinking about you. We need each other. God said the weaker people in the body or the most vital. So why do we treat them like they are nothing? Or like they are second rate or that we are better then them? Maybe because they don't have as much money as us or nice clothes like ours. You better watch how you treat that shabby man .The shabby man is the first step to discipleship. There is no pride in that shabby man and he has a contrite heart. That's who God will use. Most people think they got this and best believe God will let you have it. Don't think to highly of yourself.

Chapter thirteen Love is the best gift. So walk in it. If you don't have love the other gifts don't mean anything because you don't have God. God is Love. When you express love you are expressing God and the other gifts will come out. If you don't have love you don't have God. Cold love is a end time move. When you are cold you look nothing like God. Verse 6 explains who God is. Love never ends. It's on going like God. Love does not keep track of wrong doings. Meaning it does not keep bringing up what you did wrong. All the gifts wil stop when everything comes to completion. They won't be needed anymore. Love will still be around. Because Love is God. God will always love us. We should grow up. Right now it is like we are looking through a dirty glass. When everything is finished we will have clear vision. Faith is doing what we believe. Hope is what we expect. Love is the best because it is forever. At the end we won't need faith or hope.

Chapter fourteen We should desire spiritual gifts. We should allow love to cause us to do what we do. Verse 2 talks of tongues our prayer language. Which is like spiritual exercise. Which keeps us in shape spiritually. Prophesy helps grow the church. Because we are relaying God's message. Paul had to put order in the church when it came to prophesy. Anyone can do that one because we all can talk. The other gifts you have to really nail them. People see these or you tell them something about themselves. The world uses God's gifts better then the church. It is all about getting understanding so we should grow our gifts up so we can elevate the church. Verse 14 prayer language of tongues says we should pray in the spirit and the natural. Be innocent where evil is concerned. Don't participate in evil. Verse 21 people will know what's going on but won't listen. Verse 22 Gifts of tongues is for the unbeliever because it is the evidence of something going on. Prophecy is for the believer because it should grow us up. Speaking what God has revealed is to lead people to repentance. God's service should have order. Verse 43 says women should be silent Paul said that not God. You always have to look at whose talking and what the situation was. At the time women sat on the opposite side of church so if everyone was hollering how can they hear Paul. Also back then most men were God's forerunners and a woman can't teach a man to be a man in the natural. We all know the Holy spirit is the teacher in the spirit. What about the woman with out a husband? If you are in the spirit we are all the same. The book of Acts didn't say that because everyone was in the spirit. He probably knew if the man is in the natural man he would probably give that woman a hard way to go . If the woman is silent, God will teach her and make her a written epistle. Once God elevates her, she will be able to contend with any man. Besides the woman is God's secret weapon. Joel says women will prophecy , Jeremiah says God will do something different in that day women will protect a man and David said a army of women will announce the good news. On God's time line it is the day of the spirit. When Paul was writing it was man's day. Also Paul came from that religious sect. A Pharisee and they didn't think to much of women. Even though Paul would work with them in someone else's ministry like Pheobe and Pricilla to name a few. Peter didn't care. The men in those days were running for the Lord. Now they are scared or running after other things. You have a church full of women you don't think God wants you to use them . Guarantee you use and elevate that woman whatever man she has will follow. You know God wasn't going to reveal his secret weapon until it was time. We are in a fight and the enemy pounded the heck out of the man. Just imagine what the enemy would of did to the woman if he knew God made them the same in the beginning. The average woman has tough skin but she can be gentle when she needs to be. God told me my assignment is to train the women so they can fight. You know I took a lot of punches from believing men. Everytime God allowed me to show them I am a written epistle by him. I can fight in the spirit and I got the battle scars to prove it. I learned from God because the men in my church wouldn't allow the women to do anything. My brothers sharpened me up. In the spirit there's not enough believing men so we all have to fight together in the spirit. A fallen angel just sees a spirit not male or female. Just take everything I said to God.

Chapter fifteen Gospel of grace. The king is in us. Everything about us being restored. Bringing back everything God intended. Children of faith carry out God's orders. The workers are few because most believers are sleep. Verse 8 In the flesh not in Grace. We don't qualify for grace. It's not about our abilities. Verse 13 If the resurrection did not happen our message is worthless and means nothing. We are also liars if this did not happen. If there was no resurrection God didn't bring Christ back to life. If Christ did not come back to life sin still has power over us. Then those in Christ that have died will not rise. So what's the point of believing? If it was only for the natural . Three days after firstfruits. Not easter what does that even mean? Adam brought death Christ brought life. God will put everything back in order. Then the end will come. There will be no sin in God's new kingdom. Believers face death everyday for what we believe. If there is no resurrection we might as well be like the world. People perish because lack of knowledge. People eat up the seed which leads to life. The seed is the word which we should eat and let it grow us up. When we die our bodies are planted in the ground. Then we get a new body like Yahshuah. We have to be natural first because we have to die first to get the spirit body. The natural body's not going anywhere but in the ground. When we walk in the spirit we can experience some of the millennium. The *king is in us so we can experience it. Verse 52 Feast of trumpets. At the Rapture some will still be a live when we are evacuated out of here. Verse 25 death defeated. Verse 38 Yahshuah is what we build on.*

Chapter sixteen By faith so it will be a gift. Constantine changed God's day to Sunday. Because of one scripture where Paul said he collected money on the first day. Well we use Sunday as a day to fish. It's the spirit of it. The Sabbath was made for man not the other way around. Verse 7 feast of Pentecost Verse 11 be a cheerful giver because of how God has blessed you. If you don't want to give to God he doesn't want it. He definitely doesn't need it. Verse 13 Be alert, Be firm, In the Christian faith. Be courageous and strong. This is the same thing God told Joshua. Do everything with love this is the most important. We should commit our lives to a life of service. We should produce people that look like Christ. Verse 19 Church use to be in the house. Believers went house to house. Showing we should be close knit and know the people we fellowship with. Not just knowing their name. Verse 20 A holy kiss is a sign of affection and connection. It is all about loving God and your brother.

Second Corinthians was the second letter written by Paul. Which dealt with what Paul learned. Paul's vindication of Apostleship. Yahshuah gave us good will and peace. We have everything Yahshuah has. So we should be able to give it out freely. He suffered so what makes us think we aren't going to suffer? We have to trust God and his grace. Verse 10 God is constantly rescuing us. When more people pray they are joining in the fight. Prayer is a weapon. The angels come for our words so God will send his grace when we are fighting. It's sad most believers don't know they are fighting. Verse 12 Our minds are clear because our focus is Yahshuah. God gave us everything. Paul wrote letters so he could help the people stand and fight spiritually. Verse 19 God made the promise sure when Yahshuah died on the cross. We honor God by saying Amen. When we say amen we are in agreement with God. Verse 21 We are all connected through Christ. God set us a part for his will. Verse 22 God reconciled us back to him we know this because he gave us his spirit. It's like a deposit we are on layaway until he comes back to get us.

Chapter two Verse 7,8,9 Us feeling guilty, We should be reassured because God loves and forgave us. Verse 10 Christ became a curse so we could be blessed. Verse 11 Satan is evil with intelligence. Satan had plenty of time to study God's man. Satan knows God very well so we should want to spend more time with God. We should develop our relationship with God. Verse 16 Talks about the unsaved and how they see the saved. Verse 17 There are a lot of false teachers out there but when Paul spoke they knew he was a written epistle by God.

Chapter three The Holy spirit works inside out. It starts on the inside and flows to the outside. Inner transformation. The power of the Holy spirit changes you not us. Feed yourself the word so you can grow. Paul taught Christ from the Torah. People will be able to see if you are a written epistle. God made us who we are and we can do nothing without him. Verse 6 The law brings death but Yahshuah brings life. Verse 7 Paul is talking about the ten commandments. The ministry that brought death inscribed in stone. Then it talks about Moses face everytime he had a encounter with God. You could see God's glory on him. Then it would fade. We have God's glory. Glory is the full expression of something. We have God's glory twenty four seven. God's glory is in us. Verse 12 We are bold because we know what we have. We have Christ. Verse 14 A closed mind doesn't see Christ. A closed mind means the spirit is sleep. When you are in the spirit you are free. You are not subject to the law that was put in place until he came back. Only Christ can unveil the eyes. Even when people read the Old Testament their eyes are veiled because they don't see Christ in it. When they turn their eyes towards Christ the veil is removed. Yahshuah is all in the Torah , and I can show you where. He is in every one of the sixty six books. Verse 18 us conforming into the Image of Yahshuah. We are turning into the sons of God. People walking in the spirit God gave us our identity back. God never intended for us to be in need.

Chapter four The spirit is the light of knowledge. When God talks of treasures in jars of clay. He's talking about the Holy spirit housed in this fragile decaying body. In the son we look on God's undeserved favor. It's not because we do everything right it's what Yahshuah has done. Life will drag you under the cart when you should be on the horse. The Holy spirit is your navigator or Gps in this life. The spirit shows what to believe based on the covenant or contract it has with us. The anointing gets on you so you will do God's will. When we are in church our job is to be a body and be there for our brother. We need to come and dwell in God's house. We rather be slaves to the world. A free man knows how to manage his time

. The natural man is sleep when it comes to the things of God and awake when it comes to self. Verse 4 The blind doesn't see the light of the gospel his mind doesn't compute. It doesn't understand. God gave us a image so we know how we are suppose to look. Yahshuah did everything for us. We are constantly going to be under attack because we are not in heaven yet. The natural man is dying and getting weaker. When we were born in the natural we start dying. In the spirit it's the opposite when we are born again we start living. The spirit gets stronger. The inner transformation affects the believer's heart which consists of his mind. The way we think. Verse 13 What are attitude towards faith is . I believe so I speak. What are we declaring in the heavenlies. Our focus should be Yahshuah. We get the blessing on our actions. How do we treat our brothers? Are our brothers important to us? Do we satify our brother? If we bless our brother the blessing is on us. We need to follow Yahshuah. We need to think like him in all we do. Is my brother's cause my cause? When I look after my brother God blesses the works of my hands. How can I lend myself? How can I help the Pastor's vision? What we learned we learned from the world.

Chapter five verse 1 Talks about dying we have a weak body. We have to put on God's spirit. The natural body likes the natural and doesn't want to change. Verse 6 Now Paul talks about looking at life but not by a human point of view. Believers should have a biblical world view where only ten percent of believers do. We should do what we believe and be led by God. The church is disconnected because of the natural man. God's a spirit so how can a natural man receive from God. The natural man short circuits the power. The devil is a liar. We do what we do because it is familiar and we are use to doing it. Verse 11 God gave us the ministry of reconciliation. God reconciled us back to him and that's the ministry we should be doing. Telling his story. Also telling and showing people how they can be one with God. Verse 12 Why don't we live unto righteousness instead of putting so much emphasis on sin. The only information about God is in his word. Verse 17 Be a new creation the old one died with Christ. God restored fallen man. The message is the cross. Yahshuah was made sin on our behalf. How can we be one with Christ and not think we are worthy? If we are not honest with ourselves we will never change. The law was put in place to maintain man until Yahshuah came. Also the law showed us what sin is. The different types of sin are 1

Transgression which is sin against God like breaking a commandment 2 Trespass which is sin against your brother 3 Iniquity which is gross sin.

Chapter six Let's stop wasting time and get the word out. Isaiah sixty one verse 3 Looking like the truth no matter what. The truth is what everything is based on. Verse 10 Being happy all the time because we know what we have. We are clothed by heaven . The purpose of faith is to receive from eternity and bring it into manifested time. Once it's a reality we don't need faith. We don't have to expect anymore. Then God explains who and how we should be in relationship with. God says I will live and walk among them. I will be their God and they will be my people. God says separate yourselves from unbelievers. Have nothing to do with anyone unclean. Then I will welcome you. The Lord Almighty says I will be your father and you will be my sons and daughters.

Chapter seven We need to separate from everything that's not like God. Believers need to be united. We need to be resting in God. Verse 11 God talking about charges against his man. Which he took sounds like court to me. Now he's back to talking about the man in the first letter who was sleeping with his father's wife. Paul dealt with the church as a whole before dealing with the incident. First corporate then individual. Everyone has to be on the same page. God showed me how the disciples were corporate with him. They grew as a body with him as the head. Then they moved out individually to grow up other believers. The trickle down effect can be good or bad.

Chapter eight God want's grace on his church and the way we do that is by being gracious people. The offering is a picture of Christ. You can only give what you have. We should be sharing. God loves a cheerful giver so trust me if you don't want to give God doesn't want it .Everything we do is for us. God doesn't need it. Giving is not just money but it can be time or talent. Prosperity is not just money. Yahshuah gave us his life but he buried our old life. Telling me our old life wasn't worth to much because he didn't swap lives with us. Yahshuah made us rich so who are we working hard for. There are no have and have nots in God's church. The ones that have are the bridges for the ones who don't have. There is balance in God's church. Really church we have to stop looking like the world. We need to make sure our brother is alright. God will make sure we are alright. God has a system for everything in life. We don't work God's system. In the natural we try to work the man and every system we can. God doesn't do stuff because we need it. Don't think if you do this you will get that. If you don't sow seed you won't get a Harvest. God's system doesn't depend on the economy.

Chapter nine We should be eager to invest in the economy of God. When you give purpose in your heart you do it on purpose. God's plan is not based on necessity or someone twisting your arm to do it. It's not even based on you seeing a need and you give because of the need. God wants us constantly giving but only if we want to. God's system was implemented before the foundation of the world. Verse 9 most believers are like hoarders and have a homeless mentality. God will increase us based on his plan. People will pray for us because of what we do. There will be more people in the fight because they see what we do. As you do this your purpose wil come out.

Chapter ten Paul says God is what he needs to be when he needs to be. No human effort. Verse 4 God is doing this thing. So we need to change the way we think. God says take every thought captive. Meaning we have to make sure it lines up with God. If it doesn't we disregard it. We should build up other believers. We shouldn't care what people say about us we should be concerned about what God says about us.

Chapter eleven Paul allows you to know who he is. He talks about false prophets . Paul's trying to keep the church from being filtrated with false doctrine. Paul was trying to ground and root the believers. How people turn away. Us being pure and sincere to Yahshuah. Verse 4 This made me think about the Mormons. All the other beliefs have Yahshuah as a man. If he was just a man how could he save us. He would have been defeated. Verse 6 See Paul yielding and being used by the Holy spirit. Paul was willing to suffer and do anything for king Yahshuah. False prophets do look like the real thing but a mature believer can tell the difference. In the end everybody gets what they deserve. Verse 20 talks of how believers allow the world to do stuff to them but won't allow stuff to happen for the cause. Verse 24 Paul identifies himself with Christ. We thought we had it bad. Verse 26 Believers playing both sides of the fence. When someone goes through it's like all of us go through it. Remember we are a body. God will protect us so we can do or assignment.

Chapter twelve God allows us to see into Paul's prayer life. As Paul has a encounter with God. Verse 7 satan attacks so we won't receive a benefit. Satan wants to keep us from getting a harvest. It seems to be one thing after another. Verse 8 Paul finally gets it that God's grace is sufficient. Life will challenge you because it is at opposition to God. When I am weak I am strong because the power of the Lord rests on me. In suffering look for Christ. Verse 14 God should provide. God loves us but we have to plug into his system. Paul's intent was to grow up the believers in church. The same as mine. Verse 21 Not exalting God.

Chapter thirteen witnesses, acussations. When somebody accuses you and it isn't neeessarily true. Verse 4 Body is weak but the spirit is strong. How are we believing? We should live the way Christ did. Is our Christian faith genuine? We should be constantly praying and checking on other believers. Christ is the standard . What God ordained us to be. I know what I know but I am open. Be Christ like. We need to examine how we treat the things of God. We need to prove out what God said we are. We should be spirit filled people. Religion clothes us in religion and gives us no intimacy with God. Titles are empty. We are scared to be naked in front of God. The natural man is naked in front of God. The natural man is always trying to clothe himself with everything but God. Remember the fig leaves. Self effort never works. When Adam and Eve went to clothe themselves in the garden it wasn't good enough so God clothed with the coats. We need to put God on.

The letter of Galation is a letter of liberty. It's Asia minor and Turkey. It's by grace and not by the law that we are liberated. In Chapter one God liberated us. Verse 8 I think is pretty important. Whoever tells you good news that is different from the good news we gave you shall be condemned to hell. Even if it comes from a angel in heaven. Sounds like that angel that brought the Quran down from heaven. Verse 11 There is no physical description of Yahshuah in the bible. Yahshuah revealed himself to Paul. Then Paul tells how he was religious just like a lot of believers. Before he had a encounter with God. Then he tells the believers how he was appointed before he was born like Jeremiah. It's still beyond me how believers say they can retire from God. How do you retire from God? Or the call ? When Luke chapter nine verse 62 Says whoever starts to plow and looks back is not fit for the kingdom. Or how about this one the workers are few. Or how about Yahshuah starting with one hundred and twenty but only ending with twelve. The others went back to there lives in the world. They really didn't want God they just wanted what he could give them. It's all about the spirit. God took Paul off by himself so he could feed him. God did me like that. God downloaded in me.

Chapter two talks about no works. So why are we always trying to work and earn something. We need to identify with who he is. We need to be running on the right track. The false Christians were called Judaziers and wanted to get believers off the mark. Like I said you don't learn God like English or math. He has to reveal himself to you. When God reveals stuff to you, you can see it. Understanding is being able to see what's going on. Verse 4 God made Paul a steward when he entrusted him with his word Yahshuah. The gospel is Yahshuah. The main thing Paul wanted to do was to teach the people so they would get understanding. Verse 10 God says remember the poor. So how come we don't do it? We want to listen to everybody but God. Verse 11 Paul confronts Peter. So It's okay to disagree or correct someone. Peter was saying one thing and doing something else. Yahshuah fulfilled the law. If we go back to the law. We are saying Yahshuah didn't really save us. We were made righteous before we could do righteous. How do we value the name? If you are mindful of what you say and do you start to elevate. We have to deal with each other through God's position. God treats people based on who he is not who we are. If we don't listen to God all we can get is fallen man. Spirit and truth is real. It is the Holy spirit. God is high and elevated and wants us to recognize it. Talks more about Intimacy and maturing. Functioning as a body and responding accordingly. God talks about this a lot so it must be important. Every joint must supply meaning we must find out our part and function in the body. It's a spiritual body. God shows us natural things so we will understand spiritual things. If we understand the truth we will know what's false. So we won't be misled. Yahshuah rescued us delivered us saved and healed us. We need to desire Yahshuah . Why would Yahshuah die if we could save ourselves? God had the end on his mind. The results. God sees the end to the beginning. God gave us a clear picture of Yahshuah dying on the cross. Which is a picture of grace. Grace means loving kindness and is also a person Yahshuah. We need to understand that God is perfect and holy .

Chapter three Paul trying to figure out why the people don't understand and want to go back to their old lives. When they have the right way God's way. It's that natural man. Verse 6 Speaks about the Abraham covenant of circumcision. Which was him naturally tuning into God . We need to tune into God spiritually. Now we have circumcision of the heart. Christ did this for us. How is our transmitter and our receiver which is our heart. We have to institute believing before we do anything. Abraham believed in his heart before he did anything. God had to prove to Abraham that Abraham believed. After a while we have to do something to show we believe. If we don't do something how will people know we believe. What's our response? Us doing something is a God effort. We respond to what God has done in our lives. Righteousness is about believing . After I do I believe. I do based on what I believe. We need to approach life like we are blessed. Yahshuah is the promise. We get the promise by doing it God's way. Verse 8 God announces the Messiah to Abraham. When God talked to Abraham he seen Yahshuah because Yahshuah came out of him. ALL the people will be blessed because of Abraham. Which is now because Yahshuah came. Verse 11 Covenants don't end they just roll over. Yahshuah was condemned and punished for us. We have to understand our position. We have the spirit of God in us .God did all this so we would have the Holy spirit. Verse 15 Talks about a will which is read when a person dies. Then you get your inheritance. Your heritance is the Holy spirit. When did Yahshuah die? We need to understand we are heirs with Christ and adopted as sons into the family. Spiritually. God preached the gospel to Abraham. Verse 22 World controlled by sin because the god of this world has Adam's lease. God won't come back until the lease is up and everything runs it's course. God is a judge and he does everything by his book. God had a loop hole in the contract so he could reconcile his man back to him. That's one reason why God had to get in the ground. Verse 25 We were made God's children spiritually. Verse 28 we are all the same in the spirit. So why do most believing men have a hard time working long side a woman. I guess because they are in that natural man. When now is the day of the spirit. Yahshuah is male, Christ is neither.

Chapter four we have to make a decision to grow up. If we are babies in Christ we won't know what to do with our inheritance. Yahshuah did everything like us so there would be no mistrial. Verse 6 There is that Hebrew word again Abba. Verse 8 loving the world to much. Verse 10 Traditons of men verse 12 Paul wants them to imitate him as he imitates Christ. Verse 19 Being like Christ and making disciples. Maturing in Christ is what God says is good. If we reject Christ we have no inheritance. We don't accept the gift. Verse 21 Talks of Abraham having two sons. Hagar represents worldly bondage. Really the Law God moved from that. Sarah represents freedom in the spirit the child from the promise. Which the promise is Yahshuah. Verse 29 The natural man will always prosecute the spirit man. The natural man opposes the spirit.

Chapter five It is finished so we need to walk in the new creature. If we walk in the spirit we won't satisfy the flesh. Verse 13 Don't use grace as a excuse to do wrong. Grace is for us to live our new live and to have the ability to do our assignment. Verse 14 We ought to love each other. If we look like Yahshuah we will love. Verse 17 Sometimes we don't do what we are suppose to do because our natural man is always at war with our spirit man. If there was no fall our natural man would be sleep. You see most believers natural man is awake and their spirit man is sleep. They are operating from the wrong part of their exsistence. Verse 19 Who taught you to think the way you do? Genesis chapt six The devil really taught the man how to sin. When Adam thought like God he had so much wisdom. He wasn't thinking about sinning. Verse 22 What Yahshuah looks like in the spirit. If we look like him then people will see joy, peace patience, kindness, faithfulness, self control, gentleness, perseverance and longsuffering. Most believers look nothing like this and are down right mean. God called it fruit because it had to mature and be produced. We have to keep working on ourselves so we will produce fruit.

Chapter six we should be there for each other and share what God tells us. We reap what we sow. We have to do what's best. For everybody. God looks at us like a whole. We are the body of Yahshuah Verse 14 The cross is what is important. Believers shouldn't look like the world. The relationship to the world should be severed. All ties should be cut. Doesn't matter how we came to Christ because Yahshuah made us a new creature. Verse 16 Peace and mercy will come to those who look like Christ. Which means freedom and forgiveness. They are the spiritual Israel whoever does this. Paul talks about carrying the scars of Messiah. Meaning he recognizes with what Yahshuah did. We are always thinking of how we look or speak in the natural. With us it is a human effort when it should be a God effort. Paul's interested in being dead to this world. Our interest in the world should be dead to.

Ephesians Means body function. We need to develop our position in Christ. I don't know why no one teaches this. We are better together. Unity in church. Ephesians is the spiritual equivalent to the book of Joshua in the natural. Ephesians is us taking out satan and his gang in the heavenlies. God made a promise believe and walk it out. We deal with life through the scriptures. Do we come to church to function as a body? Or for ourselves? We need to come for each other. First we need to bless God. Verse 3 God gave us everything when he died on the cross. God did all this before the creation of the world. When God blessed us he showed us what blessing would do for us in the natural. When you are in the spirit you know the power of the blessing. Verse 8 God emptied himself out. Verse 10 To reconcile his man back and one thousand year reign. We need to move to God's plan. How can we fail and be the praise of his glory? We are to subdue the earth. Then it goes to talk about how they believe and about their relationships. Verse 17 prophesy and seeing. The process of change so you can change. It is already done in the heavenlies. We have to manifest it here on earth. The Holy spirit informs and instructs us. When we are connected to God. What we really need is a revolution. So we can change our world. We are suppose to set the captives free. The people chained to this world. I wrote this book because the world is so much wiser then God's people. Everything in this world mocks God. Just look around you in every day life. Money can be the worst pushed by the spirit of mammon. That spirit's on the dollar bill. In God we trust. Which God are you trusting in? We need to seek God's face and not his hand. I don't mind helping my siblings fight but it baffles me that believers think what I am teaching is new. This is food for the spirit. It's like Yahshuah among the Pharisees and Suducees. Which were the religious people of Yahshuah's day who had the scriptures but didn't see him in them. God taught me how to articulate his word. If we are in court there's one way not a hundred. In Isaiah God's summoning the earth and the heavenlies are the jury. Which tells me everything can hear. Well in the beginning creation heard. I just want to tell people watch what you see and hear on the idiot box which is the tv. One thing that I disagree with is when a minister may tell you to send in a certain amount of money. It's like serving money. It's like they are telling you to buy a blessing which you can't. You don't have to think you have to give God something to bless you. He's done everything and he gives freely. Also you need to seek the kingdom and all this will be added to you. Also God doesn't have prayer lines. We have to plug into God's system. Satan will always supply you with excuses. You will never see correctly. Unless you understand what God is telling you. If we have given ourselves to God why are we so busy with everything else. Yahshuah is the brains of the operation. God used his Holy spirit to bring Yahshuah back to life and seat him in the highest position in the heavenlies. Verse 21 He is far above all rulers, authorities, power, Lords and all other names that can be named. Not only in the present world but the one to come. Verse 27 God has put everything in the control of Christ. He has made Christ the head of everything, for the good of the church. Verse 28 The church is Christ's body and completes him as he fills everything in everyway. Our goal is to get in the body. God will fit us in. It's a spiritual body. Why wouldn't it be. God is a spirit. The enemy of this world blinded us for so long. God provided for us in our mother's womb. You didn't even know you exsisted. Why do we act like God changed. God set the stage for you to grow in your mother's womb and we are worrying about a electric bill. God didn't bring the storm. God calmed the storm. God holds the wind in his hand. We are all responsible for the atmosphere. What does God expect? What's God's concept? What do we really want? Nothing moves God . What is our mindset and attitude? Devil can only get you where you do wrong. People don't like to be exposed. When you do wrong the door is open for the devil to get in. It can be a little thing but the devil can kill you. The devil doesn't play fair. Adam ate then his son killed his other son. It's the cause and effect. In the Old Testament God had to deal with them good and bad. This was brought in by the tree of good and evil. The curse of the law was put on Yahshuah. It takes nothing to destroy something. It takes hard work to build something. You can paint a beautiful picture and paint a little dot on it . The whole picture is ruined. Takes work to be strong in the Lord.

Chapter two We were dead prior to Christ because of our disobedience. Verse 3 Behavior patterns were established. God saved us. Verse 10 Predestination are those works that were prepared for us to do. Verse 11 God uniting us. Verse 13 The blood of Christ brought us together. Verse 15 God rolling the commandments into himself. When he made peace he freed our spirits. Verse 16 Yahshuah finished his assignment. Verse 18 reconciling us back to the father. Verse 20 Body of Messiah is the foundation.

Chapter three God said to me he is a spirit .Yahshuah said his words are spirit filled. So why wouldn't the bible be for the spirit. We have to much natural man teaching church. You have the devil, the convert and the Judas spirit as teachers. God says the workers are few nobody's being discipled and that's what God wants. The church has been cut from it's roots. So when you are cut from your roots you eventually die. The root meaning where you came from. Our roots are Hebraic. I am here to tell you God is setting the stage for his New Testament church. No not the one down the street but the one in Acts. A church full of spirit filled people, where every need is met. Like I said understanding is seeing what's going on. We have to see as God sees through spirit filled eyes. Verse 1 to 10 Explains the foundation. Revelation , The mystery and Grace of God. Which is Yahshuah a God effort. We did nothing. Faith is us believing in God's effort. We have to trust what God has done not what we can do. God imparting his effort to us. God's effort gave us the blessing of Abraham. Live based on the promise. Are we sharing in God's plan? We all have a assignment. Verse 4 The mystery is Yahshuah which will only be revealed to you by revelation. It wasn't know back then like it is now. Because those people didn't have the spirit. Verse 6 The will of the father is the work of the son. The witness is the Holy spirit. God had our identity in mind. Since the enemy tricked us out of our identity. You don't know you. God chose to save us. Immeasurable wealth of Christ means It's limitless. God hid his plan until the appropriate time. God didn't want the enemy to know his plans. The enemy goes after God's words. We are in spiritual warfare. I guess believers don't know what that means. I am tired of people saying stuff and don't know what it means. Once again God made known the mystery by revelation. The only mystery is when you don't understand. Understanding you see what's going on. Peter says we have a more sure way because we have the Holy spirit. So we should be able to see spiritually. We need to take time and see what's in God's word. Where did the promise start?

Chapter four. We need to build a habitat for God spiritually. For God's spirit. We have to put on God's spirit. Man was created in God's image so you need to be renewed in the spirit of your mind. Are we willing to allow God to take us deep in him and search God out? You say this is the way I am .How do you know that? Who told you that? Your spirit knows the real you. God concealed his word so you could get some glory. His word being Yahshuah and his glory being his full expression. Meaning he hid Yahshuah until it was time for his assignment. After his assignment we were able to look like him again. At Salvation we get all the God we will get. We clothe ourselves with salvation the natural man doesn't receive that.

Chapter four, Work hard to keep the unity. We need to work together doing projects. If you don't help your brother you won't see God in your life. We never seen God. The stuff we have is not for us but our brother. Our jobs are not to meet our needs but to help someone else. God is our source. You can't help your brother unless you get to know him. Believers are trying to get the things of God the world's way. God says use what you have and he will multiply it. We need to move according to God's plan. God planned his plan in eternity. God did it mercifully. He planned it before us. When we complete his will we are to the praise of his glory. Verse 5 God made known the mystery through revelation. Missionaries are on a mission for the Lord. God is repetitious because he really wants us to get this. He wants the spirit man to wake up. Verse 7 God's grace is limitless. Yahshuah saved us and set us free in the spirit. Yahshuah took Abraham's busom which was in the ground. Along side hell (but you couldn't cut across) and placed it in the third heavenlies when he ascended to heaven. That's how the rich man could see Lazarous. Lazarous was a homeless man .So we should be careful how we treat homeless people. When Yahshuah took the dead people from out of the ground, people saw them walking around on earth. There was no power to get the spirit to heaven until Yahshuah came. The spirit was no longer connected to God. Yahshuah preached the gospel while in the ground. Verse 11 The fivefold are the equippers of the church. God gave them to the church as a gift. They equip the church's spiritual growth. First you have the Apostle that starts and balances the church. The prophet who sees and hears God's plan. The evangelist who tells who God is and what he's done. He travels. He just doesn't sit in the pulpit. What gets me the people in church should already be saved. They may need to be discipled. God told us to go to the lost. Then you have the pastor that takes care of the sheep. Some believe women can't be pastors. In the natural Rachel and

Rebekah took care of the sheep. So if they were in the New Testament they would be pastors. They were a foreshadow. Then you have the teacher which imparts some information. Now Paul said he did not allow women to teach. God didn't say that. You have to look and see who is talking. At that time Paul taught the gentiles who thought women were second rate. Also there were mostly men in church. A woman can't teach a man how to be a man in the natural. We are all the same in the spirit. You have to look where Paul came from he was from that religious sect. So he knew the law .He was the top man. He got Yahshuah different then Peter. Peter didn't care . Peter followed Yahshuah's lead. Paul was sent to the world. The woman is God's secret weapon .You have a whole church full of women. God's going to utilize them because it is coming down to the fight. There's not enough believing woke men in the spirit. A lot of women I know in the world will go head to toe with any man. These churches better move out of the law. Verse 12 The five fold's purpose is to perpare God's people to serve and build up the body of Christ. The five fold is a gift for the Body of Christ which is the spirit. That body is suppose to be the church. Well most churches have the pastor. Some have the pastor and the teacher. Sometime the pastor is the teacher. The pastor doesn't have to be the teacher. Just because you are a pastor doesn't make you a teacher. About seventy five percent of the churches have a evangelist. The evangelist isn't really doing what they were called to do. The prophet and apostle are rare commodities. God's bringing them back because the New Testament church is on the way. Once we understand we will be unmovable. We need to grow into what God purposed us to be. Christ is unmeasurable. Man knows measure meaning he knows limits. God has no limits. God anointed us for service and graced us so we could do our assignment. Your voice is the most authorative voice you will hear. Not God's. When the people were on the mountain and heard God's voice they acted scared but they didn't do what God said. God's about corporate success not church attendance. Everyone has a part. Don't be body ruled. Meaning thinking like the world. How much are we growing? Verse 18 People can't see because they are in the world. Verse 15 world consumed. Verse 20 the message. I wonder how many churches are teaching the message. We need to be the truth. Verse 28 Like I said our jobs are not for us but for us to help someone else. Verse 29 be encouraging . We need to look like Yahshuah. Don't disrespect things pertaining to God.

Chapter five We have to understand the will of God. We have to be careful how we live. Verse 1 God loves us so we should imitate him. Verse 2 watch what we say and do. Verse 5 talks about not inheriting the kingdom which is the life of the king. You can have the king without having the life of the king. God gave the king to the world. Now it's up to us to accept his life or reject it. Remember the bible is talking to believers. So if we are believers our lives should change .Our lives shouldn't be the same. So I wonder are we really believing? God wants us to line ourselves up with what he's done not with who we became in the world. God created us to have dominion. When death came in it started to dictate. A fool knows the word but doesn't do it. They never bother to find out what God wants for their life. We were redeemed for God. Verse 14 You need to wake up the spirit man. The light we need to follow is Christ. So we can see. It is like going in a dark room you stumble, walk into stuff and don't know where you are going until you hit the light switch. Then you can see. The church needs to turn on the lights so the church can see and be the light for the world. Let's grow up and be the church. So why is it lying? The church says they are the light but they are living in the dark portraying to be light. Isn't that crazy? Verse 15 The church and Christ became one when we believed. Verse 16 Tells you the days are evil so we have to take advantage of what God has done. We should let God navigate our lives. Then when God talks about not drinking wine he's referring to not being influenced by this world. Then God tells us what we should be doing. Verse 21 About agreement. All this is a natural perpective. So we should be the same in the spirit and in the natural. The husband and wife are a example of Yahshuah and the church. When a man and a woman marry they become one spirit. So if they are walking in the spirit they are like one. While we are on this earth we will be bouncing back and forth from the spirit to the natural. Then the rest of the chapter talks about husbands and wives loving each other and lining up with Yahshuah. All this is a natural view of how we are to be with God's church. God said he's coming back for his glorious church with out spot or wrinkle. That's the church in Acts. A church filled with spirit filled people. A full expression of God. Acts is a full grown church. Men trip on women submitting but they tend to forget they are suppose to be willing to die for her. Laying down their lives. What Yahshuah did. See how God shows us naturally.

Chapter six. God speaks upon everything. Now here's some advice for parents and children. It pays to listen. A system. God wants everything to go well with you. Verse 7 serve God. What's our approach to God. Your look at life. What do you see when you see the word? Are we doing all to stand? Verse 11 We put on spiritual armour because we don't fight against flesh and blood. That's for all those people that say you don't have to worry about the demons. Verse 12 Tells you what we fight against and you best believe they are ranked. Verse 14 The truth which everything is based on is the belt around our waist, The breastplate of righteousness is us being in right standing with God. Our gospel of readiness on our feet. Is us running and taking the gospel every where. The helmet is us being Christ minded and clothed in our right minds. Our shield is us doing what we believe. These weapons protect us from what the enemy throws at us. The only weapon we use to fight with is the sword. Which is the word of God. Yahshuah used it everytime when he said it is written. Verse 18 praying in our prayer language. Tongues is like spiritual exercise. Prayer is a weapon. It's communication with God. Be alert. Soldiers are always alert because the enemy maybe trying to use sneak tactics. We have to be for each other. Verse 21 A deacon is a servant. Know what you believe. We need to pray and stay connected to each other. God's unmerited kindness is with all of us . It's his undying love, for our Lord Yahshuah. We don't change by words of a man but by God talking to our hearts. If you are not moving after being reborn again examine yourself The purpose is to hear the spirit after someone or the Holy spirit brings it to your attention. Then the Holy spirit tells you what you heard.

Phillipians is a letter of joy. Inspite of. We have a account in heaven. We have to speak and understand the language of the kingdom. If we hear the spirit it gets down in our heart. The natural part of our exsistence is the shortest part of our exsistence. So why do we put so much emphasis on it? Essence of life to be loved by God and love someone else. How can God love you if you are never created? How can you not suffer if man is fallen? God's grace and power are his son. The enemy sowed seeds into life and he sowed them right into our character. Who we are. We fight to get blessings but if we come into the perfect will of God we will have the blessing. The goal should be to be like Yahshuah. Then we will manifest the word in the natural. Yahshuah demonstrates the love of God. We have to yield to that grace. When we are like Yahshuah we glorify God. We do that and God sees Christ in us.

Verse 8 God's will and peace are Yahshuah. It's all about relationships and fighting for the cause. You are willing to fight more for someone you love . Then for someone you don't. Verse 9 God's love allows you to know stuff. When you have insight you can see inside the situation and know what's going on. Verse 10 You will know how to live. Then we will express and give honor to God. Verse 12 people will know and believe because of what happened to us. It will help us to spread the good news. As others see us stand for the cause it will help them stand. Verse 15 Why do we tell the message? What is our motive or our intent? Paul says it doesn't matter as long as the message is told. We should be happy all the time because we know Yahshuah. Verse 19 prayer is a weapon. Verse 20 How are you living? What does Christ mean to me? Then in the rest of the chapter Paul is saying that it's better for him if he dies because he will be with Yahshuah. It is better for us if he stays so he can help grow and mature the believers. Verse 27 Unity It's power in numbers ,the blessing is there and it is hard to penetrate through a multitude. We need to be one new man.

Chapter two Act and be like God. No matter what your opposition looks like. Know you are saved. Don't think about yourself. Verse 6 Paul telling the story of Yahshuah. The story must be real important. So why isn't everyone telling the story. Verse 10 So that the name Yahshuah will be known in all of heaven ,earth and in the world below. Every knee will bow and confess that Yahshuah is Lord. To the glory of God the father. We should appreciate the gift we received. God's working in us so it's our obligation to shine. What you do gets in your mind. If you look like Yahshuah no matter what you will stand out. Hold firm to the word of life which is the tree of life. Our lives should be committed to the Lord. We should share joy with each other. Which is strength. These next few paragraphs shows the relationship Paul and Timothy have. How they were friends. Paul was more like a father figure. Then they speak of Epaphroditus. Who got sick and almost died for the cause. God had mercy on him. We should be constantly working, care and appreciate other believers.

Chapter three to know Yahshuah we have to constantly seek him. We have to beware of those that kill the body and be confident that we serve and have the spirit of God. We have to be willing to lose all things and keep looking into Christ so we can know him better. Then Paul talks of his education and physical qualifications. He knew the law perfectly. He once considered what he knew valuable and had meaning. He thought it was important. When he had a encounter with Yahshuah he found out how unimportant and meaningless everything is. No comparison. He gave it all up for Yahshuah. The most important message is what Yahshuah did for us. It was nothing we did to be accepted by Christ. We could never do anything. God's acceptance did not come from obeyng the law there's no way you could obey six hundred and thirteen laws. It's all about Yahshuah. The acceptance is based on what you believe. The power that brought Yahshuah back to life . Which is the Holy spirit. We just have to stay the course and finish the race. Know Yahshuah is the goal. Paul tells them to imitate him as he follows Christ. So many don't believe and oppose the cross. Now especially ,You see the enemy driving the people to do all kinds of things. So much perversion and sexual immortality but God tells us not to speak of what they do. The closer we get to the end the more wickedness you see. God's grace abounds more but we have to understand God's grace. Every body has a fate. How we are ambassadors and how we will get new bodies.

Chapter four talks of encouragement and fighting together. When we work we are doing God's activity or a God effort. If we keep doing God's will we will stay in the book of life. God knows what we need and everything he tells us to say and do is for us. Keep your eyes on Yahshuah and give God what he wants. Verse 10 How do we feel about other believers? Be satisfied in every situation. I can do all things in Christ that strengthens me. Verse 16 the value that we put on the offering. The measure you meet will be measured back to you. We are to take care of each other. When we stop thinking about us God will start looking out for us. If we look out for ourselves God says okay you got this. Then you can have it. Invest in the kingdom. Devest from the world. Lend to the Lord.

The Colossians had more then one belief. The letter of Colossians talks of receiving a reward . Seeking God and all his righteousness. Then God will add on to you. Love gives at the expense of yourself. Muddied water means you don't know what's what. You can't see clearly. This was the Roman province of Asia. Drink pertains to God. Influence. Stand in the Lord. Which is peace completeness,soundness well being hope. Us being reconciled back to God. Yahshuah the good news is the message of truth. This message is what everything is based on. God really allows us to know his love as we serve. Most believers won't serve anybody. Ministry means service and to supply a need. How can you serve someone sitting down? It's all about growing into the spirit man. The natural receives nothing from God who is a spirit. The light we share is Yahshuah's spirit. Believers are the only light in the world. If we don't shine in the world we walk in darkness. God brought us into Yahshuah. The power produces God's image in us. The Holy spirit. God made us heirs with Yahshuah. The owner of creation . He did it through the spirit. God has me say thinks over and over because it is important and I have to get pass your natural mind. Once it gets pass your natural mind it can get in your spirit. Verse 15 The spirit of the invisible God is the Holy spirit. God fed me all I know as I'm out professing who God is and what he has done. If you sit in a pew and think that's all to it you missed it. God has no need to give you his grace if your not doing anything. We need to keep coming towards God. God is called father because everything originated from him. No matter where, here on earth or in heaven. Verse 19 The Godhead Verse 23 Hope of gospel expect Christ. Don't drift away from the truth. Paul did everything to benefit the truth. We are suppose to be one unit. The body. Everything is in Christ. Verse 26 make disciples. Paul's growing in his anointing. So he can grow up the converts. God always increases you as you do his will. We work so we can help people understand. We are altogether in spirit whether we are together in the body are not. We need to be grounded and rooted in Christ. So we won't be moved. Word of God is in the fullest in us as the Holy spirit. We keep our strong faith by keeping our focus on Yahshuah. Verse 8 Talks about traditions of men. Which is religion which helps no one and allows you to miss God. You miss God by chasing religion. God's not in religion. There's no relationship and no truth. Verse 9 The God head Which is the three in one. God gave us circumcision of the heart and made us complete in Christ. God completed a judicial act which made us not guilty. Verse 17 God allowed us to partake in the feast so we won't be ignorant. The Old Testament is a foreshadow because it's visual. Most people need to see something in the natural. Verse 19 Talks about the worship of angels and Yahshuah said place nothing before him. It tells you a person who does this thinks like the world. When Christ is the basis for everything. Verse 20 come out the world. Verse 21 stuff perishes with the user so why do we put so much into this natural man. Verse 23 looks can be deceiving. This verse talks about harsh treatment to the body . Which means doing stuff to the body to make it line up but doing nothing about the way you think. Only the bible does something for the way you think. The only belief system that deals with your evil desires. Who better to think like than God. Changing you from that natural man into the spirit man. Put on the image of God take off earthliness. Your treasure is where your mind is. Spirit is light. You don't know what new man looks like till you put him on. You put him on by reading the word. The word shows you what you are suppose to look like. You will never get truth about you trying to get God to give you a better life. Verse 11 When we are in the spirit we are all the same. Verse 12 Tells of the fruit that should be seen in us. Verse 16 Be forgiving thankful and know you are free. Remember your behavior is tied to this earth so you have to pull him off. Everything is done on purpose so don't be scared to check yourself. Don't get tired why you are waiting for God's answer. God's not subject to time. You figure when you pray the angels come for you words. They take your words up to heaven and bring your answers down. So say what God says. That's where the angels are descending and ascending come from. The fallen angels are constanly fighting these angels. Just think of Daniel, the king of Persia hindered his prayers for twenty one days. The king of Persia was a fallen angel that had Persia as his territory. When you talk and sing to God it gets into your heart and changes you.

The end of chapter three tells us how to be in relationship with our families. God has a system for everything and puts everything in order after the fall. We need to pray all the time and for each other. We should get the word out and think about everything we say. So we will make sense when we answer people. We should be people of integrity. The whole bible is about relationship. The disciples use to go house to house. We have to stay connected and help people become mature believers. We should remember Yahshuah is with us. So we can be bold because we know who is in us.

In the letter of First Thessolonians they thought Yahshuah was coming right back. So they went to work really doing the things of God. Such as caring for one another. They are doing what they believe. Verse 5 Yahshuah came with power. The Holy spirit power. This church was suffering but they still walked in the word. What you do speaks for itself. We should be a model and set a example. Some stop what they were doing for God and were physically waiting for Yahshuah to come back.

Chapter two they didn't waste time and spoke the word inspite of Opposition. They had endurance and didn't do it for money. Why do we? Or please God. God knows why we do what we do. We may hide it from people but we can't hide it from God. They shared everything and this church was nurturing. They worked hard in the things of God. They were concerned about growing up the believers. Thankful for what God did. We are the spiritual Israel so we should look at the spirit. We are going to go through stuff because Christ did. We have enemies. Verse 18 Satan is always trying to stop the word. Satan doesn't think much of God's man and wants him to go to hell. Satan has workers working so the word won't get out. It's all about relationship and family. Whatever we go through we should go through together. When God says sisters and brothers it's like we are siblings. Everything in this world God did first. The world made everything perversed especially love. We should go to our heavenly father and allow him to teach us. Verse 10 Every joint supply is us bringing our part. We give what is needed. We need to always pray and allow God to grow us up. Verse 13 When Yahshuah comes with all his holy people he's talking about the millennium.

Chapter four tells us to go the extra mile for God. Tells us how to find a partner not through lustful desires like the world. We should be holy and love should be our goal. Verse 11 Here's for all those busy bodies. God says live quietly,do your work and earn your own living. Then your way of life will earn respect. Verse 13 Telling us not to grieve like the rest of the world. Because we know we will see our love ones again if they believed. If not they will be erased from our memory. The dead in Christ will rise first. Then us. Verse 16 The trumpet will sound are evacuation call. The rapture. Yahshuah will be in the air and we will be out of here.

Chapter five We don't need times and dates , we just follow God's time line the feasts. We just don't know which one but we should be alert. The world is still going to be doing what they do. They will be caught off guard. Just like in the times of Noah. So we need to keep our spirit man woke. We need to help each other on our walk Verse 12 we need to appreciate our leadership. Verse 14 Tells us how we should be. We shouldn't do wrong for wrong. You keep your spirit lit by joy praying and thanksgiving. Verse 21 We need to test every spirit and make sure it lines up with God. Verse 23 The whole you the spirit ,soul and body. Even though most people live by the body part. The lower part of their exsistence or the world. The answer to the body of death is renewing your mind. If you don't renew your mind you won't see. God's answer in your life which is the Holy spirit. The renewed mind is the mind of Christ. Our decisions should be bible based. We have to stir up the spirit. We shouldn't be the same person. Our gifts are in us but are for everybody else not us. Just like our faces aren't for us. You can't see your face unless you look in the mirror. So we should smile. We need to stay in the feasts. Then we know what we have. People like money to much. God wants to meet our needs but he's not our slave. Verse 26 holy kiss means deep affection. Verse 27 Lord's name represents authority and power. Verse 28 Yahshuah be with us.

Second Thessalonians They are still waiting for the Lord to come back. They were enduring and expecting. Verse 6 God will take care of everyone for what they have done. God will help us do everything he says is good through his Holy spirit. Our desire should be God.

Chapter two talks about a sign to know the day he comes. We need to pay attention. So we aren't deceived. First it will be a rebellion. The man of sin will be revealed. He will be in God's temple saying he is God. Right now there is no temple. He opposes everything of God or related to God. It's getting there. The believers are still here. The Holy spirit is that one new man that's holding sin at bay. When we are raptured out the Holy spirit will be gone and then you will see this stuff happening. Even though most believers don't believe right it is still to much light. Only ten percent of believers have a biblical world view. I believe it's increasing. It will increase enough to get God's New Testament Glorious church here. Before we are raptured up. The enemy wants you to think it's not coming . I'm telling you it's coming. Satan has powers and he will be behind the man of sin. If you walk in the spirit of God you will recognize a false spirit. God gave us the Holy spirit so we could defeat the devil but we have to be a body. God made satan but he didn't make him the way he is. We all have freewill. Everyone doesn't choose Yahshuah. Verse 15 Hold on to the word. God loves us. God chose us. God called us but few answer the call. If God was like us none of us would be saved. We wouldn't of died we would be like I will go save them tomorrow or maybe I will just make some new people. I don't feel like it or I don't want to go through all of that. Do I really love them like that? All of this is a human point of view.

Chapter three We should be constantly praying and allow God to direct us. Verse 6 says we shouldn't associate with believers who are one way in church and another way out side of church. We need to imitate Christ. Paul supported himself but in verse 9 he says he has the right to be supported by the gospel. Paul didn't want any excuses for anyone not excepting the gospel. At the end of this chapter you have people that stopped working and had other believers supporting them . They thought Yahshuah was coming right back. God wants us to keep working and doing what we are suppose to be doing moving in the things of God. We shouldn't get tired and stay alert. Some people won't listen but we are still nice to them. Verse 16 Paul is continually praying for the believers.

First Timothy is a letter about church care. Which refers to the natural. It tells us how to live as a church family. God always wants us to be a family. So I don't see why we always want to be separate. Where did we get that? Who taught us that? Verse 3 talks about opposing views. Verse 4 talks about teaching false doctrine and history. God's on his own time line and it's about the spirit. So the natural man always wants to prove stuff. Verse 5 Is talking about your mind doing what you believe. People don't know what they are talking about and don't see Yahshuah. Verse 8 If we have Yahshuah we supercede the law and we are dead to sin. A dead man is not subject to the law. Because he's dead. We should pass everything down. The law was so we would know what sin is. Verse 12 Paul talks of how he prosecuted the church. Yahshuah had mercy on him. Verse 15 Yahshuah came to save us. Verse 18 What they believed governed the way they thought meaning what you believe will be the way you act.

Chapter two if we pray for everybody we are in the fight. The more people fighting the harder for the enemy to penetrate us. We should be telling the truth. The message never changes. Focus should be Yahshuah the message the cross and no world in God's church. Verse 8 There shouldn't be any distractions. Verse 12 Paul said he doesn't allow women to teach. God didn't say that. In Corinthians he says you decide. Paul came from the religious sect. Peter didn't care. In the spirit we are all the same. In the churches back then the women and men sat on opposite sides. So it be pretty hard to teach with wives and husbands yelling back and forth. Well a woman can't teach a man how to be a man in the natural and most men were down for the cause back then. Of course God allowed the woman to be down played. She's his secret weapon. The Holy spirit's the teacher in the spirit.

Chapter three verses 1 and 2 These are natural positions. How many women had more than one husband in the bible? Some one asked me about a woman being a bishop. Who am I to question another man's servant? Back then more men where in church. The secret's out. Verse 16 Yahshuah manifested in the flesh. Support of the truth. Spiritually Christ's writing to the church. Coming back to get us. How to conduct ourselves in church. The mystery of truth is those coming in knowing what the truth is about. It's not personal .God's looking corporately. When we do that it benefits individually.

Chapter four people leaving the faith. What they believe. Verse 3 stopping people from getting married sounds like the catholic religion to me. The priest in the bible could marry. Look at Zachriah John Baptist's father for one or look at Aaron. Then it talks about eating what you want. Verse 7 old wise tales, fables Verse 8 outside appearances although the inside is more important. Verse 10 making our body line up with our condition. From verse 12 down what we are suppose to be doing in church. When we do what we are suppose to do the gifts start coming out.

Chapter five respect and love taking care of each other especially the woman with no husband. Family-family-family Telling us how to live. Verse 13 Don't be a busybody which is a gossip. Verse 14 don't give the enemy any room to get into our lives. Verse 17 honoring our leaders for doing what they are suppose to do. Verse 18 never stop those working for the Lord. Workers should get paid for what they do. Verse 21 To end of chapter five keep yourself right or aligned with God. Verse 23 Yahshuah should be your influence. Everything's in the spirit. Verse 24 Some sins you see like homosexuality and some you don't like wickedness in the heart. Everything comes to light and God will judge.

Chapter six lead by example. You do it in the natural first. Be and live the truth to avoid strife. Be happy and content. Can't take anything with you. Verse 9 Talks about chasing money. If you make money don't let it master you make it your servant. Anything that takes you away from God becomes your master and you can only get death and destruction. Not the life God attended for you. Verse 11 Tells us what man of God should look like. Who God is and what he has done. Verse 17 How rich people think their riches will sustain them. Most rich people won't do anything for anybody. Verse 20 stand on the word and don't waste your time on stuff that sounds good but isn't true. Just keep telling the story and do what you believe.

Second Timothy Paul's final word. Verse 3 Paul was like Timothy's mentor. Verse 5 Timothy's mother and grandmother enstilled the word in him. Something we should be doing for our kids. Verse 6 anointed for service so activate the gifts. Verse 1 God gave us a spirit of power, love, and good judgement. So why do believers act like they don't have anything. God did everything before the foundation of the world. Verse 10 He has to be revealed. Christ took the sting out of death. Christ was before death. Verse 13 We have to show the world we believe. It's not enough to say it. We prove it through our worship and lives.

Chapter two Grace verse 2 the discipleship process. Have to be willing to die. Present the evidence. We have to be committed to the cause. That's why they could lay down their lives. If you think about yourself you won't fight hard. Verse 8 brought back to life. Descendant of David. Verse 10 God chose us. We need to be there for our brother not self Verse 11 We need to recognize and bury our old lives. Verse 14 don't trip over words Verse 17 If you preach anything preach the truth. It will spread like cancer. Like Easter and xmas. That's what you call the blind leading the blind. Blind means you don't see spiritually. Verse 19 God knows who belongs to him. Verse 20 need to put on new man. Verse 21 come out of the world. Pursue God. Everytime we study God we are breathing into the natural man to grow the spirit man. The end of this chapter talks about being a teacher.

Chapter three verse 1 talks of violence and people loving money in the last days sounds like today. They will have no respect. They will be God depraved. They will love the world over God. They will appear to have God when they really don't. They will deny God's Holy spirit. Verse 6 men who take advantage of weak women. Verse 8 the wordly teacher. People see right through them. Verse 11 people really walking with God will be prosecuted. All the others will get worse. As you grow in the word you will know whose who. Verse 16 God breathed in same substance in Genesis in his word which is his Holy spirit. Verse 17 The Holy spirit empowers us because it is God's power.

Chapter four verse 2 duties of a soldier Verse 4 talks about people grabbing hold of myths and not listening to the truth. Like grabbing hold of easter and xmas. Verse 5 A evangelist professes who God is and what he has done. The evangelist tells the story the truth. A field soldier. We need to stand steady and not be afraid. We need to bring others to Christ. Verse 6 Paul's going to die soon. Our goal Yahshuah. We run to get Yahshuah out. We just keep getting Yahshuah's story out and we will get the prize at death. Which is eternal life. Verse 9 people left the faith back then because they loved the world. There's nothing different today. Verse 14 Alexander made idols. He opposed Yahshuah if you believed in Yahshuah you wouldn't buy a idol. They traveled miles to get the word out. They walked we won't even drive. We won't even come out of the four walls.

Titus was the man they sent out for tough tasks. He was tough and not about foolishness. Titus was dependable reliable and diligent. Are we like that? If I changed you should be able to see the change in me. When we get the new life we have to realize we have the new life so we can benefit from it. Paul's constantly telling the story. God can't lie whatever God says it comes to be. Then Paul goes on to say how spiritual leaders should be. He says spiritual because they should be led by the spirit. People need to be discipled. What we say should match our behaviors.

Chapter two We should live by the word. Make our lives examples for others. We should have good moral values. Verse 11 God came for our benefit. To give us back the spirit so we can live. The spirit freed us from the world. We should heed to the rules of the government. God's government. God doesn't lower his standards.

Chapter three verse 4 Regeneration is when we have the life of the king. Righteousness is a gift. God doesn't expect us to sin. People walk in condemnation thinking about sin. Law of firstfruit is where you see it first or where it happens first. Cleansing from sin which is renewal and rebirth. A renewed mind is the washing of the mind from filth. The filth is the world which is getting filthier. Verse 10 God tells us not to bother with people who don't teach the truth. A righteous life allows or needs to be met. I said righteous which means being in right standing with God. I did not say religious. If you are religious you miss God. These letters are basic instructions to teach people. People think serving God is a inconvience. Prayer enlightens us of who we are.

Philemon was a slave owner who became a believer. Philemon had a slave named Onesimus who committed a crime that landed him in jail with Paul. Onesimus became a believer and later on in life became a bishop of a church. If Paul never reached down Onesiumus would of never been lifted up. We were all runaway slaves disobedient and willing to run. All of us sinned. We were converted run away slaves who were running from God. We were held in bondage by our sins. We were fugitives. The perfect mercy of Yahshuah set us free. We need to share our faith with others. What we believe will grip their lives. Onesimus a run away slave found Christ through Paul. If we don't share our faith many will still be run away slaves. Paul wrote a letter to Philemon and expressed how valuable Onesimus was to the work of the gospel. Getting the message out. Onesimus could share his faith with others like Paul. Paul was willing to lay his life down for his new found brother. You can look at laying down your life as taking up for your brother. Or being there for your brother. Believers are suppose to be a body. The body of Christ the anointed one. Anointed means set apart. His anointing, his Holy spirit. What part of the body are you? Yahshuah removes the burden which is sin and destroys the yolk what holds us to sin this world. If you don't repent you don't receive the king or the kingdom. Repent means to turn or change direction.

Hebrews is a book about believers that wanted to give up and quit the cause. They were being prosecuted. They were Messianic Jews. A N was put on their door which means their possessions could be confiscated because they followed that Nazarene. Believers are the only ones who get prosecuted so. Why? The enemy wants to stomp out the Holy spirit so we would have no power to defeat him. Yahshuah never said he was a Christian he said he was of the way. The way back to God. After Adam and Eve sinned God had to make away back to him. So how can there be more than one way? Angels are to go where needed. Servant flames are us. We received salvation and we need to be passionate about the cause, driven. Yahshuah is our standard there is no comparison. Christ is the mediator of the New Covenant. Which means contract. I was talking to a friend today and God dropped something about the ark of the covenant on me. Earlier in my book I told you ark meant coffin which represents death and a covenant is a contract. God was showing his people about the death contract. Him dying for us. The ark had the ten commandments in it which represented Yahshuah and then you had the two angels on the side which guarded Christ. The seat of the chest was gold which represent the mercy seat where the blood would lay. Gold is for a king. Kings go to war. Old covenants just roll over. The New covenant is between God and a resurrected man which was Yahshuah. All the other covenants couldn't be kept. Verse 3 God is shaking this world today. Meaning he's letting his hands go and the hedge is coming down. God said if we don't want him he won't be our God. God comes where he is desired. Three in one. The son who Is Yahshuah, God in the flesh, God's glory and power is his Holy spirit and God's being which is the father. Verse 5 throws the Mormons out when they say the devil and Yahshuah are brothers. Do people even read the bible to see what God said? God never called any angel son. The bible defines itself. Verse 6 Yahshuah was with God before anything was created. Verse 17 Angels are messengers and go where God sends them. You might not see them but you know they are there like the wind. We should get brighter because we have Yahshuah. Verse 8 To all those who said God isn't God But God said about his son Your throne God is forever. God is not his name God is what he does. God wants to bring us to maturity. Christ is God's last word. The staff represents authority. Verse 9 says that why God your God anointed you, rather then your companions with the oil of joy. God poured out more gladness on you because he is perfect. The oil represents the Holy spirit. Verse 11 and 12 Everything will end but God. Verse 14 For the saved

    Chapter two Angels put the law into affect. In misdt of congregation declare his name. Verse 4 We need to watch the way we hear. Verse 5 What is man that you are mindful of *him? Which is Christ. The son of man that you care for him. You being the father crowned him with glory and honor. Which is the spirit. Verse 8 Yahshuah broke the power of the devil when he established authority over death. We need to pay attention and trust God Verse 11 Spiritual adoption Verse 13 take power so you can become who God ordained you to be. Power comes to influence you. Once Yahshuah eliminated death there is no bondage. Speak from spirit into this age. Verse 14 honor Christ in people Verse 18 temptation comes to all of us since Yahshuah beat temptation he can show us how to do it.*

Chapter three when you declare something you make it known formally. Look at the mystery of creation, seek God out. You see a comparison Moses as a servant and Yahshuah as the son. Yahshuah is the blueprint or the negative of a picture, the owner which shows you how things should be done. Moses is the worker made off the blueprint or the picture off the negative. When I say foundation I mean support. We shouldn't think the way we think because we don't see a opportunity. Yahshuah lives in us. Verse 7 don't lean to your own understanding Verse 8 talking about Israel. Verse 10 It's not personal God has a system and if you don't do the system you won't get the results. Verse 13 While we are still here we need to encourage each other. We need to provoke one another to trust Verse 16 the world brings us something and we repeat the cycles of destruction which are rebellion oppression capitivity and deliverance. Verse 18 Israel didn't enter God's rest naturally because of disobedience. If we don't obey God we won't enter his rest spiritually which is the Holy spirit. We have to seize from our work and allow God's effort to work. If Joshua had given them rest then Yahshuah wouldn't have taken us into the kingdom. If we don't believe in Christ we won't partake of his rest. We are constantly being filled. Life starts at the cross. Cross means forgiveness no cross means no forgiveness. We need to preach the word and mean it and preach on what everything is based on . That's what sincerity and truth means. We need to restore and recognize what we have. Salvation Is God's gift to the world. The Holy spirit is God's gift to his children. You get the gift by believing and receiving. When you labor you obey God's word. Examples are giving and taking care of your brother. You can't only guard your heart. Have to watch out for evil with intelligence. We have to walk in the word. We are in a life long war. Which refers to now. Recognize God is faithful. God is now. God's ultimate power is stronger than the flesh. There is no such thing as a small act of obedience or disobedience. God consummated us through his blood.

Chapter four God's not telling us to work for it. We need activity to receive it. We have a enemy, our bodies which are under resistance. We have to resist what we were taught. The enemy had along time to teach this flesh. We have come to the end of man's way. Enter into God's rest which is the Holy spirit. It's not to qualify. How can we qualify when God gave us everything. How can we ever be good enough? Joshua wanted to enter into the promise land. They didn't, they were scared. The natural man is always going to be weak and scared. It's all about believing. Verse 3 God's wrath prior to Yahshuah. If you don't believe you will be hindered from God's rest. We have to come into agreement with God. God gives us examples so we won't make the same mistakes. God's word is alive and doesn't miss anything. God's word can do everything and sees all. We need Christ he did it all. If we don't grow in him we can't live. We aren't strong enough to possess our life because we are not strong enough to hold on to it. We learned from Adam when he gave his lease to the enemy and God gave him dominion.

Chapter five Yahshuah is our high priest , God called him to be. Look to the power of the seventh day. The seventh day points to rest which points to the Holy spirit which is rest. All before the law. The Sabbath which points to rest was made for man. Moses was a type and shadow of Christ. Verse 6 Melchizedek supercedes the law. He had no genealogy meaning no history. He was a priest and a king that stepped in time and set the order for Yahshuah to be a king and priest even though Yahshuah came from the tribe of Judah. Yahshuah took on humanity. When we respect God we yield to God. Verse 11 Talks about how believers aren't getting the principles or the foundation. Which is Yahshuah. God wants us to go into the deep things of him. Which is more than preaching, singing and scratching the surface. We have to anchor our soul and guard our heart. God wants a body of believers that function like a body. If you never go to church how are you going to function as a body? I know it's a effort to get out the bed. We go to church for each other . God is preparing us to do what he ordained us to do. When we have faith towards God we attend to God's needs. We pray and preach to get the lost saved. When you are on the road to promise the advasary comes after you. What are you thinking about? Perfection or Maturity?

Chapter six repentance from dead works means reversal in thinking, changing direction changing your mind walking away from sin and going towards God. Understand and believe in the mercy of God. In the economy of God we have to do what we hear. We should be mature not babies. How much strength do babies have? We think spiritual time is like natural time. The way we prove we know something is we do it. We just can't run to God when we are in trouble. Everything you do for the kingdom has a reward. Verse 8 talks about believers that left the truth. Going back to the world and unbelief. Verse 7 What fruit are you producing? Verse 9 We need to go on to perfection. God gave us grace to endure so we need to keep moving in him. Verse 13 Abraham understood blood covenant. Where you would make a agreement or draw up a contract and seal it in blood. If the contract wasn't honored the person was penalized or killed. We all know God is faithful and true. The covenant spoken in Jeremiah 31 verse 31 speaks of our contract with God which is between God and a resurrected man. Which was sealed with God and Yahshuah's blood who is God. See what happens when you get understanding which means you see what's going on. Verse 18 God can't lie Verse 20 Melchizedek had no geanology so we know Christ stepped down in time to set the order.

Chapter seven verse 2 Tithing the first time you see this in the bible sets the order. Melchizedek's name means king of righteousness and king of salem. Which means king of peace which means freedom and priest forever. Priests did sacrifices and Yahshuah offered himself up as the last sacrifice. There is no remission of sin with out the blood. This was four hundred and thirty years before the law and before the Levitical priest hood was set up. They were still in Abraham's loins while he tithed to Melchizedek. Natural priests received a tenth of what God got but they would eventually die. They would go in the holy of holies once a year to atone for sin. They could only cover up sin until Yahshuah came .Yahshuah had to become a priest so he could offer himself up as a sacrifice. Grace prompted God to offer a new land in the natural. Exodus chapter twelve verse 25 Which was a foreshadow of the spirit. That gave us eternal life. Verse 26 Yahshuah was the last and ultimate sacrifice. He was made sin because he had no sin.

Chapter eight Yahshuah sits at the right hand of God which represents power and authority. Everything was set in heaven before it happened on earth. Heaven is the blueprint for everything . Yahshuah gave us a better promise. The last paragraph of this chapter is God putting the Holy spirit back in the man.

Chapter nine Atonement deals with the way you think. Why would Yahshuah tell you, you have something and not give it to you? Your inheritance is in eternity but you get it here by the Holy spirit. The power of God. Verse 2 through 5 describes the tabernacle tent of meeting Verse 6 explains what priests do. Rituals couldn't make anyone perfect. They do nothing about the sin factor. Verse 8 the tent was in use because the way had not been made yet. The way is Yahshuah. Verse 11 Christ went through the tent in heaven and interceded for us. Verse 12 Christ used his own blood because there is no remission of sin with out blood. Blood of bulls and goats do nothing for the way you think. Abel still speaks because Cain shed his innocent blood for nothing. The enemy thought Abel was the seed that's why Cain killed him. Yahshuah's blood was better than Abel's because it was shed for a reason . The reason for the remission of sin and to give us back the Holy spirit. You can't see God functioning but you know he is. We have to have a hearing ear. Why do we think we don't have to have faith? When we meditate it helps us to see. We get to see what's going to come to pass. Noah listened even though he didn't see. That's faith. Abraham was another one who listened but didn't see. I wonder how well we hear God? Verse 13 Knew this earth isn't home. I will say it again the job of the believer is to believe. Verse 37 and 38 Dying for the cause and how the world didn't deserve these people of God. They believed and they didn't receive what God promised on earth. Yahshuah. So we should see them as examples and not cave in. They were before the cross so we should be like them and not faint. We should be good soldiers. We need to let God reveal himself. The attitude of our hearts dictates the quality of the relationship. Quality meaning value. We should place value on God's divine image. God's not moved by emotions but by his word. The joy of the cross is what Yahshuah gave us. Joy means strength which God's strength is his Holy spirit. He died so we would have God's presence in our lives. He was born to die. We don't need to know when he manifested in the flesh. God's presence is the fullnest of joy. The Holy spirit is the glory of God. If we don't apply the word to our lives we have no power. God's weakness on the cross is more powerful then the strength of man. God wants us to partake of his finished work not sit in church, twenty or thirty years and suffer. We can't be confident and apply scriptures to our lives if we think it is dumb or weak. God gave us his wisdom but we magnify singing and church attendance. Stuff we can do instead of what God can do through us. Word of God should be our speech. Eternity is greater then time speaking. Time said what are you going to do? Do the truth. Salvation is the door to Yahshuah. This is where my heart should be. Your treasure is where your heart is. Who are you serving? Where is your money, and time going? God wants the world to know that we are wise people. Not that we come to a building and not do bad things. The kingdom will touch those no one wants to touch. So why is it believers aren't willing to touch those undesirables? We need to receive the kingdom. So we can impact and change soceity. You can't earn anything. God won't have flesh glorify in his presence. How can I respond to someone I haven't had a revelation of. The natural man is tied to the old creature which is Adam and satan goes after him. If I live from the old creature that is defeated how can I be risen? We don't need to be distracted. Stay on course. We need to value Yahshuah and accept correction. We are corrected so we can stay lined up with Yahshuah. Next few verses God tells us how to live. Verse 18 Our hearts and lips are suppose to be one with God. Verse 25 It is important to listen to God. Verse 26 God's talking about shaking the earth. He's doing it now. Letting his hands go because we are disobedient. The only things that won't shake are the things connected to God and people walking in the spirit. We need to respect ,please and thank God.

Chapter thirteen Love and we may be entertaining angels. Also walking in someone else's shoes so you know how to treat people. Verse 4 marriage is honorable. God looks at the husband and wife as the natural covenant and Yahshuah and the church having a spiritual covenant. Verse 5 Be happy don't make money your master. What can man do to me besides harm or kill my natural body which isn't the real me. Verse 8 don't do it man's way. God was and is merciful. Verse 9 We praise God and sacrifice to him because when you value something there's a cost or else ir doesn't mean anything. If you desire something you will do *anything to get it. It brings you closer to God. As you get closer to God he gets closer to you. We should honor a king. Where do we get clapping from? We need to research the scriptures and see how they worshipped . They lifted their hands, they danced, twirled and sung and verbally spoke praise to God. They declared who God is and what he's done. What do you think fruit of the lips is? So if we are suppose to say something how come we never do? Who taught us that?*

James talks about true faith. Living out faith. Does your walk match the bible. The way to God is to walk with God. James was writing to believers who weren't acting like believers. Our faith should be genuine and our walk authentic. If you say you believe like you do why do you behave the way you do? James Yahshuah's brother didn't have faith in him before the resurrection. Yahshuah wants us to be mature believers. So we will be able to stand while being prosecuted. You can see what we believe when we do something. James speaks of Abraham at a different point in his life. He had been walking with the Lord for awhile. God accredited his righteousness to him believing but after walking awhile we see Abraham serving. Doing what he believed. Then it goes back to saying how you treat people. Verse 7 and 8 talks about a double minded man. That's a person who can't make his mind up. Verse 9 humble means you are thankful for what you have. Verse 12 through 15 teaches us how to quit and it has nothing to do with God. We get a idea we think about it and we do it. Natural thoughts. Carnal thoughts which is the body producing works of the flesh. Us taking our belly over God. Remember Esau. What we want. If we want the best possible results we have to listen and do God's word. God's word is a mirror when we look and study we see our identity. We get to know who we are. Religion is man's way to reach God but James says true religion is taking care of the widow ,orpan and not polluting your body. See God always wants the fatherless and husbandless to be taken care of. That polluting the body is being worldly. We need to examine ourselves.

Chapter two treat everybody the same. You don't know what God's doing with that Shabby man. God told me that's the first step to discipleship. I was that shabby person in church. God won't use you if you are prideful. You have to be humble and have a contrite heart. If you are prideful it is all about you. Yahshuah came as a servant to show us, It's not about us. If you disobey part of the law . You break the whole law. So just be like Yahshuah. Mercy supercedes the law. God rather have us forgiving. Abraham responds to the promise so God takes him to the promise. James uses Genesis twenty two partakers of Israel the blessing is through Christ. Paul referenced to Genesis fifthteen which talks about Abraham at a different stage of his life. It shows growth. The first part of Abraham's life he only believed. As he walked with God he had to show he believed. If you never do anything how do you actually know you believe. Is it really believing if you don't do anything? God gave the promise but there has to be some corresponding action to give our faith life. The way we respond to God. Verse 26 says a body that doesn't breathe is dead. Just look at a person in a coffin. Their body is lifeless when the spirit leaves.

Chapter three what comes out of the heart is important. God gave us the blessing which is a empowerment to succeed. Grace is Yahshuah. Faith works for every one. All you have to do is act on what you believe. The more you know the more you will be held accountable for. Verses 4,5,6,7, talks about how small your tongue is but how much power it has. People didn't know there inward power. There are power in words so choose your words wisely. We shouldn't be cursing and blessing out of the same mouth. We should have God's wisdom. Speak God's words because God's words give life. Be the truth.

Chapter four We fight because we want our way. What are our motives when we pray? If we are just shooting empty words in the air our prayers mean nothing and accomplish nothing. Why do you want the things you pray for? Is it of any value to the kingdom. We should be doing God's will which is God's word. The only think the devil can't handle is God's word. Verse 7 Here's the key submit to God, resist the devil and he will flee. God made the devil so he can handle him. He didn't make the devil act the way he does . The devil has free will. God used his Holy spirit power to throw the devil out of heaven. God used his word to do it. That's where that saying came from power in words. You know God had power in words by looking at creation. Believers need to think. We need to yield and allow God to use us. We need to stop talking about each other and inspire one another. I don't know why we are so prideful we have no control over our lives. We don't know the next second and this life is like a vapor. We have no power without God. Sin is if we aren't in right standing with God and don't want to do what God says. Sin is disbelief. When you believe you do. You do what you believe.

Chapter five talks of how rich people think their money will sustain them. You can't take your money with you but so many rich people are so unwilling to help. Verse 4 might of fact they want to take advantage of the people who work for them. Not paying the workers what they are worth. They don't think God sees it all. They made money their master. They had no reason to not give the workers. What they deserved. They just didn't want to. I see a whole lot of this in the area I live in. In this country you have one percent of the people who control the wealth and the other ninety nine percent work-work-work. That's not God's system. You see how the middle class is weeded out and the older unemployed worker can't find work. So what we see is the super rich or the super poor. We better plug into God. I asked myself how come they never teach kids about the stock market or finances in school. They want kids to learn how to be consumers. No understanding about money. That was a little food for thought. I grew a little sick of people doing stuff because they can. No reason but they can. So I said to God I love you and I'm plugged in. I don't care what it looks like I'm following you. I'm patient I expect and I look forward to the end result. Job had a great end result. Verse 12 don't feel bad just do what you say and say what you mean. Verse 13 talk to God. Believe what you say and why. God's forgiving. We have so many sins we can't remember. God said he will remember our sins no more. We are going to have this sinful nature until we die. What value do we place on God?

So now we get to the first letter of Peter. Peter's talking to a church under heavy prosecution. It's tough being a believer. You have to preservere and continue. Yahshuah the Holy spirit is better in Peter than when he walked with him in the natural. That's because God's power moved in Peter. Judgement is a result from a decision we made. Peter says we are scarcely saved. Meaning are we willing to endure for the cause? When you read that verse it sounds like he almost didn't save us. Or he had a hard time he almost couldn't get us out. No it means we like the world to much and can't decide if we want to be worldly or not. Do we really want to follow Yahshuah? It is better to suffer for the Lord then be a evil doer.

Chapter one verse 1 Temporary residents could this mean it's not our home. So why are we so comfortable here? God knows us and tells us how to live. God gave us his grace and freedom. God's professing what he has done. Verse 6 and 7 If you are for real God will start pruning you. Taking stuff off you. So you will be prepared to do the work he ordained you to do. Believe believe believe believe believe believe Verse 12 God has to be revealed not studied. Like taking off the covers or pulling up the shades. Or removing the veil. Verse 13 don't be worldy. Honor ,respect, and value the Lord. Be ready for service. God always tells us how to do something. God wouldn't tell us to do something he has not done himself. We should look like our father since we say he's our father. You know how you get your eyes or your nose from your parents. God gave us his image. His image is the Holy spirit. So shouldn't we look like our daddy. We couldn't redeem ourselves the natural man's defeated. So how could a defeated man redeem his spirit. The real us is the spirit. The enemy is higher than a defeated man so we need to walk in the spirit. We weren't redeemed from our natural fathers so why do we put so much focus on them. They just had to get us here. We could have had good or bad fathers in the natural but our focus should be Yahshuah. Our father in the spirit. We need to learn from God in all areas of our lives. Even if our parents rejected us we need to look towards God. This world is so perverse, so why would we look towards the world when God is the answer. Perversion came in when Adam and Eve opened the door to sin. We need to know what our redemption is based on. The word of God is eternal. We need to hunger and thirst for the word.

Chapter two We need to crave the word like a baby craves milk. Especially the milk that comes from the breast first. A baby has to eat to grow. So why do we think we don't need to grow as believers. We need to thirst for the word so we can be discipled. Verse 4 They rejected Christ. So how do you think they feel about us. Everything is done in the spirit. The people are mad and trip over Christ because they don't believe. Verse 9 God says we are a chosen people, a royal priesthood and a holy nation that belong to him. God forgave us. Verse 11 We are foreigners. The world's constantly against us. The world accuses us of doing wrong when God says we are doing right. They will say God is good when they see God help us. So we just need to stay in right standing with God. Verse 19 don't let life dictate to you. Yahshuah showed us how to navigate through this sinful world so we can live. We have to live righteously on purpose. We need to be dead to sin in the way we think and act. Yahshuah took the power out of sin. So why is sin our focus instead of righteousness? We should respond to God not people.

Chapter three God's talking about natural position. Sometimes you can win a person without saying anything. What's inside a person counts more then what's on the outside. When God talks about the woman being weaker then the man it's physically. God's grace gives us the ability to live in harmony. If we are married and in the spirit we are one with God. We should be in agreement with each other if we are in agreement with God. So I don't know how we can spend time with God and go off on our mate. I guess people don't know this can hinder your prayer because your not in agreement. The blessing is in unity. Verse 8 don't do things to people because they did something to you. We must focus on Yahshuah and do God's will. Verse 12 Says the Lord's eyes are on those who does what he approves and his ears hear their prayers meaning God doesn't hear or answer every prayer. So how can we ask God for stuff when we are in trouble and we aren't connected to God. Do you think God actually hears you? Should we wonder what happens? Uphold your integrity no matter what. Verse 19 Yahshuah preached to those in hell. Eight were saved in Noah's ark . Eight points to eternity. Baptism allows us to recognize with what Christ has done. We also get to show all the heavenly hosts what we believe. We need to leave that old man behind.

Chapter four If we think and act the way Christ did we won't satisfy our flesh. Then God talks about all the stuff we did in the world. Everybody will be held accountable for their actions. People want to live two different lives that's why God says we are scarely saved. When you love somebody the stuff they have done doesn't matter. God tells us how to serve. If we suffer for Christ you know we are suffering for the cause. If we suffer for any other reason it's worthless and meaningless. When God starts judging it's going to start with his house. Now the judgement can be good or bad. A judgement is a sentence that can be for or against you. So if we don't want to get judged with the world we better not look like them. When God say worshipping idols it can be anything that takes us from God or we spend more time with then God.

Chapter five spiritual leaders should be skilled warriors. They should be intimate worshippers and combat ready. We should all be discipled by someone so we can become mature believers. Our focus should be Yahshuah. He's the brains of the operation. The enemy is always on the prowl and trying to prick us off. Yahshuah has all authority. Verse 13 when he talks about Babylon he's referring to the world. When he says kiss that represents intimacy. When we have the father we can access grace which is Yahshuah. Don't worry about your sin. God's concerned about your faith. Faith deals with sin. You have to access what God has given you. We have to respond to God's grace. Faith is the spiritual force to access what God has kept for us.

The second letter Peter wrote was about getting understanding. So they would understand God's power and wisdom. We have to look deeper in our hearts. Yahshuah gave Peter the key to unlock our faith. Meaning he can unlock the way people think.

Chapter one verse 3 through knowledge of Yahshuah we get our divine nature. Why is it some of us are scared to say Yahshuah ? I can say Yahshuah all day long. He's all we need. We have his spirit. We have to come out of the world's system. We get the promises because we have the promise. Yahshuah. Verse 5 What and how are we standing? People should be able to see Yahshuah in us. Verse 10 We should be grounded and rooted. So we need to do everything so we can be like that. We need to remind ourselves constantly with the word. Peter's getting ready to be put to death so he's enstilling some things in the believers. Believers died horribly then and they are still dying for the cause. The enemy is constanty trying to stomp our lights out. The enemy doesn't want the Holy spirit on this earth. Everything was made to yield to the Holy spirit even the enemy. He doesn't want anyone discipled and placed in a body. The more disciples, the more soldiers. The harder it will be to penetrate us. It's all spiritual. Where do we think all these fallen angels went? They are all around. All those voices in the land are them. Everything in this world is a dillusion. The enemy wants you to think its about color. You missed it, if you think that. The soul is colorless. We need to know who we are. We need to be committed soldiers. Peter talks about a falling away. We already fell away. Why do you think Peter was willing to die? Really as believers we should be asking ourselves questions. We need to ask God questions. We have a majestic

God. Everything is revealed by the spirit. Verse 19 The prophets had visions and dreams. Yahshuah filled some of the prophesies. Yahshuah gave us the spirit so we can see. Peter says we have a more sure way because we see prophesy playing out. It's more sure than us hearing God's voice out the sky. You don't know what God's voice sounds like. We have to match God's voice up with God's word.

Chapter two talks about false prophets if they don't say what God says you know they are false. The Holy spirit will let you know. They will sound good for money. We have to read and spend time with God. If you go other places in the world they can't read their bibles. They pass a round one page of the bible among a hundred people. And we don't want to read. They have to hide and read. What are we doing? As believers we should be roused up. Yeah I know everybody will have their case heard in front of God the judge. I want to hear God say good and faithful servant. I don't want him to ask me what I did with his ministry. Verse 9 God knows how to rescue us because he already has. Verse 10 false prophets insult God all day long. When do we stand up? They are clueless and have no understanding. Going by their sinful nature. We as believers are just as bad . We need to stand together. False prophets don't care what they say how they say it or what they do. I am tired of believers having the balaam spirit which is the spirit of compromise. These false teachers produce no fruit. I guess some believers don't produce any fruit either. Verse 18 They appeal to people who want to do what they want to do. Especially where sex is concerned. Verse 20 We can escape the world through Yahshuah. If we backslide it's worse on us. It's better if we never knew Yahshuah then to go back to the old man. Or old life. It's like giving up everything for nothing. At least if you never knew Yashuah you can't miss him because you never had him.

Chapter three repeats so they can remember. We have to get the word to sink in and get pass the natural man. Verse 3 people who want to believe what they want to believe. The ones that know everything but what they are suppose to. Verse 4 Tells what's going to happen to the unsaved and the heaven and the earth. Verse 8 God's not subject to time. So it doesn't matter when it's going to happen. We just need to know it's going to happen. God's probably taking his time because he wants everybody to be saved. So shouldn't we be out there working. I know the workers are few. Verse 10 people will do what they do so they won't recognize when God comes. When they try to realize it, it will be to late. After the end God will bring down a new heaven and a new earth for us. Sin won't be a issue. There will be no darkness. The only light we need is God. Verse 14 So we should be living from our source the Holy spirit. Peter still spoke nice about Paul even though Paul corrected him. Paul corrected him when he was acting funny towards the Gentiles when the Jewish people were around. Gentile means uncovenant. If it were us we probably would of let Paul have it or say don't judge me. So we don't need to be carried away or follow what people do. What we need to do is follow God. We need to grow in the word and our relationship with Yahshuah. Let's stay in agreement.

John the Apostle was called the revelator. We have to put Messiah over this flesh and walk in the light. We live through him by declaring our righteousness. We have to walk in love and witness Christ .

Chapter one talks about the word always being here. The Holy spirit has been revealed to us so we should get the word out. The most important relationship is father and son. We should be speaking and looking like the same message. It's all about the light. We know what Yahshuah has done. We know we have a sinful nature thanks to Adam but if we confess we are forgiven. Yahshuah paid the price for our sins. He is the mediator for us. Yahshuah sits at the right hand of God in heaven. We know we have Christ if we do what he says. The more we walk in the word the brighter we get. Verse 12 God's believers come from all walks of life. So don't love the world that's perishing. In verse 16 you see the world can give you stuff to. The world's system Pride of life which is self, lust of the eyes you want what you see, lust of the flesh giving your body what it wants. Verse 10 It's the end of time. The anti christs started coming on the scene when Yahshuah did. The devil's such a copy cat or counterfeiter. Verse 20 allow Holy spirit to teach you. Verse 22 Says whoever rejects Yahshuah as the Messiah is the antichrist. This verse says if they don't have the son they don't have the father either. They are one and the same. I made some people mad when I said this. We need to be confident in who we are.

Chapter two verse 8 the son of God appeared to destroy the works of the devil. The works of the devil is sin. Whatever isn't like God is sin. We have to do what is right and love other believers. We shouldn't be surprised to find out the world hates us. The world hated Yahshuah.

Chapter three verse 17 How can a person who has enough not care about his brother who doesn't. That's the samething that was going on in Isaiah's time and it's happening today. The way the world knows that we are Yahshuah disciples because of our love for one another. We show this by what we do not empty words. God knows everything. We need to be loving and kind. We have to test all spirits because they're not all from God. We need to understand God's love and we won't be scared of it. We will respect it. God's love has no flaws so we need to trust it . We never seen God so we love other people to show we love him. We need to follow Yahshuah's lead. Chapter five obeying God isn't hard. Yashuah was washed and cleansed before he shed any blood. He did it first in predestined time. Then John did it. Yahshuah was represented by the lamb in the Old Testament. The Holy spirit verified this because it was there with the father . At least two witnesses were needed. I can't understand how we can accept a human testimony and not God's. The disciples wrote letters to keep the believers encouraged. They wanted them to keep remembering. The law of exchange. Whenever you are in a relationship you give. We are like when I don't get I'm out. We are always about us. God's not like that. When I should know I get to give and it comes back to me. Reaping and sowing. Scriptural error is darkness calling it light. The sin that leads to death is not believing on Yahshuah's name. In the Old Testament cursing --- then you would die.

The second letter of John was to a church that was walking in the truth. The truth is what everything is based on. The church cared for each other and Yahshuah was it's foundation. They continued to teach what Christ taught. If you allow someone to teach wrong teaching and don't stop it your just as bad because you didn't stop it. John wanted to pay them a visit so he could help them stay strong. God wants believers to be like siblings or family. God has one family in two locations.

The third letter John wrote was about doing what you believe even if you are burdened. Messiah's anointing is the spirit of God. How do we go to church? By observation or revelation? When we receive our bag of seeds what do we do with them? We have to have a revelation so we can advance and grow. This letter is a reflection of John's workers. Verse 2 What John commanded them to do. Command means the best possible way to live. Verse 5 live the way God told us to live. Verse 8 supporting other believers in spreading the word. Verse 9 Diotrephes was self righteous. We have some of those in church. All about him. He was misusing his position and power hungry. John was going to deal with him when he got there. It's alright to expose a person because it is the truth. When you expose darkness to light it is dispelled. On the other hand Demetrius another believer looked just like the light. You could see the truth in him. He didn't have to say a word he portrayed the word. He looked like the word. Life speaks for it self. We should strive to look like the word. We need to do what's right in the face of opposition.

Jude was the half brother of Yahshuah. His letter talks about dealing with false teachers. Holding on to your faith. He was defending the church. Jude said there are evil people among us. We need to expose deceivers with there ungodly motives. They twist God's words for their own desires. We need to examine each spirit. Are we honest? What's the quality and quantity of our time? Verse 1 If you are called how do you retire from God? It also talks about us being saved. Staying encouraged and fighting for the cause. Verse 4 false teachers infiltrated the church and changed some of the doctrine. That's the only way the enemy could weaken the church. Prosecution, taking their stuff or killing them didn't do it. The church just got stronger and united even more. The church did positive things with Yahshuah's anointing. The world will do anything to stop God's spirit. The Holy spirit can handle the enemy. A defeated man can't. Since the enemy's time is not complete God can only come through us. God's a judge so he's legal and does everything by his law his bible. The enemy is really pouring it on so I don't finish this book. But I got God's grace, Thank God for his grace. Verse 5 through 8 Are a few examples of what disobedience gets Verse 9 The infiltrators do all kinds of things. Contaminating their bodies, not acknowledging God as God and denying God's power. Verse 9 Micheal and the devil argue over Moses bones. Micheal didn't judge the devil because he's already judged. There is no redemption for angels. People that have no understanding follow the wrong. They can't see what's going on. Verse 12 Talking about the sader. Then it talks about the shepherds which mean pastors that are only thinking of themselves. They don't care about the sheep. These pastors produce no fruit and aren't making disciples. They look nothing like Yahshuah. They are spiritually dead have no light and can't see Yahshuah. There wrong doing out weighs their anointing. We see they are anointed but that doesn't matter compared to the wrong they do. God will take care of them. Enoch spoke of them Verse 16 These people say what you want to hear and then get over on you. These people care about what they want and none of what they want has to do with God. These people divide the truth. These people are about what you can see. Verse 20 Act on what you believe. It's all about your response. God gave us the ability to see what he has done and not to qualify. Verse 20 the verse stained by their sinful lives doing what they do. Satan will get you to focus on you. All satan does is present your life to you. And we fall for it. Satan uses the same tricks and we fall for them. What we need to do is keep our focus on Yahshuah. Remember Yahshuah gave us the mininstry of reconciliation. Remember you have the convert teaching church who can't make disciples. You can't make something you aren't. You have the devil teaching church so you know he's not going to make sense. Then you have the Judas spirit who can make disciples but his focus is money. I know there are still some pastors who are walking in the word but it's few. Yahshuah loved and died for us. I'm almost finished.

Chapter 16
The End

After I go through Revelations I'm going to throw some notes in the back of the book. Revelations is the book of unveiling. The unveiling of Yahshuah. Most people won't touch this book. God says you will be blessed if you read this book. This book allows you to see what's going on right now. God's house is cleaned up first. Before he addresses the world. Revelations shows us what's to happen. It unfolds the story.

Chapter one what John seen. Chapter two and three what John sees now. Chapter four to twenty two what will happen. The Jewish people understood the candlestick was the only light in the temple. Sounds like Yahshuah in us. The candlestick is called the manure. The manure represents Yahshuah. Yahshuah should be the only light in the church. They understood there were no out side lights. We need to live from the risen savior. Remember God has happened God is happening and God will happen all at the same time. The scroll is man's redemption plan. No one but Yahshuah can open the scroll. He completed the assignment and everyone else is sinful. At the ultimate trumpet It will be the end and Yahshuah will be revealed. The book of Revelations is a book of signs. Signs are to show us something. We should follow the signs. Revelations means appearing or coming. Verse 53 God says blessed is the one who reads also the one who hears the words of this prophesy and pays attention to what is written in it. Because the time is near. The time is closer. So if it's such a blessing how come no one's reading it. God always let's you know what's going on. There's no mystery in him. God is strictly by his word. The bible is all the disclosed evidence. You can go through all the evidence when ever you want. It won't be any mistrial. If your not in the spirit how can you be a accredited witness? What are you a witness to? I *am a witness to his testimony which is this bible. The Holy spirit is in me and it was there in predestined time when he died. So I'm a witness. If you weren't there how can you be a creditable witness. God said bear witness with his spirit. When you bear you carry. So I'm carrying his spirit in me. The natural man is a opposition to God. Meaning it's always fighting against him. God says the natural man receives nothing from him. God's a spirit. So how can all these other beliefs be his witnesses? They would be thrown right out of court. They can't say I heard it either. The judge won't accept hearsay in his court either. If you add or take away from the evidence that's like tampering with it. The bible is about the Holy Spirit. You have to be like someone to associate with them. We have the spirit. My opening statement should have been let there be light and my closing statement it is finished. God took the wrap and redeemed his man. Not the body but the spirit. I really don't care what people believe but I was a little tired of believers not knowing what they believe. So I hope this book helps. I tell people if you are confident your belief will get you to heaven then fine. I just want people to think. I know God told me to write this book . The other beliefs always take out what God said or what the person was doing. Which was important especially in the court room. If we don't hear or see anything how can we be a witness.*

God's tired of the clickiness, phoniness and foolishness of his believers. God's ready to bring his New Testament church. When God did a covenant that's a legal contract. Just listen to how God talks like a judge not a religious person. God would seal his contracts with blood. Even the husband and wife sealed their contract with the blood from the hymen. We are so far away from God. All the other beliefs changed the book and tried to weaken the bible. This is so the spirit in the believer wouldn't grow. Only mature believers know what to do with their inheritance or how to fight. When does a person get a inheritance? Yes when someone dies. These other beliefs use our bible as a aid they are steady pulling from our bible but they don't want our spirit. I'm like this don't use my bible.

The bible is a form of government for the people of the one true living God Yahveh. The w was a error that we as believers ran with . There is no w in Hebrew. So it would be Hebrev. God told me not to trip on words. The bible is the basic instructions before leaving earth. The bible is prophetic and for the spirit . I don't care what version of the bible you have the spirit man can understand it once you wake him up. There is a difference, I know because it happened to me. God showed me where he just closed the book on man's day and now it's the spirit's day. We really need to push with that spirit man.

The book of Ezekiel is unfolding now. My book is to enlighten the believer. My book isn't for everybody some believers are happy being lukewarm and just hearing a message. I am passionate about the cause and I want to take out the enemy. It's only going to be a remnant because everybody's not going to be walking in the spirit. We have to be willing to die for the cause. I asked God why didn't the believers use his anointing to get out of predicaments. God told me his anointing was for positiveness and not selfishness. The apostles used the anointing for others such as to heal. The enemy is always trying to prick us off. It's easier for the enemy to get us when we are by ourselves. There is power in numbers. It is harder to penetrate us when there are more of us.

It's a spiritual fight that will be going on till Yahshuah comes back. That's why he says occupy till I come back. He's talking spiritually. I was reading how they placed Peter in a nine feet hole. With his hands over his head. He couldn't change his clothes so you know he defecated on himself. I just want to know when does the believer get roused up. You know people rather torture the believer then kill them. Talk about going through for the cause. The more you walk with God the higher he takes you. The bigger the devils and the harder the fight. I thank God for his grace. God often touches my spirit when he increases me. I have pretty tough skin. Later Peter was crucified on a cross upside down.

Back to Revelations. The seven churches represent seven periods of time in church history. Good will and peace. Which mean Yahshuah and freedom. From the one who is the one who was and the one who is coming. God is everything all at the same time. God sees the end to the beginning. The seven spirits refer to completion. Yahshuah's the first to come back meaning there's more to follow. He has authority over everything and freed us with his blood. Verse 7 Our relationship should be with the son. He's coming the same way he left. He won't be hiding. Yahshuah made everything final. Everything starts with Yahshuah. He was the light in the beginning. Yahshuah has a hold on everything all the time. Only God can do that. God made man so he could fellowship with his man. Yahshuah is a resurrected man representing us in heaven. God's original intent was for us to be like him. Verse 8 Almighty represents God's power. We should share and endure in each other's suffering because of Yahshuah. John was exciled to Patmos. God wouldn't allow him to be killed until his assignment was complete. Some say he was dipped in tar and set on fire but he didn't die . God allowed him to live so he could write this book. John wrote this book which is a testimony about Yahshuah. Testimony meaning evidence based on observation or knowledge. An outward sign a solemn declaration made by a witness under oath in court. Evidence is the confirmation or proof of a testament. Declaration means to make know formally or to announce. Proclaim or publish. Testament is like a will. Testament means deposition. The will isn't read until after someone dies. Deposition is the transfer or control to another. Yahshuah transferred the spirit back to us.

The Holy spirit came on John on the Sabbath. God gave John a revelation. .John was seeing. The gift of seeing and hearing are a little different. God said to me all seers are prophets but not all prophets can see. God blessed me with the ability to see and told me I was the Prophetess in the plans. God blessed me with insight.

The seven gold lampstands are the seven churches Verse 13 points to Yahshuah's humanity stage son of man Then God goes on to describe Yahshuah's transformation state verse 14 Where it says his eyes are like flames of fire. Shows his passion for his church. Yahshuah lights us .We have to let the bible define it self. The seven stars are the seven angels. Who are ascending and descending on Jacob's ladder with our prayers. It talks about God's word coming out of his mouth and how powerful it is. His face is like the sun in all it's brightness at it highest point. The churches ,picture seven periods or stages in church history. Christians are being martyrd all over the world.   The ten days of prosecution consists of ten literal periods of suffering. Persia is Iran,Iraq and Syria. Assyria is Asia and Babylon is The Roman Empire Babylon the great is political and is probably the U.S Verse 17 bowed at Yahshuah's feet.

Yahshuah laid his right hand on John which represents power and authority. Yahshuah is saying he's God when he says he is the first and the last. Yahshuah says he's living was dead and says he lives forever. To those other witnesses when did he die? Yahshuah has the keys.

Keys point to authority. Yahshuah has the keys over heaven and earth. God used the example of the manure because Hebraic people understood it to be the only light in the temple. Like Yahshuah should be the only light in us. We need to stand up and not compromise.

Chapter two the church of Ephesus, God will tell you what you do right then he will let you know what you do wrong. Now this church worked hard at church activities. They didn't tolerate wickedness and tested every spirit. They would go through and not stop. But this church lacked intimacy. They were to busy to have a relationship or spend time with God. God loves us . We work because he loves us. It's all about what God can do through us. We need to work with God not for him. At first the church did all this . They didn't compromise what they were doing. Even though they left God. God tells them to listen to the Holy spirit not themselves. Most church people are about self. If we do it God's way and let the Holy spirit guide us God says we will partake of his life. Stand with him and be victorious.

The church of Smyrna was a church that was poor and suffering. They didn't know what they had. They claimed to be believers but didn't really believe the power. They were double minded. God was encouraging them. The ten days are a period of prosecution. The important thing here is to hear the spirit. The second death is the great white throne of judgement. This is where God tells you why you are going to hell. The first death is when you die in the natural. We should come to church to manifest the body of Christ. Satan trained God's people to be distracted. If we understood God's mind we would make better decisions. We are suppose to be advancing God's kingdom. Waiting on the Lord is not like waiting on the bus. Where you are stopped at the bus stop. When you wait on God you are steadily moving in the things of God.

Now Pergamus was like a mixed marriage. The church being married to the world. Worldly religion. This is where satan has his throne. God's not going to share his throne. Either you want God or you don't. The people were faithful to false teachings. Antpas was killed for the cause. The church had the balaam spirit which is the spirit of compromise. It was a lot of backsliding. Then God tells them what's going to happen, to them. All God has to do is use his word from his mouth to fight. So it's so important to hear the spirit. That's why you have two ears so you can hear twice as much. The hidden manna is Yahshuah. It was hidden until the time because we have a enemy. The manna is natural food where Yahshuah is the bread in the spirit. The white stone represents our acquittal with God. God gives us a new name when he sets us free. We will get the new name when we get to heaven. God is the head we have no say in the matter.

Thyatira First God is talking about who he is . This was a worldly church. They condemned false teaching. But they tolerated the teaching of Jezebel which was opposite of God's teachings. Sexual perversion. What you eat matters even though it doesn't because it is going to come out. They suffered because of what they do. Maybe that's why we see more sexually transmitted diseases. Her children are her followers. Her followers are a product of her. She produced what she is. When God uses his power, they will know it's him. Verse 26 through 28 talks about when we come back and rule and reign with him. During his millenial reign.

Sardis this church was all about appearance. They appeared to be one way but were spiritually dead. God wants them to stop compromising because he doesn't want to condemn them. Or find them guilty when he calls them up. Verse 5 talks about erasing names in the book of life. Which tells me that everybody's name is in the book of life until they come to the age of accountability. Where you can make a decision.

The church of Philadelphia Verse 7 is Isaiah twenty two verse twenty two this church was faithful and had access to God. They spread the gospel. They were the city of God. I guess that's how they coined the name the city of brotherly love. Verse 9 putting satan under our feet. Our strength is in Yahshuah .God will protect us during the tribulation. So we have to occupy until he comes back. Verse 12 If we do what God says we will be victorious. We are strong in God. We are the temple for the Holy spirit. We have God's name. In the Old testament God told Aaron to put his name on the people. Do we know what God's name represents? There will be a new heaven and earth and Yahshuah will have a new name. It is important to hear and it is important how you hear.

The church of Laodicea was prosperous. They made eye ointment. They were in between. Worldly. They reaped the benefits and forgot the focus. You couldn't tell if they believed or not. God's telling them to have energy when they are corrected and stop losing spirit when they are corrected. Going from spirit to natural. They needed to get the spirit in their heart so they would know how to be. Verse 20 We need to recognize the harvest which is Yahshuah. Then walk in it. All about overcoming. God demands enthusiasm. Total commitment. God wants us to be his people. To be his people we have to cooperate with him. Satan will use every relationship to nullify or cancel us out and mutilate us. Religion binds people up and doesn't allow them to enter God's rest.

Chapter four Trumpet means awakening. We better wake up. Verse 2 Holy spirit is the power of God. The rainbow seals a covenant just like God made with Noah. Everything God has is like precious jewels. Verse 4 The twenty four thrones represent the twelve tribes and the twelve disciples. Verse 5 shows power . Seven spirits of God shows completion and perfection. Verse 6 The four living creatures represent the gospels. Verse 7 The lion represents Yahshuah being the king. The bull represents servitude, because oxen normally work. A human for humanity and a eagle for diety. Everything is done in predestined time. That's why things are around the throne in this. Wings represent covering and six is man's number. We should always be praising God. Verse 8 Holy holy holy is the Lord Almighty all power who was who is and who is coming. God is constantly revealing himself. Verse 9 Is how God wants us to look at him. With power, glory and honor. Verse 11 God created everything from nothing.

Chapter five the scroll is man's redemption. The right hand means authority. Yahshuah was the only one that could open the scroll. Everyone else was sinful and under the curse. God redeemed man and got Adam's lease back. Verse 12 Lion from tribe of Judah. Kings came from Judah. The root of David has won the victory. Root meaning David came from him. Something grows from a root first. Most believers can't grow because they were cut from their Hebraic roots. Yahshuah will sit on the throne. Verse 6 The lamb represents Yahshuah in predestined time. Seven horns means he is head of all. Seven eyes means he sees all. And seven spirits means he has all power. Seven represents completion. The four living creatures are the gospels. Verse 8 The lamb is Yahshuah , the scroll is man's seven step redemption plan. The twenty four leaders are the twelve tribes and the twelve apostles. The incense is for death of the overcomers. Everything is complete and finished. Verse 9 Tells the story how he completed and united all his people. Verse 11 All creation will know because everything can hear. The story being told again. The lamb deserves to receive power wealth strength honor glory and praise. Verse 4 All of God's creation in agreement and order.

Chapter six seals mark a document as authentic. Prepare for earthquakes, frantic, chaotic, no love, panic of the four seals more intense as each seal is opened. People after what you have a piece of bread or a cup of water. Verse 1 Catholism world church Verse 3 communism will take peace out of the world Verse 5 capitalism U.S wine and oil is the influence of the spirit. Verse 7 socialism muslims Verse 9 martyrds people killed for the cause Verse 11 overcomers had to wait for everyone else before the end Verse 12 end time Signs are in place to show us something the blood moons we had four in a row two on Passover and two on tabernacles. Representing Yahshuah's death and him being together with us. God gave us signs and seasons to tell us something. We better pay attention to God's calender. All this is definitely end time stuff. If we aren't connected to God we will be shook with the world. The church is gone before the tribulation period. God wants to spare us from going through it. Then Yahveh is going to deal with his bride Israel. It's going to be real bad. Where people will want to die but can't and wishing the rocks will fall on them. God's going to close up heaven so their prayers won't be heard. God's adjourning the court. God will shorten the period so his people can endure but you will still have people that won't acknowledge God. The day of the Lord is when God passes his sentence.

Chapter seven the four corners represent north, south, east, and west. God sealed his people meaning his word is in their minds. The church is gone so the light is gone so there is nothing but darkness. God is going to be calling all his Hebraic people from all corners of the earth. The 144,000 are from the twelve tribes and they will evangelize Israel. They are virgins meaning they weren't corrupted by the world. The prime minister from Denmark is starting to call them back. They found a tribe in Africa linked to Aaron through DNA. Yes they are black. There are black Jewish people. Verse 9 These people are the church , Yahshuah's bride. We will be in heaven then we will come back with Yahshuah for his one thousand year reign. Palm branches represent victory. Verse 11 Everyone will bow and acknowledge the king. Verse 13 John or the prophets didn't know the church they saw right pass the church to Israel. Yahshuah grafted the church in. Yahshuah wanted all men to be saved. Then it talks about the believers that stood and knew they were covered by the blood. Yahshuah will take care of them fully and nothing will ever hurt them again.

Chapter eight After the Great tribulation there will be silence in heaven for half an hour. God adjourned the court now he's going to pronounce the sentence. You know it must be loud in heaven and like a party praising God. And we don't want to open our mouths in church. Now this chapter speaks of judgement and the Great Tribulation. The prayers of all God's people that have died come up to God. Now God's ready to pass judgement on the world. Verse 2 On the Atlas a third of the continents equals what will be burned up during the Great Tribulation. Each trumpet gets worse then the previous one. Verse 13 A eagle flying over head is a symbol of God's judgement.

Chapter nine The beasts political and religious power. Spirit of Islam rising. The Pit of hell opened. The enemy has a well ranked army. They are under rule of the god of this world. Verse 11 fallen angels released verse 16 fallen angels in people over people areas and nations. Euprates river is Iraq ,Syria and Red China? Verse 16 war in the middle east verse 20 people still didn't want to change the way they think. They still did what they wanted and still didn't want to come to God. Verse 23 people were still influenced by the world ,murder, sinning sexually, practicing witchcraft and sorcery. Sorcery means pharmaceutical in Greek. Which you can link to drugs and drug addiction. If believers just dig a little bit they would ground themselves where they won't waiver.

Chapter ten verse 1 Authority of Yahshuah Verse 2 man's lease. His right foot on the sea and his left foot on land shows his authority over everything . Lion represents king Seven always represents completion Verse 7 Yahshuah's assignment is complete. Verse 9 The scroll John ate was the word of God. God's word through study and application. Some parts of God's word are sweet where other parts are bitter. A angel told John to speak what was revealed.

Chapter eleven spiritual life of Israel. This is when the peace treaty is made. Israel will go back to doing sacrifices since they don't believe Yahshuah came. The arrangement will be reneged. Israel will be mad. They will trample Jerusalem for forty two months. God's two witnesses will be speaking with God's power. They will speak 1260 days. I believe the two witnesses will be Elijah and Enoch. Neither one of then died. Elijah was a prophet and Enoch instituted writing. So Moses could write the law. Alot of people thought one of the witnesses might be Moses. Maybe that's why the devil argued with Michael over the bones of Moses. You know the devil is on top of everything God says. Elijah and Enoch represented the law and the prophets. God allowed the Holy spirit to flow through these witnesses until there assignment was complete. Their testimony was Yahshuah. The beast that was fueled by the devil killed the two witnesses. The beast was a alliance of nations that had power. The witnesses, dead bodies laid in the street where Yahshuah was crucified. The people wouldn't allow the witnesses to be buried. The people were happy the prophets were dead. What they did to these two prophets could be called gross iniquity. They say the whole world will see. The internet made that possible. After three and a half days the Holy spirit entered the witnesses. The people were scared. God called the two witnesses up to heaven. Verse 15 Everything put under Yahshuah's feet. Verse 17 Us being thankful and God judging and sentencing the world. Verse 19 God opened heaven after judgement. The ark of the covenant a portable chest that had the ten commandments in it which represents Yahshuah were inside the temple.

Chapter twelve Lucifer use to be the light bearer next to the throne. No wonder the devil is called the angel of light. God gives us freewill the power of choice. Lucifer had the ability to choose. The story of satan and how God protected Yahshuah. Satan always makes war and is always going after the seed. Satan doesn't want anything to grow and he knows how God operates. Verse 10 All of heaven knows Yahshuah has authority. The accuser of the brotheren is satan. The people overcame by the blood of Yahshuah, the testimony and not loving their lives to much that they would not lay it down. The devil knows he has little time so he wants to devour the world. Verse 13 The woman is Israel. The ones that keep the testimony of Yahshuah are the believers. Satan always goes after the seed. Satan is at war with the seed in you. Doesn't want you to use or grow your seed which will take you to your future. Your seed came from God. God gives a body to every seed. The enemy came to kill, steal and destroy. If you reject the seed you reject your future. If you don't grow your seed you look like a person with no confidence. Your not happy or joyful. We need to trust in the system and look like people that trust God. We need to ponder on God's word and see what he is saying. Your seed is growing before you see anything. What we know God does something with everything. How much confidence do you have in your seed? God gave us a lifestyle. We need to show righteousness as a harvest in our lives.

Chapter thirteen New World Order. The ten horns may be the Soviet Union, Leopard more likely Germany, Bear probably Russia and the Lion Great Britain. They say the lion has a big mouth because English is the Global language. This union is fueled by satan. They are physically strong. Forty two months in authority the beast rages war on the world. Everyone worshipped the beast whose name isn't in the book of life. Verse 8 Yahshuah did the work. No human effort before the foundation of the world. Before the world was created or man exsisted the lamb did everything. Verse 11 the unholy trinity The antichrist, the false prophet and the devil. The devil has power and can do things. Not like God does. The devil deceived and made the people get It's mark. People couldn't buy or trade without it. Verse 18 We will have to have the Holy spirit and understand and know God to be able to see.

Chapter fourteen The original tribes with Yahshuah. Verse 4 They were undefiled. Verse 6 people on earth that will be judged. Verse 8 The fall of the world church. Drink the wine refers to the influence the world church had on the earth. The beast statue. Statue is something that is worshipped the statue probably is money. The alliance of these nations worshipped this statue. God's going to punish the beast and it's followers with hell fire. God gave his people endurance. Verse 13 The people who have died believing are blessed because we have Yahshuah. Yahushuah gave us eternal life. Entering into God's rest which is the Holy spirit. Shows Yahshuah on the throne. Verse 15 God gathering up the believers. Then another angel gathered up the people that were going to hell. Stadia is a survey measure for distance.

Chapter fifthteen Signs shows us things. Signs are to shows us things that we should see. Now these are the plagues. The final expression of God's wrath . The believers in Israel.

Whoever came sung unto the Lord. We're suppose to profess who he is and what he's done. Verse 5 testimony and way made in heaven. God's throne symbolizes grace and mercy. The temple was shut until all the judgements were done. All the sentences were pronounced.

Chapter sixteen the seven bowls. The bowls seem similar to what the Eyptians got. Verse 5 We need to examine our relationship with God. Verse 8 God is a true and fair Judge. Even going through with people who didn't want to believe like Pharaoh. Verse 12 Iraq and Syria road for the kings of the east. The authority of the east. MIDDLE EAST. The evil spirits were demons so the serpent, beast and false prophet were demon possessed. These demons could do miracles. They went around and recruited for their army. Verse 15 We need to be alert and don't take Yahshuah the Holy spirit for granted. We are supposed to be clothed with God. The natural man is naked and always trying to clothe himself with the things of the world. The kings gathered at Armagedden(another Hebrew word.)for the last war. Then creation took a hit from a earth quake . The most powerful one ever. Jerusalem split in three like when Israel split in the old Testament. Israel- Judah –Aram Everything's falling and experiencing God's wrath.

Chapter seventeen the world church Some of the churches today are setting the stage for the world church. This church is the complete opposite from the church in Acts. Verse 7 new world order. The world system, the world church is the church in Rome. Which the man of perdition will go south on them. Which is the false prophet. Like Muhummad went south on the church in Rome. Everybody will come against Israel and that is when Yahshuah will put his feet on the ground.

Chapter eighteen talks about the fall of the political system. The world fell because of the demonic influence and the light of the church was gone. Verse 4 God's constantly telling the people to come out of the world so they won't be judged with the world. God uses the femine personification because in the natural a woman is physically weaker then a man. Verse 11 crash of the whole system. Never to rise again . Everything destroyed because of the enemy's influence.

Chapter nineteen Yahshuah's marriage to the church in heaven then we come back and reign with Yahshuah for a thousand years. Which is the millenium. The devil is chained up for the thousand years. The false prophet and anti Christ are in hell. People will be born and there will be peace and little sickness on earth. When the enemy is unchained he will get followers from the people on earth. How do you know someone loves you if they can't choose to love you? Verse 4 The tribes, Apostles and the creature that represent the gospels worship and praise God. Verse 6 through 8 church and Yahshuah in heaven. The church has the marriage to Yahshuah in heaven and the wedding reception on earth. The purpose of prophesy is to tell about Yahshuah. Verse 11 white horse faithful and true is Yahshuah. Yahshuah is passionate and victorious. Verse 13 Yahshuah's name is the word of God and he wears his shed blood. Yahshuah defeats his enemy with his word. Yahshuah was on earth to bring salvation . He defeated the devil with his word. It is written. On his thighs his name was written king of kings and Lord of Lords. The false prophet and the antichrist received hell fire. All of their followers God allowed the birds to eat their flesh.

Chapter twenty After the one thousand years satan was released. Verse 4 believers had to get their heads cut off because they wouldn't take the mark of the beast. Or denounce Yahshuah or the word. Thanks to the internet we see believers getting their heads cut off around the world. Everyone that was dead ruled with Yahshuah during the millennium. The people who died during the millennium stayed dead until it was over. Verse 8 satan is released and gathers up a army. Gog and magog which I believe may be Russia. Who ever it is they have a real big army. Russia may link up with China. God sent down fire to consume them all. Verse 11 White throne judgement Is where God is telling you why you are going to hell. You will be raised from the dead put back in your body and stand before the judge. Books were open telling me there is more then one book. If you are a man God is going to see how you were as a father, husband, son, worker, how you treated people etc. The same for the women. If your name is not in the book of life you are thrown into the lake of fire.

Chapter 21 God gives a new heaven and earth because sin isn't a issue anymore. Then God sent down a new holy Jerusalem his bride. God is reconciled back to his people. There will be no need to cry. There is no need for the sun because God is the only light we need.

There is no more darkness. God made everything and everything is influenced by him again. God is the beginning and the end. Whoever overcomes will receive these things. God will be our God and everyone else will receive the lake of fire. Now God talks about the new Jerusalem which is perfect. At it's gates are the names of the twelve tribes. There was no physical temple because the spirit of God and the lamb are the temple. Our housing. The gates stay open all day because there is no enemy. Everything that was taken from the first holy city will be given back. Once something is placed in the sea you don't see it anymore. We need to walk in the truth, God's word. The word is light and we should focus on it. The word should be lit up in my life. Jerusalem is glorious meaning it is a full expression of God. Yahshuah wanted us to see through John's eyes of the future so we would avoid the end. There is no sin in the new heaven and the new earth. Only the names that are written in the book of life will enter into the kingdom. Meaning having God's life.

Chapter twenty two water of life is the Holy spirit . God always wants to give us life. Now we see one tree the tree of life. Unguarded. No sin. We get to constantly choose life. The tree produced fruit for the twelve nations representing the twelve tribes and the twelve Apostles. There is only one set of twelve here showing unity. God brought the Jewish and Gentile together. Meaning his covenant people and the people he grafted in. The leaves on the tree of life have healing properties in them. God took care of everything. We will see the Lord's face and worship God. We will be his people and he will be our God. The Lord is coming to fill the unfulfilled in his bible. The time is closer then we think. Verse 12 Everyone will get there just rewards. Verse 14 Is about repenting. God always wants us to change our direction. God doesn't want anyone to perish. He wants all of us to partake of his finished work. But we have a right to choose. He's not going to make us. God doesn't want robots. Verse 16 Yahshuah sent his testimony , his story to the churches through a angel. So how come no one tells the story. We have gotten so far away from the story. Yahshuah says he is the root of David. Meaning David came from him. Everything grows from the root. Yahshuah's a descendant of David through his humanity side. He says he is the bright morning star. Which a star guides you. He's our guide and light. Verse 17 It is important that we hear. Are we hearing? Did we hear the message? It is not enough to say we are hungry , thirsty and want the gift. If we don't hear the message or know how to get it. Verse 18 God wants everyone to hear this prophesy about Yahshuah.

Now God says who adds to this book he will strike him with the plaques in this book. This is for all you religious folk that felt they had to add to God's bible. The plaques happen through the Great Tribulation. So that means if you add to this book and you are living your going through the Great Tribulation. The others who added to God's book and died maybe going through the plaques in hell. Verse 19 Now God says anyone that takes away from his word ,he will take away their portion of the tree of life. Everything pertaining to life is on that tree. So things may be taken from your life. Yahshuah's testimony. He's coming soon. At the end of Revelations it will be another Eden.

It's something how God used things in the garden to tell a story. Then he used the court room to tell it another way. God's sure amazing. John was inspired by God to see revelations and through his eyes we were able to see what God wanted us to. Just as God inspired me to allow you to see through my spiritual eyes the accredited witness

CHAPTER 17
FOOTNOTES

Tidbits

I thought you should know

The remnant will be people walking in the spirit

Elect are God's chosen

Tashuva is God's New Year

Hidden manna is word of God in the natural

Culture is the way you live

Doctrine is teaching

Dress is cultural

God supercedes culture

Jews and kings come from the tribe of Judah

All God's light is suppose to shine so don't be conformed to the world

Yashuah lighted the way so we wouldn't walk in darkness

What is darkness? Us looking like the world. When we don't do God's will. When we function under the law instead of Grace. You think God gave us the light so we would *walk in darkness. Everything Yahshuah did was in our face. We are prisoners of world culture. The enemy came in God's house and changed his people.*

If you seek Yahshuah from man when do you ever get a revelation of who Yahshuah is. Man has different views.

The early church met where Messiah will return. We gather where Messiah won't go. What has invaded our mind? The first thing the enemy attacks is the mind. The spirit is suppose to represent the church.

The shepherd protects the relationship. A shepherd lays down his life for the sheep. He is suppose to establish them in love and support. Us being for each other.

What king dominates your temple?

Hebraic Roots, God's moving End times

1948 prophesy Israel became a nation in one day. The people are being called back from all over the world. Prior to 1947 Israel wasn't a nation. Four blood moons a tetrarch. Two on Passover two on tabernacles. The beginning and end. No temple, Rome destroyed the temple. Yashuah prophesied about the temple being destroyed. Seventy years after Yahshuah said it, it was destroyed. Israel was dispersed. They are being called back home. They have everything but the temple. They may even have the red heifer.

The adamant spirit infiltrated little by little into the church. That's why we have what we have in church. You see what our nation has given us

Pastors aren't seeking God so they won't prosper.

Flesh was under the curse. Yahshuah was before the law so he wasn't under any curse.

What's your vision? God said people perish if they don't have a vision. Vision allows you to see. People without vision are naked. It's who you know not what you know. You study God's word to know. We as believers need to start gaining ground which is the soul.

Why don't we live like we are favored?

Enemy's trying to stop reflection of Yahshuah. What's influencing you?

The soul has no color when you make it about color you missed God.

God doesn't want us divided

We can't change people. People change when they have a encounter with God.

The Sabbath was put in place so we understand God's rest.

If my life is so good why didn't God ask for a exchange instead of laying his life down. Satan fabricated this life and deceived us into believing we have something.

We associate more with sin then righteousness.

You can't teach someone about somebody you don't know

Trumpet means a coronation of a king. Man came into earth coronated as a king. What satan took from Adam, God got it back.

Yom Terah-Feast of trumpets, Yon Kippur-day of Atonement, Sukkot-feast of Tabernacles, Hanukkah –feast of lights

Why not meet with God at his appointed times

The Roman church changed Sabbath to Sunday because of a verse in the bible where they collected money from a church on a Sunday.

Battering ram-Was a war machine .I think Israel got this idea from the Trojan horse. Showing us we need to know what's going on in the world.

Apocalyptic-Revelation

The church has no voice . We are called the angelicans. If we showed the world wisdom they would have direction. The world looks to the Pope.

If the church lies about Yahshuah's birthday maybe the world thinks we are lying about his exsistence.

God never wanted his people to be pagan. Hebrew culture believes death is better then life.

Baptize means to emerse. Believing qualifies you to be baptized. It's us identifying with Christ .When Phillip baptized the Eunich. It didn't say he sprinkled water on him.

I'm a evangelist called by God. So I'm of the way charged up and on fire. My father owns the electric company so I better be charged up.

Shikinah cloud-God's glory.

The Quran expresses crucifixon as the punishment permitted for enemies of Islam. Chapter 9 of the Quran instructs muslims to fight Christians and Jews. The prophet who the muslim people exalt imposed these rules and owned slaves. We know the Quran was translated. The word Christian didn't come about until Yahuah was dead a hundred years and he never called himself a Christian. He said he was of the way. Every time you see someone going to the altar they were doing a sacrifice. So how do you atone for sin without a sacrifice?

The Holy spirit is like our immune system in the spirit world. We need to get proper rest, partake in God's finish work, Get proper water and food which is God's word. Our immune system becomes weak without proper nourishment. Religion is like a temporary fix. Like medicine. Believers need to wake up in the spirit.

We need to build up our spirit man. When God says occupy until I come back. He's talking about in the spirit. We are that one new man holding back the enemy. Which are spiritual enemies.

The mission should be our focus in church not our stuff.

Yahshuah never said people would love us but we are always looking for someone to love us.

If I am in a relationship with the master why don't I understand his message. We think we really have to perform and settle into culture. This western culture tells me we need to meet our needs and not walk in this finished work. When your in a relationship you don't think about you. We are who we are because of Christ. How do we buy into the world's system and think it will really work. Racism, Classism, sexism age etc. We don't even know these people but we think this system will work.

You think just because you have a good job ,money and a house you have a successful life.

Satan blinded us from the message of our father spiritually.

God gave us the blessing which is a empowerment to succeed. To get true wealth which isn't just money.

God's calendar is based on the moon.

This world made man a junkie. Man craves and lusts after the things in this world. We are addicts looking for the next high. Instead of being in God's presence.

The Lord doesn't take sides you have to come on his side.

The world is miserable and looks for another spirit to get high like alcohol or drugs.

End times beginning of end days when Yahshuah came. Earth is groaning, Romans chapter eight waiting for us to manifest who we are.

Signs false prophets, wars, famines, earthquakes, tribulations, The Elements God created are out of order because men sinned.

Yahshuah didn't use power for himself. He developed a system to help the weak. No man left behind came from God not the military. If you don't prepare for enemy he is at the door.

You have a preacher so you can hear something in the spirit.

Scavengers of the sea are shrimp, crabs, and lobsters, which are like mice, roaches,and rats in a house.

Romans sent Christians to the lions den for sport. It was just like going to a boxing match.

Issac dug the well of his father. Meaning he did what his father did. Jewish boys ask questions. God talked to them.

Black Jews were traced through the line of Aaron through DNA. Yahshuah was middle eastern. He has no color in the bible. You have to look at the land to tell the color of the people.

A rainbow was a everlasting covenant , that God wouldn't destroy the whole earth by water again. Only way to get out of a covenant is to die. God is merciful he gave us a new one.

Social media waters down friendship. Your brother is suppose to go through your trial with you.

Title is what you do not who you are.

Religion confined to four walls. Holy spirit has no limits.

Believer is a accredited witness

Exclusia called out to carry will and plan of God.

When you wrestle with the devil you suppress your flesh and watch your words mind and emotional state

Loves not a emotion it's a decision. Issac decided to marry his wife then he loved her.

Praying for other people is based on what we believe. How do you see yourself?.

God is Christ centered not man centered. The devil gets you focused on you.

Your first ministry is a personal relationship with God. Your second ministry is wife and kids. The third is the operating function in the church family and the fourth is the job and the community.

Fallen world is under attack.

System for success word determines what I say not my situation. My life lines up with what I say. Thoughts control the body. Crusades killed people not people of the way. God didn't tell them to do it. Just because people say they are believers doesn't mean they are.

Hashem (The Name) Yahshuah fulfilled over two hundred prophecies in the bible.

God brought Israel out like a army. Every soldier is trained. Word is our weapon. We made church like a social gathering.

Cold is a sinner. A saint can't be cold. If you are luke warm we don't know what you are, when you are hot you give everything and are passionate. Cold love is a end time move.

God's goodness leads to repentance

Law established on Mt Sinai 3000 died, under the law you die. God gave us grace and took the penalty.

Why do we say we know you can do it, God but will you do it for me?

Forty is the number of preparation. Moses had forty days on the mountain. Yahshuah had forty days in the wilderness.

Church is about intimacy. Communion came from the body. We received the blood and we received the blessing . It's about us being together. We need to look at scriptures as love letters to us.

We should acknowledge events on God's calendar.

We have words of life if we don't tell anyone these words they die with us.

America we are powerful and spiritually blind like Samson. Sansom took what God gave him for granted like us.

Agobbi is sacrificial love

Mesopotamia was Iraq. Abraham was called out of there and introduced to the one true living God. Abraham knew God by God Almighty his power. Whatever God showed

Abraham it impacted his life. Abraham was worshipping the sun god when the true God called him out. I explained this in my book.

Come out of the old man . The old man will make you poor. We are so busy trying to make a living we can't make a living.

We want God to move but we won't read God's word. God already moved.

God will go to hell for you but he doesn't abide there.

When you receive Christ you already became what you are.

The World did a number on us.

God's about the fight. Angels hearken to God's command. The word. God wants us to establish the kingdom

Why do we labor to be rich. We learn to live from a perverse world.

Some end time signs growth of knowledge, gospel out, financial collapse, moral decline, spiritualism, pervasive teaching, growing band of perverse teachings, New world order

Some of best men in church are women

Me being black doesn't supercede kingdom of heaven

Satan prevents light from shining by attacking your mind

Even though you don't feel anything doesn't mean God isn't doing anything

Faith can be rocked but not love. Religion says you have to qualify. Just like you can love someone without any money or on drugs God loves you unconditionally.

Silence isn't golden when It's time to talk especially during a trial.

Religion produces rituals, traditions and separation

Relationship produces intimacy

The older you are the more time satan had to work on you. A little child just left heaven so he knows exactly who he is.

Yahshuah is male Christ is neither

David put tears in a bottle. God recorded your tears in his book. You had not one wasted tear. God cares and he heard everytime you cried.

The leper took from Yahshuah and was restored to original state.

Yahshuah saw joy beyond the cross

Millienium enjoying earth in it's fullness

God worked his way back in the earth through a man. If every man sinned what man is qualified? What we perceive is what we think.

Seven words from the cross

Father forgive them for they don't know what they do

Assurely I say to you today you will be with me in paradise

Woman behold your son, behold your mother

Eli eli lama Sahachtham my God my God why have you forsaken me

I thirst, the spirit thirst to win spiritual battle over evil and the natural body thirsted for water

It is finished, it is complete

Father into your hands I commend my spirit. The only way you get good at something is if you practice. You go to church to work the family business.

Spiritual blessings in Christ(Ephesians)

He Blessed us in the heavenly realms with every spiritual blessing in Christ

He chose us in him before the creation of the world

Predestined us

Glory and grace freely given to us

Forgiveness of sins in accordance with riches of God's grace that he lavished on us with all wisdom and understanding

Made known mystery of his will

Judaizers=Legalistic gospels-rejects God's grace and insists on works of righteousness

Food for thought love kept Yahshuah on the cross

Illumination the acts of being enlightened with the truths of God's word

Lazy hands makes you poor

Moses---------------------Prophets-------------------------= Yahshuah

Torah-------------------dreams, visions-------------------= Torah., finished

The fix is in one world government, Top countries meeting masses are distracted, setting world up for man of sin, shake the earth

Fat Christian is faithful, available and teachable

God's new year celebrates when man was created

World's connection to God is church

Doctrines of Christ-Repentance, Faith towards God, Baptisms, Laying of hands, Resurrection, Eternal judgement

Cycles of blessings-double portion, Abundance, No lack, favor, restoration, God's presence

I will see the goodness of the Lord in the land of the living

God- agreements, triology,direction sun and moon, grace, man, completion, eternity, new beginning, prosperity,double blessing ,hand service

Trumpet awakenings- discipleship, teaching, laying on of hands, creativity, God's presence

If we live out God's word nothing can come but favor

Satan can touch anything in this world

All hard work brings a profit but more talk leads to poverty

Church people forever learning never coming to the knowledge of the truth

Our trumpet word of God,watch men are the five fold ministry. Stronghold are thoughts that build up in my mind and start to dictate to me

Isaiah fifty nine verse 12 through 17 government of vengeance not putting up with anything

God speaks to creation not gender. If your moved by what you see you are captured by the enemy. Life happens so you keep moving until you hear something else. God won't rain down money he's not a counterfeiter but he will rain down a idea.

If you are in the pursuit of God you can't be brought down. Don't jump ahead. When a nation is vulnerable and it doesn't apply kingdom principles it falls. If we don't apply kingdom principles we will fall with it. Never seek something on the way to something else.

We are responsible for God's atmosphere.

If you don't obey God's word It's going to be real hard to hear in the spirit. If you don't get understanding you will suffer all the way to heaven.

When life hits you what are you going to do? Champions know what to do. Satan has more confidence in deceiving you then you serving God.

Honey from a rock is every hard thing in our life sweet.

We want rights but we don't want to give rights

When you think something your body doesn't know it isn't happening. Change your mood by what you hear.

A Almond tree is a sign of diligence to enter into God's work by laying down self effort

The Faith book which is the bible is the face if God

Greek culture tried to stamp out Yahshuah

Prayer- communication with God

Yahshuah sweat drips of blood in the garden to redeem the land. Remember Adam sweated from his brow over the land because it didn't yield to him. Yahshuah redeemed the land. So it would yield to us.

Israel is Caanan land. Our land is living in Messiah

The Body doesn't change the mind does.

I Never seen a soldier look for comfort in a war.

You think it's bad now when the hedge comes down it's going to be a lot worse.

Tabernacles is the engathering of the nations.

We value more of what we can do then what God's done

We value our position over God's position. We think the key to receiving is based on what we can do.

Time doesn't make a person improve it's the person.

When they say father they are talking about father, grandfather, greatgrandfather, generations

Sojourners are just passing through

God sees the whole parade

Isis is burying babies alive, and cutting teenagers in half because they wouldn't denounce Yahshuah. It's nothing new under the sun. People sacrificed their chidren to the false god Molech and Tammuz was a false god who was a transvestite. Believers walk miles to a church with no roof and we won't even drive.

The western culture thinks God is suppose to elevate our lives like the rich and famous when we are suppose to bring the kingdom

Yahshuah defeated death, hell and the grave

Grace is unexplainable and not of human origin

A veil covers your sight

We need to do everything like Yahshuah is with us

A unsaved love one sees you better than you see you. Flesh can only be moved by tradgedy

What does a blessed person look like? Happy, fortunate and prosperous

Dead sea scrolls are five hundred scrolls and fragment of scrolls which were found in 1947 in eleven caves. This is before Israel became a nation. The whole scroll of Isaiah is intact. Wonder why?

Immanuel means God with us. There are many types of muslims but they talk about us having different versions of the bible.

Your secret place is your heart.

First Corinthians chapter ten verse 13 No temptation has ever taken you except what is common to man meaning that what happens to you can happen to anybody. Because we are all in this world. God doesn't tempt anybody. Why would he need to? He knows what's going to happen. Everything happens because this world is fallen. Satan's the one who does the tempting.

1967- Was a six day war miracles happened Israel was so worried about being a nation they stopped fighting even though God wanted them to keep fighting. How much do we fight for the kingdom? The Enemy is advancing . We don't need to be impacted by the economy. God's not subject to man's economy.

Simon the Zealot one of Yahshuah's disciples was a descendant of Ham. Ham was Noah's son that came out of the lineage of Adam's son Seth not Cain. Simon the Zealot was probably a man of color even though color means nothing to God.

Some martyrds for the cause

Antipas - was roasted alive in a hallow life size bull with a bonfire under its belly because he refused to denounce the faith.

Isaiah - sawed in half long ways

Simon sawed asunder (in little pieces)

Mark - rope placed around his neck and dragged in the streets

Simon Peter - crucified upside down on a cross

Andrew - crucified on a x shaped cross

James - first of the twelve Apostles to be put to death

Bartholomew - flagged and crucified upside down

Thomas - killed in India

Zachariah - killed on the side of the altar

Paul - was beheaded

Many Christians were fed to the lions, or set on fire, dipped in tar, skinned, dragged, sawed in half, beat, whipped with a cat's tail. The Whip was a whip that had glass and metal pieces so when it hit you it would rip skin out of your back.

Chapter 18
Legally speaking

Testimony - Evidence based on knowledge or observation(through the Holy spirit) A truthful statement made in court

Testament - Is a deposition of a will to be released after a person dies, Two parts of the bible

Declaration - To make know formally, To affirm to be true

Litigator - A lawyer who argues a case

Accredited - Credentials from God A written epistle

Witness - person who furnishes proof

Eyewitness - seen first hand like the Apostles

Verdict - finding of the decision

Weight and scales - being just and fair

Precept - A rule for moral conduct

Statues - Way of God or person on the throne, A law inacted by a legislative body

Ordinances - Charges against

Counsel - Advisors

Oath - promise to tell the truth, hand on the bible

Countersuit - To respond to a lawsuit against some one

Arraignment - To call to account before a criminal court to hear and answer the charge made against him or her

Dismissal - A official notice to discharge

Argument – Debate A discussion where the parties disagree

Jury - A body of persons selected to decide a verdict in a legal case.

Trial - A proceeding in which opposing parties in a dispute present evidence and make arguments on the application of the law before a judge or a jury.

Brobono - for free

Conspiracy - an agreement to perform together an illegal or wrongful act.

Public defender - An attorney employed by the government to represent needy defendants in criminal cases

District Attorney - (Holy spirit) A public officer who prosecutes cases especially criminal cases on behalf of a state.

Evidence - proof, verification

Preliminary - preparing for the main matter

Affirm - Agree with or set of things helpful in forming a conclusion or judgement

Counterfeit - Illusion , magic, trick

Disclose - Allow to be seen, make known

Mistrial - A trial rendered invalid through an error in the proceeding

Cross examination - The examination of a witness to check their acredibility

Prosecution - *the conduct of legal proceeding against someone in respect of a criminal charge*

Conscience - *The way we think*

Virtue - *What you stand for*

Objective - *A thing aimed at, Not influenced by a personal feeling I was told I was a Extremist wouldn't you want the best possible defense if you were on trial.*

Accuse - *Charge with a offense or crime that you don't know is true*

Expose - *make , visible, true*

Plead the fifth-Grace - *protects a person from being a witness against himself*

Contempt of court - *The offense of being disobedient or disrespectful to a court of law*

Condemned - *Guilty*

Sworn statement or Testimony - *Is a document that recites facts appropriate to a legal proceeding the bible*

Approach the bench - *Satan approach God's bench in Job so you know Satan has a entrance to God*

Sabbath - *Rest, Before the law understanding God's finished work. A gift to us from God*

Discovery - *pretrial disclosure of evidence*

Judgement - *A sentence for your actions can be either good or bad*

Sentence - *could be either good or bad, The assigned punishment to a defendant found guilty in a court of law.*

Bailiff - *The angel are officials assigned in court Opening statement let there be light and closing statement it is finished*

Just cause - Why, A reasonable and lawful ground of action

Collateral - Something pledged as security for repayment of a loan to be forfeited in the event of a default.

Bear witness - Providing the evidence which is the Holy spirit. The holy spirit was there. Bear means to carry and we carry the Holy spirit in us.

Judge - A public official appointed to decide cases in a court of law

Decrees - A official order issued by a legal authority

Order - An authoritative command, direction, or instruction

Acquitted - made not guilty

Supeona - A summons to come to court

Judgement seat of Christ - Rewards for believers what we did with Yahshuah's ministry

White Throne Judgement - Why you are going to hell

Mercy - forgiveness

Court - Place where justice is administrated

God says in Isaiah the jury is the heavenlies and he's summoning the earth.

Minister means service and it starts at home. Jerusalem, Judea and Samaria

Adjourn means to suspend the meeting like when God closed up heaven for half an hour.

Acknowledgement and thanks

I thank my God Yahveh for entrusting me with his word and choosing me to write this book.

I like to thank my family for being there for me

My mom and dad Charles and Ruby Harvey

My siblings

William and Sandra Christmas

Terri Robinson

Charles and Charolette Harvey

Eric Harvey and Elyana Dudley

My children Reyna, Rachel and Racquel

Special thanks to my mentors and teachers

Reverend Darryl Pratt and Reverend Mark Merrill and all of my Ihim family

I like to send specials thanks to my friends who inspired me . I couldn't of done it with out you guys.

Miss Darlene Jones, My sister in Christ Miss Patricia Poteat, and Mr Robert Jones. I love you guys

I also wanted to think my love and other half Mr Troy Wimbish for being there for me. I love you.

Reference sources

Yahveh, God, Almighty. Comparative Study Bible. Grand Rapids: Zondervan, 1988. Print.

Spangler, Ann. The Names of God Bible. Grand Rapids:Revell, 1995. Print.

Syswerda, Jean E. The Women of Faith: Study Bible. Grand Rapids: Zondervan, 2001 Print. Illustrated Dictionary of the Bible Herbert Lockyer, Sr. Editor with F.F Bruce and R. K. Harrison Copyright 1986 by Thomas Nelson Publishers

www.ingramcontent.com/pod-product-compliance
Lightning Source LLC
Chambersburg PA
CBHW080517030426
42337CB00023B/4551